—*Kaslo*—
The first 100 years
(The oldest incorporated municipality in the Kootenays)

by
George McCuaig

Consulting Editor
Martin Lynch

Dedication
to the volunteers of our community

*This book is dedicated to all those who have, over 100
years, shared their talents and molded Kaslo
into a special and caring community.
May the spirit which inspired them find a place
in the hearts of those who follow.*

Tom McKinnon,
Kaslo, B.C.

Published by
Semco Press, Kaslo, British Columbia,

under the auspices of
the Seniors Centennial Book Committee.

*Printed in Canada
by Hignell Printing Ltd., Winnipeg, Manitoba*

ISBN 0 - 9696413 - 0 - 3

• Contents •

Kaslo Village Hall, library and fire hall in1992. Photo courtesy of G.D. McCuaig.

• Photographs •

Cover photo: Kaslo from Easter Lily. Donated by Dieter Arndt Photography, Kaslo, B.C.
Back cover photo: After the fire of 1894. KLHSA no. 988.40.329

Mayor's message

The celebration of a birthday is the time to reflect on the past; at the events and people that have shaped our lives. This is what the authors of this book have done. Kaslo has seen prosperity and depression; peace and wars; flood, fire and other disasters and yet the people you will read about were able to face the adversities and keep their spirits high. As we start Kaslo's second century it is this spirit that will sustain us through the coming years.

It is with pride as the mayor of this wonderful village, that I congratulate all of those responsible for this book and wish Kaslo a very happy one hundredth birthday.

Gordon Gaskell
Mayor

Acknowledgements

The Kaslo Senior Citizens' Association Centennial Book Committee was comprised of: chairman Stan Leathwood, secretary-treasurer Dot Morris, writer George McCuaig, and researchers Jack Morris, Shelagh Leathwood, Isabel Butler, Mary Johnson, Joyce Davidson, Catherine Douglas, Joe Scarbo, Dave May and Teresa May.

The Centennial Book Committee would like to thank the following organizations for their financial contributions toward the printing of this book:

The Royal Canadian Legion Branch 74 | West Kootenay Power
Corporation of the Village of Kaslo | Kaslo Boat Club
J.V. Humphries School | Kaslo Bay Marine Club
Kaslo and District Chamber of Commerce | Kaslo Bowling Club
Kaslo Golf and Country Club | Kootenay Lake Farmers' Institute
St. Mark's Anglican Church | Kaslo Curling Club
St. Andrew's United Church | Village of Kaslo Grant in Aid
Kaslo Recreation Commission | Economic Development Commission
Kootenay Lake Historical Society | Kaslo and District Senior Citizens Associatio
Kaslo Riding Club | Meadow Creek Cedar

Cover Photo: Donated by Dieter Arndt Photography, Kaslo, B.C.
Back Photo: Courtesy of Kootenay Lake Historical Society Archives.

The Kaslo Senior Citizens' Centennial Book Committee would also like to acknowledge the financial assistance of the The New Horizon Seniors Program and the Seniors Lottery. Without their assistance this book would not have been possible.

The committee would like to express their appreciation to the Kootenay Lake Historical Society Archives and archivist Elizabeth Scarlett for her assistance in locating many hard-to-find news items and photographs in the course of this project.

A special note of appreciation goes to Shutty Bench resident and editor Martin Lynch, who spent much time and made many phone calls to ensure this book is as accurate and readable as possible. Without the benefit of his considerable experience the compilation of this book would have been a much longer process.

Geographical Location

British Columbia has been described in the past as hundreds of Switzerlands rolled into one. In the West Kootenay area, especially around Kootenay Lake with its rugged ore-rich mountains, all Switzerland and its tourist hotels would become lost in the great ranges of mountains.

Kootenay Lake splits the Selkirk mountain range into two chains, the eastern range being known as the Purcells. The peaks range from twenty-three hundred to thirty-four hundred metres, and the highest peak visible from Kaslo is Mount Loki, on the east side of the lake, which rises twenty-seven hundred and seventy-one metres into the clouds. Its peak rises majestically, reminiscent of a church spire, and there have been many years when it is not entirely free of last year's snowpack when the coming winter dusts it again with fresh snow. To the southwest lies the famous Kokanee Glacier, easily accessible from either Kaslo or Nelson. Numerous small, jewel-like alpine lakes nestle within the peaks, and many creeks, some almost large enough to be called rivers, tumble down the steep watersheds to empty into the lake. The scenic beauty of Kaslo is one of its greatest assets—completely unsurpassed even to this day.

Kootenay Lake, lying almost directly north and south, is over a hundred and fifty metres deep in places and more than a hundred kilometres in length, and up to six kilometres in width. The "Main Lake," as it was known to the pioneers, extends from Lardeau at the north end to Kootenay Landing at the south. The West Arm is a variably narrowing channel from

3

Procter to Nelson. From there, the Kootenay River flows in a southwesterly direction for more than forty kilometres to Castlegar, where it joins the Columbia River.

Kaslo is situated at the mouth of the Kaslo River on the west shore of Kootenay Lake, about sixty-two kilometres north of Nelson. Touted as "the Lucerne of North America" in pioneer days, it is ideally situated on one of the few good-sized sheltered bays on the lake. Lower Kaslo is virtually flat; built on an alluvial fan (delta) extending into the lake, meeting it with an inviting sandy beach that stretches from the north side of the Kaslo River to the drydocked sternwheeler S.S. *Moyie*, which is a national historic site. Upper Kaslo, a portion of which was once known as "Nob Hill," extends to the foot of Mount Buchanan, and is joined to the rest of the town by a short steep hill that gives a quick thirty-metre jump in elevation to that bench of land adjoining the mountain that bears the name of one of Kaslo's most influential pioneers. Across the lake, the sharp mountain spires tower; their rocky teeth seem to take a bite right out of the sky.

Sturgeon-nosed Kootenay Indian canoe
KLHSA no. 988.40.724

Early History

There is abundant evidence that the Kootenay Lake valley was a breadbasket for the original inhabitants, the Kutenai Indians. These people used the valley as their seasonal hunting-gathering grounds for thousands of years before the area was "discovered" by any white explorers. They would journey up the lake in their unique sturgeon-nosed canoes from winter camps near the Idaho-Canada border south of Creston, B.C., setting up summer camps from which the women and children would forage for herbs, fish and berries while the men undertook hunting expeditions of several days or weeks into the surrounding mountains and valleys to procure the coming winter's food supply.

Hundreds of arrowheads and spearheads have been and occasionally still are found on the shores of the lake. Indian pictographs are still legible at various places on the north and south arm of the lake, their messages and meaning lost in the mist of time.

Exactly who the first white men to visit the Kootenay Lake area were is still somewhat of a mystery—it is known that the great explorer David Thompson reached the south end of Kootenay Lake via the Kootenay River in 1808, but turned back on the advice of the natives there, as winter was fast approaching. He then headed back overland along the Goat River to Moyie Pass, returning to Windermere Lake, from where he continued his explorations along the Columbia River system.

The next documented white visitors were trapper/traders from the North West Company, or Nor'Westers as they were called. They mostly traded with the natives, not bothering to explore the lake in any detail. The Hudson's Bay Company absorbed the North West Company in 1821, and there was not a detailed description of the lake area itself until 1825, when William Kittson, from Fort Colvile, was told by George Simpson to discover why Kootenay Lake was not widely used for travel. His journal is in the Hudson's Bay Company Archives, and it describes the area's rugged and magnificent beauty—but this first literate explorer didn't head up into the north arm of the lake—instead, he headed west toward the Kootenay River and the journal is testimony to the dangers encountered once the fragile canoes hit the vigorous rapids west of present-day Nelson.

The Hudson's Bay Company trappers, probably following a lead from the natives, discovered galena (and consequently lead) at the site of the Bluebell Mine in present-day Riondel, which they put to good use making bullets. And where there is galena, there is a good chance that there is silver somewhere nearby.

In the spring of 1882, Robert Evan Sproule staked a claim to a fifty-foot vein of silver he found on a cliff face in the area. He was unable to register this property and lost it to Thomas Hammil, who was working for Captain George J. Ainsworth and his brother of Portland, Oregon. This led to hard feelings and harder action—Sproule's mind snapped and he shot and killed Hammil from ambush. This was the first documented murder in the Kootenay Lake area. After a lengthy pursuit, Sproule was captured and paid for his crime on the gallows at Victoria.

A year later, the Ainsworths were crown-granted 160 acres of land across from the Bluebell mine site, where Ainsworth now stands. By 1884 it was a small town. Four years later, it was plotted out into lots. A. D. Wheeler was a pioneer and the first store was operated there by G. B. Wright, George Ainsworth's brother-in law, in 1888. That first store still stands, an arts and crafts store now, and has been restored to its heritage look.

The Beginnings of Kaslo

In 1887, George Thomas Kane was sent to the Kootenays by the Waterous Engine Works of Brantford, Ontario, to install their machinery in a Canal Flats sawmill. The mill was being built there to facilitate the construction of a canal between the Kootenay and Columbia waterways. It was around this time, possibly as he was en route to report to the Waterous agents in Victoria, that he first passed through the north arm of Kootenay Lake. The man had vision—he was probably the first pioneer to recognize the potential of the Kaslo River delta as a townsite.

In 1888 Kane was again sent to Kootenay Lake by Nicholles & Renouf, the Victoria-based Waterous agents, to select one or more millsites for Joshua Davies of the Sayward Mill Company, who had purchased Waterous milling machinery. On his return to the lake, Kane selected two 300-acre sites, one at Pilot Bay, the other at Kaslo, and applied to the authorities for both. Davies chose the Pilot Bay location and dropped all rights to the Kaslo site, whereupon Kane took it for himself.

Kane was not the only one who became interested in the flat land and sheltered bay. George Owen Buchanan, most commonly known as "G.O.," arrived in late October 1889 after rowing there with Tom McMurray from his recently constructed sawmill in Harrop, then known as "the Outlet." He had received a tip that there were good stands of timber there from Government Agent G.M. Sproat in Revelstoke a year earlier. Sproat in turn had got the tip from the late R.E. Sproule, who had by that time been hanged. Buchanan didn't think much of the timber after he and McMurray cruised the area, but nonetheless, just before he headed back to Harrop, he drove a stake just above the shore of Kaslo Bay and posted a notice of application for a lease covering one and a half miles west and one mile south, accounting for about 960 acres. This was the first stake driven on the site of what was to become Kaslo.

George Kane returned to Kaslo in the spring of 1890. He applied to purchase 8,000 acres covering the shore to the south of Buchanan's staking. Becoming more deeply interested in the site, Kane next applied for a preemption on the shore front. He got this, subject to G.O. Buchanan's rights, and sent for his younger brother, David, to live on the pre-emption while he went to the coast to organize the Kaslo-Kootenay Land Company.

David Kane built a log cabin almost on the corner of what is now Front and Third Streets. He lived there alone all summer, with only a small dog and a tame bear for company. As the only means of transportation was a rowboat and the nearest supply centre was many miles away, he did not make many trips. He lived mainly on such foods as could be obtained from fishing and hunting, and from the abundant supply of berries to be found in the hills around. Later, when prospectors were arriving daily in every type of small boat, the bear would meander down to the shore to greet the newcomers. However, it developed a fatal appetite for small dogs and had to be destroyed.

In the spring of '91, Buchanan again visited Kaslo, this time accompanied by his wife. They had breakfast in the log cabin with Dave Kane and his clearing gang. Mrs. Buchanan was the first white woman to set foot in Kaslo.

There has been much difference of opinion as to the origin of the name of Kaslo. One opinion was that it was named after an Indian, 'Old Caslo,' who, while working for Richard Fry (fur trader and general factotum of Bonner's Ferry, Idaho) had spent a winter trapping on what was later known as the Kaslo River. This was years before any white man came. Another version was that it was derived from an Indian word—"Asassaloe" meaning "home of the blackberry," and shortened first to Akasloe, then Kaslo. Yet another account is that given by David Kane in a radio broadcast from Spokane in October 1933. He says:

"The name is derived from the river which runs through the city. The stream was named for John Kasleau, who arrived in the Kootenay in the '80s with a Hudson's Bay party, to secure lead for bullets from the outcrop of the present Bluebell mine. His name, spelled Kasleau, was later shortened to K-a-s-l-o."

The site was also known for some time as Kane's Landing. The theory about John Kasleau is as yet unproven, as are the rest, and it is likely that the true origin of Kaslo's name will, like the messages of the native pictographs, remain lost in history.

Prospectors Open the Kootenays

The summer of 1891 was to be a banner year for the neophyte settlement. Prospectors Andrew Jardine, "Lardo Jack" MacDonald and Jack Allen staked the Beaver claim on what is now Mount Jardine, located about 30 kilometres northwest of the community. MacDonald and Allen had seen the potential of the present townsite on a previous trip through the area and decided to put their ideas into action on their return. Allen was an American citizen, and therefore could not pre-empt the land on his first trip through. When they found that the land had been taken up by the Kane brothers, they staked an addition to the townsite on the west side, calling it "Allen's Addition," and an area on the north side which they called "MacDonald's Addition." The two areas are known by the same names to this day.

These men left their marks in more than one place—the mountain southwest of Kaslo reminded Allen of his home in Virginia and he named it Blue Ridge after the Blue Ridge Mountains of his home territory. Another mountain, just south of Kasl,o was named "True Blue." Allen and Jardine also named Bear Lake and Fish Lake near Retallack. However, there is some dispute as to which small lake is which now, due to a (possible) signage error made in the past by the Highways Department of the provincial government.

In any event, once the news got out about the Beaver claim, a rush of prospecting and mining began in the Kaslo-Slocan district. Ainsworth-based assayer A.E. Bryan was kept busy with rich silver and lead samples from claims bearing fanciful, hopeful names. The Ibex was located by Jim Pringle and Jim Brennan, and the Payne by Eli Carpenter in 1892. The group known as the Noble Five—Bill and Jack Hennessy, Jack McGuigan, Jack Seaton and Frank Flint—located a number of successful claims, among them the Noble Five and the Last Chance.

E.H. Kamplan located the famous Whitewater mine the same year. At first it showed nothing on the surface but an oxidized iron stain in the slate on a cliff top, only a few feet high. Kamplan had little confidence in his find and let it be known that he would accept any offer. Men with money—capitalists—were induced to investigate the claim. In order to reach the top of the cliff, one of these men used a prospecting pick to assist his ascent. His weight dislodged and exposed a forty-pound chunk of galena. J. C. Eaton, with several partners, then paid $200 for the claim.

These men knew how to get their money's worth. With one pole pick, which was never sharpened during the work, one man graded about a mile of trail and mined over seven tons of ore, which when smelted netted over $900. Extensive work did not commence until 1896, when the Whitewater became the banner mine of the central Kaslo-Slocan district. By 1897, $240,000 had been paid in dividends, at which time a two-third interest was sold to an English company. A fine concentrator was built and the mine operated successfully for many years. Since then, it has changed hands several times but has produced many thousand tons of ore through the years.

The Utica was located by Paddy McCue, for whom Paddy's Peak was named. Paddy was a young Irish lad cooking for a group of prospectors. Occasionally he would do a bit of prospecting in his spare time and was teased unmercifully by the other men, who told him not to mind his failure as a prospector as they would give him an extension. However, more by good luck than good judgment, Paddy located the claim that later became the Utica Mine (named after Utica, New York, whence Paddy came). Where-upon, Paddy, who stammered badly, said: "N-now I have the m-m-mine and

Whitewater mine concentrator
KLHSA no.988.40.688

I w-will g-give you g-guys the extension," Later it was sold to George Hughes, and after that to Charles F. Caldwell. The ore was rich in silver and paid rich dividends to its various leasers. It has been reopened several times since then.

The Lucky Jim, also located in '92, has had a checkered career. Staked originally as a silver-lead mine, the property, after a fruitless expenditure, was practically abandoned owing to its troublesome zinc content. Then George Hughes took it over and made a small fortune from the high-grade zinc he shipped to American zinc smelters. The American zinc producers took such action as insured a prohibitive tariff against all Canadian zinc ore. Next, G. Weaver Loper, an astute promoter, formed a company with many prominent Manitobans as stockholders. He induced the CPR to spend $175,000 on the construction of a spur from Three Forks to Bear Lake. Since then, it has had many ups and downs, and belonged to various companies. The ore was low grade and was mainly zinc with little lead or silver, but it could be mined in such large quantities that it has produced millions of dollars since it was located a century ago.

The Cork mine was located by Ben Briggs and his brother. Briggs

Creek, which empties into the south fork of the Kaslo River, was named after them. They did little development work and it was taken over by a syndicate of French promoters called the Selkirk Mining and Milling Company with Captain A. Fournier as its mining engineer. A mill was built in 1904 and ore was shipped for several years. It was closed for a time but reopened in 1912 when most of the work was done on No. 1 vein on which the Province mine was also located. During the winter the snow became very deep and miners working at the Cork related, with great glee, how a "green" foreman had attempted to remove the snow from the roof of one of the buildings by setting off a charge of dynamite inside it with disastrous results to the building and contents. Later W. E. Zwicky was in charge of mining operations. The ore was not high grade and when the price of metal deteriorated it was closed for many years. Charles Lind and a crew of men reopened it in 1948. It was operated by Base Metals Mining Corporation and then by London Pride Silver Mines until it closed in 1966. There were many other mines too numerous to mention.

The mining techniques used in the early days were, as one might expect, extremely primitive. Drilling was done by "single jack" if the ore was not too hard, or "double jack" if it was too difficult. The former was a miner who worked alone, and the latter was a two-man team, one holding the steel chisel while the other hit it with an eight-pound hammer—a great builder of faith in one's partner. The ore was loaded into ore cars—sometimes pulled by horses—and taken to the outside where it was transported down the mountain to the road by packtrain in summer, and "rawhided" down in winter. There it was put into ore sacks and taken to the nearest shipping point via ore wagons.

"Rawhiding" ore was a method in which the ore was placed on raw steer hides, laced up, and then pulled down the mountains by horses. Old-timers tell of many instances when the horses would ride the rawhide down the trail. On very steep inclines, the rawhide would slide into the horses' hind legs, whereupon they would sit back on it and, steering themselves with their front feet, would slide serenely down the mountain. Many horses became so accustomed to their novel job that they knew exactly what to do without any direction from the driver on the long trip down the mountain. When the snow became deep, the horses were fitted with wooden snowshoes, or ore-sacks filled with brush were tied to their feet. These snowshoes were approximately ten inches by twelve inches and had cleats under them to prevent the horse from slipping. They were clamped to their feet and a small bolt kept them secure. The horses soon became accustomed to these and often refused to venture forth without them. Soon the snow would become so hard on the surface that four-horse teams would pull loads weighing seven and a half tons over twenty feet of snow without sinking in. The ore wagons made the trip from Kaslo to Bear Lake in one day, usually stopping at the Ten Mile

Rawhiding
KLHSA no. 988.40.1429

House for dinner. This was a boarding house equipped with a saloon and also a barn for the horses. It was operated for years by Bob and Neil MacDonald.

All this mining activity greatly increased the prospects of Kaslo's becoming a successful town. On the strength of this, and on general optimism, George Kane organized the Kaslo-Kootenay Land Company and later the Kaslo & Slocan Railway Company with the aid of promoters from New Westminster and Victoria. In the spring of '91, the first house was constructed in the new town. This was a frame building at the lower end of what is now Front Street. Here David Kane lived.

When the miners and prospectors began to arrive in ever-growing numbers, he hired a cook to feed all the newcomers who were arriving daily by various means of transportation. While many arrived in small boats, the *Galena*, a twin-screw boat, and the S.S. *Nelson*, Kootenay Lake's first sternwheeler, were bringing in huge boatloads of prospectors and mining men of every description. Men came from many points in the United States and Canada, but the largest number were from Spokane, Coeur d'Alene, and the surrounding district, who arrived via Bonner's Ferry.

Good News Brings Commerce and Civilization

Attracted by the wild tales of rich mines being discovered almost daily, miners, prospectors, saloon men and gamblers poured in and land that only a short time before was covered with heavy timber was now being sold at fabulous prices for choice building lots. George Kane had sent in John Keen, a civil engineer, to lay out the prospective city into lots; a total of 160 acres was set aside for this. Keen made surveys and also took levels for a railway to mining properties up the Kaslo River.

Although Kaslo was still a settlement of tents and cabins, a few permanent buildings began to make their appearance. J. B. Wilson opened the first general store at the corner of Front and Third Streets in front of David Kane's original log cabin. This was an excellent location as the boats landed on the beach almost directly in front of the store, which served also as a post office. A blacksmith's shop had been opened and construction was started on a new store for Samuel H. and Robert F. Green, on Front Street. The Green brothers, who were staunch Conservatives, had been operating a general store at Ainsworth for some time. Men were working on a new floating wharf on the present location of the bathing beach at the lower end of Front Street, and nine miles of the Kaslo-Slocan trail had been completed. In the fall, the Kane brothers' mother arrived with her large family to take up residence in Dave Kane's new house. Mrs. Kane and her daughters were the first white women to live in Kaslo.

One daughter, Stella, often related their experiences on this trip. They came from Eastern Canada by rail, and eventually along the Northern

A.T. Garland Store
KLHSA No.988.40.421

Pacific Railway line to Kootenai Station on the north shores of Pend Oreille Lake in Idaho, and from there by stage along a rough wagon road to Bonner's Ferry. At this point they embarked on a small wood-burning tug for the trip down the Kootenay River to Kootenay Lake, and then up to Kaslo. The tug had a large load of freight, beside the passengers, so they had to replenish its fuel supply from woodpiles stacked at intervals along the bank for this purpose. On this particular trip, the wood must have been of inferior quality; steam started to go down before the next woodpile was in sight. Knowing this would probably entail a wait of several hours before other river traffic would be along to give him a tow, the captain looked around in desperation for any type of fuel that would serve to take him to his next source of supply. Spying a stack of prime hams in the freight, he knew his problem was solved; so upon his orders, the fireman proceeded to stoke his fires with several of these hams (which then sold for less than two dollars each), and the tug proceeded on its course with gathering speed plus a strong odor of burning ham. Stella Kane was the first white woman to set foot on the new wharf.

By the spring of '92, the town was really booming. The steamer S.S. *Nelson* was loaded to capacity every trip. The *Spokane*, which had been built at Bonner's Ferry and seen duty in the construction of railway lines, was

13

purchased by the Columbia & Kootenay Steam Navigation Company "to ply the lake between Kaslo and Bonner's Ferry, Idaho." A few months later, the *State of Idaho,* which had been renamed the *Alberta,* was added to the lake fleet. Soon the excitement of the day was the arrival of the boats. A crowd, which included practically every man in camp, welcomed every boat. The receptions were rough at times—an example is the first "plug" or top hats to brave Kaslo's interested welcoming committee. The hats were worn by two tinhorn gamblers attracted by the prospect of easy money, and a shout of delight rose from the crowd as they came down the gangplank from the boat. The instant they hit shore, their hats were smashed down over expostulating eyes. Then both visitors were shoved roughly from one man to another up the long human chain that led to Front Street. No record exists of the length of their stay in Kaslo.

The population was made up mostly of men, although a few families had arrived. There were few sidewalks and no electric lights. The streets were in complete darkness at night and people found their way about using miners' lamps or "bugs" made from a tomato can with a small piece of candle inside and a piece of haywire for a handle. The more prosperous used lanterns burning coal oil. There were no waterworks, so fresh water from the Kaslo River was sold from two hogsheads on a wagon drawn by a team of horses. This was delivered daily for twenty-five cents a barrel to the downtown residents, while the unfortunate ones living out of town had to pay double that price.

The town grew rapidly, as more stores, together with saloons and barber shops, made their appearance on what was now known as Front Street. Early in the year, Henry Giegerich had opened a general store. For the past year, he had been operating a store at Ainsworth. Later he owned one at Three Forks; it was moved to Sandon some years after. W. B. Livingstone started a leather goods store. There were several hotels and boarding houses.

The first hotel, the Grand Central, was built by Archibald Fletcher. G. O. Buchanan built a sawmill on Kaslo Bay and abandoned his old site at Harrop. So great a demand for lumber was there that it was purchased as it came from the mill and buildings were constructed immediately with the green lumber. Although these buildings kept the snow off one's head, the wood shrank as it dried, and cracks big enough for snow to blow through appeared in the walls.

The first ore from the area went out that summer through the Slocan Valley. It was from the Freddie Lee mine and was packed out by Jim Wardner to Nakusp. Wardner's feat illustrated the need for a road from Kaslo up to the mines, and towards that end the Kaslo people worked night and day until their trail reached the Dardanelles mine. E. E. Coy, then a prominent figure in Kaslo life, packed out 10 tons of ore. He went with it to Tacoma and returned with $5,000 in gold in canvas sacks. Wardner switched

Kaslo Transfer Company Express, Dray and Moving Wagons.
KLHSA No. 988.40.1078

his packtrain to the Kaslo route, and $10,000 was subscribed of the $33,000 necessary to convert the trail into a road. When the winter of 1891-92 was over, the 30-mile wagon road was ready. However, this was not accomplished without overcoming what seemed, at times, insurmountable difficulties. Once when the committee was hard up for ready money for a payroll, Coy offered some of his sacks of gold for the committee's use.

Besides subscribing their money, the pioneers of Kaslo gave many hours of voluntary labour to this project, setting the groundwork for a community spirit that has lasted to this day. Time and again residents of this community have proved their ability and resourcefulness in solving their own problems.

Before the building of the road ore had been rawhided or packed down to the trail, loaded into sacks, and brought out by packtrain. The first packtrain left on May 4, 1892, with eleven men accompanying it. This method continued until the completion of the road—then ore wagons and, in winter, ore sleighs, pulled by four-or even six-horse teams replaced them. This was much more efficient. William English drove one of these ore wagons. He described the determination of the drivers to get their loads through regardless of adverse weather conditions. In winter, the snow would be so deep it would be up to a horse's belly but the trips were kept to schedule and nothing was allowed to interfere. Many mines were producing now and a warehouse was built down on the waterfront where the sacks of ore could be stored until they were loaded on the steamboats, which were soon making daily trips. A small amount of ore from the more inaccessible mines still had to be brought in by packtrain but with the road completed, the main method of transportation was by the ore wagons. Before long, a stage drawn by two sturdy teams of horses left Kaslo for the mines each morning loaded with prospectors and supplies.

The First May Day Celebration

In May 1892 the population was about 600, consisting mainly of miners and prospectors. When the idea of a celebration on the 24th, the Queen's birthday, was put forth, it was received favourably by everyone and soon a committee was formed and plans were made. In a short time $350 had been subscribed. A committee meeting was held in the Greens' store with G. O. Buchanan as chairman, and for formality and parliamentary style no meeting was ever conducted more decorously. All were comparative strangers to each other, all took part and the business of arranging the program for the following day was quickly and harmoniousy transacted. A program of mucking and drilling contests, log sawing competitions and various races was being drawn up when the question of enforcing order was brought before the meeting.

The first Maypole Dancers in May, 1923
KLHSA No.988.40.188

It was pointed out there were two justices of the peace present (R. F. Green and G.O. Buchanan), and special constables could be sworn in to keep the peace. This idea did not meet with favour and one man, a sort of leader in the proceedings, spoke up, and the applause with which his remarks were received showed that he voiced the unexpressed sentiment of the meeting. He said, "Mr. Chairman and gentlemen, I am opposed to the appointment of special constables. It is a reflection on the moral standing of this camp! (laughter and applause) We do not require officers of the law to keep us in order (hear, hear). I don't think there will be any need of anyone to keep order. We all know enough to behave ourselves. In case, however, some outsider should come in and raise a row or disturb the peace, I think it would be just as well to have a vigilance committee. There is no need of any swearin' business. Tom Norquay, Bill Jones, Ed McQueen, Sam Edwards and me will act in that capacity if agreeable to the meeting. We'll be around handy all day and if any person starts any funny work or kicks up a row, which is not likely, we'll simply collar him, march him down and throw him in the bay (tremendous applause)." The speaker's predictions proved to be true. Nobody was spoiling for a fight the next day, and although there was great enthusiasm, many keenly contested events, and considerable betting, there seemed to be a general understanding that order was essential. The duties of the self-appointed vigilance committee were light and with the exception of assisting a man overcome by drink to a shady place on a plank behind a big log, their services were not called into requisition. This reflects great credit on the character of those present at this first celebration.

Succeeding celebrations improved each year, and the events were many and varied. Huge piles of trees were cut and hauled down from the hills

May Day 1897, looking west on Front Street.
KLHSA no. 988.40.466

Activities at the halfway house to the Payne mine.
KLHSA no. 988.40.612

to decorate the main streets—Front Street naturally receiving the most attention. Banners and streamers with "Welcome" written on them were strung at intervals across the streets and flags were everywhere. A huge pavilion was erected at the corner of Front and Fourth streets where people danced all day and practically all night to the music supplied by the local band. Horseracing up Front Street was the main attraction at all these early celebrations. Prizes as high as $250 were awarded to the winners and many horses were brought in from outside points. For variety an occasional mule race with shovels as whips was introduced. Many humourous incidents occurred and the rider was lucky indeed whose animal continued from the starting point to the end of the street without either stopping for a rest or exploring the side streets. Rock drilling, mucking contests, races with wheelbarrows of ore, and log sawing contests were held besides the usual sports.

An innovation one year was a "Prospectors' Race." Many prospectors, including Lardo Jack himself, were lined up on the street with their entire camping equipment. During the race, they had to pitch their tents, set up their cooking equipment and light a campfire, and according to custom, had to mix their bannock right in their sack of flour. The first man to produce a well-cooked bannock (cooked in a skillet, of course) was the winner. This produced much fun and excitement, particularly when one prospector, finding his bannock raw in the middle, punched a hole in it producing what appeared to be a giant doughnut.

The steamboats ran excursion trips from Nelson and called at every lake point along the way. People arrived in every type of boat and conveyance, and each year the crowds increased immensely. The tradition of out-of-town celebrants visiting Kaslo during the May Day celebration has continued to this day—although most people now arrive by car, the population swells to almost double its normal size, and logging sports and madcap bed races have taken the place of the mining-based competitions of the past.

After the waterworks were installed in 1896, hose-reel competitions were held. Kaslo had a famous hose-reel team, which travelled to Nelson, Rossland and other cities to compete. The teams, starting from a given point, ran their hose to its full length, connected it to the hydrant, and the first to have water coming from their hose was the winner. Ball games and boat races also added to the pleasures of the day. Many people never missed "Empire Day at Kaslo" for years. "Big John," quite a famous character from Nelson, would bring his hack up on the steamboat just for the big day, and never lacked customers for "a ride in my hack." The "taffy man" in his white apron with his tray of toffee was a familiar sight each year.

The first May Queen was crowned in 1921 and this event soon became one of the main attractions of the festival, continuing to the present. Another May Day institution, the Maypole Dance, was instituted by Mrs. John Keen in 1923. This tradition has continued to this day as one of the highlights, preceding the official ceremonies in which the politicians and other important townspeople get to speak their piece. There has been speculation that this age-old ritual has more than a little to do with Kaslo's continued good fortune, although it is unlikely to be proved unless the tradition ceases.

Baby shows were an innovation some years, although it was reported the judges "took to the hills" for some time afterward to avoid the reprisals of rebuffed mothers. Although the type of entertainment has varied with the years, and there is no sternwheeler to make excursion trips, the Kaslo May Day celebration—in later years called May Days—is still one of the most popular events in the Kootenays.

Firsts in Kaslo

Kaslo continued to grow during the next year. More families had arrived and it soon became evident there were enough children for a school. A one-room building had been constructed on the lot east of the present site of the United Church. This was being used as a church hall, and in October 1892 became the first school until the proposed new one across the creek could be constructed by the government. Annie McLennan was the first teacher, but remained only one term. John J. Miller taught during the 1893-1894 school term. In the fall of 1894 when classes reopened, Stella Kane, later to be Mrs. John Keenan, was in charge and she taught for the next two school years. James Hislop, who replaced Miss Kane as teacher in 1896, became the school's first principal when the school was expanded to two rooms in 1897 and three rooms in 1898. Other teachers during these early years were the red-haired, tempestuous Bella McTaggart and Bibianne Moore. The first trustees were George Kane, William Goodwin and Tom Norquay. After James Hislop left to take up teaching duties at Fort Steele, school staff beginning in 1901 consisted of the principal, Alexander J. Dove, and teachers Annie Ketcheson and Minnie English. A strict disciplinarian and excellent scholar, Mr. Dove did much to raise Kaslo school standards before he was appointed a school inspector. A successor, George Hindle, maintained these standards.

Although other ministers and missionaries had visited Kaslo and conducted services in various buildings, the Rev. D. M. Martin, a Presbyterian minister, was the first to take up residence in Kaslo. He was a popular man, liked and respected by everyone. His first church was the one-room building previously described that was used both as a church and a school. Here Mr. Martin conducted services every Sunday, but during the week he worked his mineral claim near Bear Lake. He often rode with the ore wagons and came to know the teamsters and miners very well. However, he soon decided Kaslo needed a bigger and better church, and with donations from miners and townspeople, a fairly large amount of his own money, and practically all volunteer labour, the building now known as St. Andrew's United Church was completed by '93 on the lot west of the little church-school building. Several other denominations were holding services in various other places at this time, but their churches were not built until later.

Dr. Bruner was the first doctor. When he returned to the States Dr. J.F.B. Rogers took his place and remained for several years. Dr. Gilbert Hartin came in '96. His willingness to do all in his power to alleviate the suffering in the surrounding area, and his genial good nature, won him many friends. He was at one time mayor and later alderman and health officer in Kaslo. He built a small hospital east of the present site of the Government Building, and also the building on Front Street now known as the Kootenaian Building. With Frederick E. Archer, he built the Archer-Hartin Block, later selling out to Mr. Archer. When he moved to Nelson to take up practice there, the best wishes of the whole community went with him. His son, Dr. David Hartin, was an eye specialist in Spokane for many years. Before Dr. Hartin's little hospital, several other buildings had been used—the Harris house at 242 D Avenue, Dr. Rogers' home at 417 A Avenue, and for a short time the Anderson home on A Avenue. However, Dr. Hartin's was the only real hospital until the hospital at 320 A Avenue on the hill was built under the auspices of the Victorian Order of Nurses in 1903. The first newspaper, the *Kaslo-Slocan Examiner*, with Mark Musgrove as editor, came into existence in the summer of '92. Several of the first copies were printed on silk—presumably for the archives at Victoria.

Among the advertisements at this time were the various hotels—the Ottawa House, McAndrew and Murchison, proprietors; the Palace Hotel, Mahoney and Lundberg; Leland House, Devlin and Mackay; Dardanelles Hotel, Mrs. E. E. Coy; and the Grand Central Hotel, and J. Fletcher. Other advertisers were Horace Bucke, lawyer; DeForest Gile, notary public; W. A. Jowett, auctioneer; Langton W. Todd, architect; C. D. Kinnee, tonsorial artist; also the Can Can Chop House, the Noble Five Bath House, and Kemp's Therapeutic Mineral Water (from the mineral springs later occupied by the Gas-Ice Corporation).

Marsh Adams was the first policeman and was very successful in keeping law and order among the rather rough population of early days. There were no serious crimes, and about the only use to which the small jail on B Avenue was put was to house overnight the occasional drunk who had become a little too noisy. In the spring of '93, when the population was estimated at 3,000, the police force consisted of only two men—the chief and one constable. Although there were over twenty saloons at this time, the inhabitants were surprisingly orderly, and the policemen found their duties light. Of course, arguments were settled occasionally with fist fights instead of words, but at these times, the local police could be found looking very hard in the opposite direction and things were soon settled to everyone's

A play at the Theatre Comique
KLHSA No. 988.40.78

satisfaction. With such a large and varied population, the fact that only two policemen were necessary is a compliment to Kaslo's early citizens.

The Theatre Comique (315 A Avenue), a branch of the old Comique Variety Show in Spokane, was the centre of excitement each night. Three storeys high, with a saloon on each floor, it employed eighty girls, known locally as "boxrustlers," and a staff of fifteen. A variety of vaudeville entertainment on the revolving stage was provided and it held great appeal for the rougher element. However, this big barn-like structure on A Avenue, with its dubious inhabitants, was an eyesore to the respectable citizens, and one of the tasks of the first City Council was to deal with a petition and delegation headed by teetotaller G. O. Buchanan, to deal with "that nuisance the Theatre Comique." This was done in short order.

The Kaslo Transportation Company had stages running daily to Bear Lake, leaving Kaslo at 7:00 a.m. and Bear Lake at 8:00 a.m. They guaranteed "fast time and good service."

Jerry Bell owned the first dairy. It was down by the creek in the vicinity of the Timms family's house (247 E Avenue). The next year this was taken over by T. M. Steele. Riedel and Kuester had the first bakery at 331 Front Street and operated as grocers in the R & K Block. Wilson and Perdue owned a fine butcher shop at 335 Front Street. John Reuter managed this shop. In a short time, this was purchased by Pat Burns of P. Burns & Co. and became one of the first retail stores owned by that famous company. It was on the south side of Front Street west of the R & K Block, now known as the 1896 Building. Mr. Reuter managed this shop for the Burns company for several years. Later he left the butcher business to become co-proprietor with Edward Latham in the Maze Saloon until 1911 when the partners took over the St. Pancras Inn, which they renamed the King George Hotel. This they ran successfully for many years.

T. A. Garland had opened a drygoods and men's wear store in the building that was later to become the Maze Saloon. In April 1893, his son, A. T. Garland, became manager of this store. The next year the younger Mr. Garland built his own store at the corner of Front and Fourth Streets, and remained in business there until his death in 1939. During the years he lived in Kaslo, "A.T." as he was known locally, was very interested in civic affairs, serving as mayor and alderman. He was an officer of the Rocky Mountain Rangers, and was instrumental in starting the Cadet Corps; he also was a director of the Board of Trade and a school trustee.

Frederick E. Archer arrived in Kaslo on January 15, 1891. He opened a tinsmith's shop and continued in business for many years. He served as mayor thirteen terms; also as alderman, and was always very interested in anything concerning Kaslo. With Dr. Gilbert Hartin, he constructed the Archer-Hartin block at Front and Fourth Streets, later purchasing Dr. Hartin's interest. In May 1903, while serving as mayor, Mr. Archer, by invitation, went to Spokane to meet the President of the United States, Theodore Roosevelt. With him were the mayors of Rossland and Grand Forks. A newspaper account of the meeting says: "President Roosevelt gave each of these gentlemen a hearty handshake and seemed particularly taken with Mr. Archer's magnetic personality. In a five-minute conversation with him, the President said he had been up and around the Kootenay country as early as 1889, having paddled up Kootenay Lake in a dugout from Bonner's Ferry to the Bluebell mine in company with Dr. Hendry, enjoying some good shooting along the shores of the lake. He believed the Kootenay country had a great future before it."

Even during these pioneer times, the Kaslo area may have had a global impact. In a letter dated November 9, 1947, Stuart Brown wrote to Kaslo Mayor George S. Baker, requesting confirmation for a "tall tale" dating back to the turn of the century. He tells how he captured a mountain goat with a lasso in the Deer Creek watershed and, with the help of twelve men, got it back to Kaslo and shipped it to Washington, with the goat's final destination being the London Zoo. Corroborators of the story were Jack Reuter, Fred Archer, F.S. Chandler, R.A. Chester, Clarence White and Basil (Bab) Palmer. The letter also tells of how Brown and Arthur Cody caught ". . .a young grizzly up the South Fork. Teddy Roosevelt was in Colorado after bear. He heard of our cub, bought it and we sent it to him in Washington. It was a very popular little cub, and some German envisioned the doll idea, and as it was Teddy's Bear, hence the Teddy prefix. I would appreciate it if you can send me the goat story confirmation as I want to use the item in a speech I am to make , and such a 'tall' story needs confirmation. . . ." Well, teddy bears are certainly known throughout the world now, and to think that the original one came from Kaslo shows the effect that a little community can have on the world.

Mr. Archer had the honour of owning the first car in Kaslo in 1913. In 1898, he donated the mayor's chair, which still has a place of honour in council chambers, and a drinking fountain at Front and Fourth streets that was used for many years.

The boom is born

During the early 1890s, mining activities were expanding and many new claims were registered. It was in 1892 that the famous "Big Boulder" was discovered. The following news item from the *Kaslo-Slocan Examiner* was headed "A 120-Ton Boulder of Solid Mineral." The article read ". . .Mr. W. D. Middaugh of Minneapolis, Minn., has purchased from Mr. James W. Cockle, of the Morning Sun mine, a very valuable boulder of solid galena which was found on the Morning Sun on the 14th of July last. Mr. Cockle stepped outside of his camp to cut a tent pole; he secured the pole and turned around to retrace his steps, when a rock in front of him attracted his attention. He struck the rock a smart blow with his axe and was astonished to see a piece of pure galena drop at his feet. He examined the boulder carefully and found it was seven and a half by three by nine feet, and engineers estimated its weight at 120 tons of solid galena ore in one boulder. Four assays have been had as follows: Two of which went 126 ounces each, the third 142 ounces and the fourth 196 ounces per ton. It averages about 60 per cent lead. This immense piece of fine ore is probably the largest single chunk of galena ore ever discovered. It is the intention of Mr. Middaugh to remove his purchase to Chicago for the World's Columbia Exposition."

J. Will Cockle of Kaslo, the discoverer of the big chunk of galena, received $2,000 cash. It is claimed it eventually produced $20,000 worth of silver and lead. Thinking he had stumbled on the outcrop of a wonderful mine, Mr. Cockle immediately staked claim. Subsequent development, however, proved that the piece of ore had become detached and rolled down from the Slocan Star vein farther up the mountain.

By the spring of '93, the price of silver was high and the depression had not yet set in. Boat after boat coming to Kaslo brought loads of men numbering from 125 to 150 a load. Accommodation was at a premium. There were three men for every bed, so beds were used in shifts. Hotels were built in a month's time. The Slocan Hotel, one of Kaslo's finest, was constructed in 30 days with wet lumber, used as it was sawn. The hotel boasted 70 rooms, and 75 carpenters were used in its construction. When the timber dried out, there was little privacy in the hotel rooms.

The Pirate Raid of 1893

Mining promoter John M. Burke, a Virginian who'd headed west after the Civil War, was known locally as "Governor" Burke although he was unsuccessful in his bid for office in the state of Idaho's first statewide elections. In May of '93 Burke, who was also known as Colonel Burke, led a "pirate raid" to Nelson on a chartered steamer. The purpose of the raid was to capture the newly organized South Kootenay or Nelson Board of Trade, and make Kaslo its habitat. The forty-two pirates consisted mainly of Kaslo businessmen with a few from Pilot Bay, Lardeau and Ainsworth. Their plan was simple—taking out membership in the Board of Trade and, when they had the majority, voting to move it to Kaslo. This failed only because of the quick wit of President Bob Lemon. When the Kaslo motion was offered, he looked around the room to see every Kaslo man wearing a wide grin, which advertised what was afoot. He made a ruling that the motion was not in order as it was in conflict with the bylaws. This was promptly overthrown by a vote of the meeting. The president shot a glance at Secretary Bigelow, and picking up a huge volume that was beside his hand, sent it crashing at the

The Brick factory located in the little valley in upper Kaslo
KLHSA no. 988.40.270

lamp, shattering it and plunging the room into darkness. When the Kaslo men looked over the scene with the aid of matches, the officers, the minute book, and the $450 membership paid by the new members was gone.

Next morning, the expedition had to return to Kaslo to report failure. Honorably enough, they would not press the matter to a legal test, admitting they would not have won it in a "fair fight," and only such a victory was worth having.

Instead, the Kaslo Board of Trade was formed and began working for the welfare of Kaslo. One of the first matters to occupy the attention of the new Board was the necessity of a fire engine and a competent group of firemen. Their president, G. O. Buchanan, went on to become president of the Associated Boards of Trade of Eastern British Columbia for many years.

On May 12, Robert Thornton Lowery, known in the Kootenays as Colonel Lowery (the colonelcy was an honorary Kentucky one), published the first issue of the *Kaslo Claim;* now Kaslo had two newspapers. During the spring and early summer months of 1893, Kaslo remained the mining centre of the Kootenays and gradually took on more frills of civilization. Saloons of low and high degree lined the streets. There were 14 barber shops, where the "tonsorial artists" plied their trade. A bank had been opened by the aforementioned Colonel Burke, backed by a then-famous financier— Colonel E. L. Mims.

Buchanan's sawmill was humming day and night at the head of Kaslo Bay; steamboats were landing passengers at all times of the day and night; stories of fabulous finds were still trickling in from the hills, and real estate was very active. Times were bright—it looked as though each holder of a likely claim back in the hills held a winning ticket in the lottery of fortune.

Meanwhile, the first clouds of the devastating financial storm of that year were gathering on the horizon. In one day, five leading banks failed in Spokane, the financial centre of the Kaslo-Slocan movement, and almost overnight money became scarce, development in all directions was stopped and property payments were postponed or options surrendered. It now seemed certain that the Sherman Silver Purchase Act would be repealed by the United States Congress, and silver began to decline precipitously. From an average of well over a dollar, the quotation had receded to below seventy-five cents per ounce to three and one-half cents. The boom was punctured.

Many with enough money departed for the "outside" and before winter came, dollars looked as large as cartwheels. The situation was brought home to Kasloites one fine Monday morning in July when Burke's Bank failed to open its doors. The Colonel had been in Spokane for some weeks seeking help and incidental liquid fortitude, but threw up the sponge when the big crash practically deprived Spokane of banking accommodations. It didn't help matters that the cashier had also departed the previous Saturday night without the formality of saying goodbye.

The failure tied up every spare dollar in town and before the depression had run its course, the steamboats were hauling out passengers for anything they could spare, or "for free." As far as is known, only one depositor of the bank ever collected his money in full. That was Joe Davis, a long, lank Missourian from the Coeur d'Alene, docile as a kitten until aroused and then a quietly dangerous man. Immediately after the failure, he borrowed enough money to take him as far as Spokane to recover his $700, all he had in the world. After a prolonged search, he located Burke and with as few words as possible, demanded his money in full. When the Colonel insisted he was broke, Joe quietly reached into his hip pocket and deposited a murderous-looking six-shooter on the table beside him. Next morning, the Colonel met Joe, as requested, with the money in full. Rumour had it that the money was the Colonel's entire poker winnings from the previous evening.

The reverberations of the bank failure were still echoing in the hills when the *Kaslo Claim* blew up with a loud report on August 25, 1893. The last edition was as unique as its "editor and financier," as Colonel Lowery styled himself. On the front page, edged in black, was a huge tombstone with the caption "Busted, by Gosh." On the tombstone, "Keep off the grass, sacred to the memory of the Kaslo Claim. Born May 12, 1893; died August 25, 1893. Aged sixteen weeks. Let her R.I.P." [It was actually fifteen weeks, but the Colonel wasn't strong on Mathematics.] And then the verse:

This monument upon the primal page,
Speaks in sad words of the impending gloom,
Tells of the battles that the Claim did wage
To save the town of Kaslo from the tomb.
But all its loyal efforts are as naught,
Its pennant now is trailing in the dust,
By the financial flurry it was caught,
And like the town of Kaslo, it is 'Bust'.

Other pages of this final edition proved novel, too. All advertisements that had been paid for were printed in the usual manner; those partly paid for were printed horizontally; and those not paid for were printed upside down.

The prediction that Kaslo was "bust" proved untrue, however, although for many months the future looked extremely dark. The population dropped to less than a thousand—close to what Kaslo's population is today. Many restaurants, saloons and other businesses were forced to close their doors, and many of the mines closed down or reduced their crews to a minimum.

Civic Progress

It was during these troubled times that Kaslo incorporated as a city. The more serious-minded inhabitants saw the need to guide the rapid growth of the town by providing solid leadership and set to the task of making Kaslo a legal entity. Under the Municipal Act of 1892, the charter of the City of Kaslo was granted on August 14, 1893, although it was not until September 14 that it was recorded at Victoria.

Nomination Day was September 30, and amidst intense interest Robert F. Green and George Kane were nominated for the position of mayor. John Retallack was appointed returning officer. When election day, October 7, arrived the number of votes cast was very small as so few could qualify as voters, not having owned property for the year required by law. It is interesting to note that the election had a partisan edge to it—the Kane brothers were as militant Liberals as the Green brothers were militant Conservatives, and this fact no doubt heightened the excitement of the crowd that gathered to hear the results of that first civic election. The final count showed Green—28; Kane—22; so Robert F. Green was Kaslo's first mayor.

The town's first council was composed of Alfred Cameron, David Kane, Thomas E. Devlin, Adam McKay and Samuel H. Green. At first, meetings were held in the dining room of the Palace Hotel until suitable council chambers could be obtained. The city hall was not built until five years later. Starting a bureacracy from scratch required much work—the amount of business to be dealt with was enormous. At times several meetings a week were necessary. However, committees were appointed and civic offices were filled. The heads of those first committees were: Finance, Samuel H. Green; Police and Lights, Adam McKay; Fire, Thomas E. Devlin; Streets, David P. Kane; Water, Alfred Cameron and Adam McKay. Many applications for the various positions were received and after careful consideration by the Council, the following were appointed: City Solicitor, C. W. McAnn; City Clerk, Henry Anderson, (he died three weeks after his appointment and was succeeded by S. P. Tuck); Police Chief, Alfred Sherwood; Junior Constable, C. Murchison, who was soon replaced by A. Hughes; Night Watchman, Thomas Harris; City Engineer, Charles Trumbull; Police Magistrate, A. W. Wright. Archibald Fletcher and John Walmsley were requested by the council to form a volunteer fire brigade. This was done and Walmsley was appointed as the first fire chief. Kaslo has been served by a volunteer fire brigade ever since and a remarkable record of efficiency and service is to their credit. The fire brigade has been fortunate to have the benefit of capable leaders throughout the years, and the current Kaslo Fire Department is still a source of pride to the town's citizens.

Three months after the first civic election, a second one was held on January 11, 1894—the municipal terms of office were yearly at that time. The same two men were nominated as mayor, but this time the final count showed Kane—111 votes, Green—103, with over four times the number of voters casting their ballots than at the first election. The second council consisted of Francis Beattie, Samuel H. Green, Andrew Jardine, David P. Kane and Adam McKay. These two first councils were the guiding hands that launched Kaslo's civic history.

Disasters Galore

It's a good thing that such steady hands were at the helm, because Kaslo's enduring legacy of intestinal fortitude was about to be tested, and shaped. Before Kaslo had recovered from the mining depression, a series of major disasters struck. The first occurred in late February—a fire that destroyed almost an entire block of Front Street.

On Sunday, February 25, 1894, at 2:30 a.m., the fire alarm sounded. When the volunteer fire brigade responded, they found a large blaze at the Bon Ton Restaurant, which was situated on what is now the *Moyie* site . In the five weeks previous to this, three attempts had been made to destroy the town by fire. On one occasion, a pile of wood in the basement of a store building was saturated with coal oil, ignited and left to burn. Fortunately, it was discovered before serious damage was done. On two other occasions, fire broke out in the same locality, in the vicinity of Goldstein's store and the Coeur d'Alene Hotel (322 Front Street). Citizens suspected firebugs and the city employed a special night watchman in an attempt to prevent further conflagrations.

In spite of the efforts of the firemen and practically every able-bodied man in town, the fire spread rapidly. A bucket brigade was formed down to the lake, but it soon became apparent that this was useless as the fire spread to the buildings on either side of the restaurant. However, the firefighters continued to fight the blaze with every means at their disposal. Blankets from the local stores were soaked with water and spread over the roofs of nearby buildings. Merchandise of every description was hurriedly removed from hotels, saloons and stores in the path of the fire. This was put into huge piles in the snow and covered with blankets, carpets or mattresses soaked with water.

By now, the fire was burning on both sides of the street. A light snow was falling and it was bitterly cold, freezing the wet clothing of the firefighters. Men were stationed on the roofs of all the nearby houses and buildings, to keep the sparks from starting additional fires. This kept the fire confined to Front Street, but it soon became apparent that desperate measures were necessary. At about 4:30 a.m., a group of men made preparations to blow up the Byers Hardware Store (304 Front Street), which was directly in the path of the fire. A case of dynamite was suspended by a rope from the ceiling and a fuse attached to it. The store blew up with a terrific explosion, shattering most of the glass in the surrounding buildings. Several smaller buildings were hastily pulled down and the clear space checked the fire for the first time. A few people were slightly injured by flying glass and some slight burns were suffered, but there were no other casualties.

From the start of the fire, people had been removing their belongings from their houses and carrying them to safe places, for it was generally believed that the town was doomed. Salvation came in the form of a strong south wind blowing up and sweeping the flames out toward the lake.

Almost every man in Kaslo fought the fire all night, and some found time to sample the "merchandise" which the various saloon owners had stacked out in the street to prevent it from being burned. Next morning some of the teamsters needed a little assistance mounting the ore wagons, but once in position, they were able to proceed on their journey (probably because the horses knew the way by themselves).

Daylight broke on a sorry sight—practically the entire lower half of Front Street had been destroyed, with the exception of the John Keen building (302 Third Street) and the Kane house at the foot of the street. Some roofs of houses on the nearby streets had been scorched, or partly burned, but the hotels and stores of Front Street suffered the principal loss, which was estimated at over $100,000. Some insurance had been carried on a few of the buildings, but others were a total loss. Many of the tenants lost heavily and only a few were able to save any of their belongings. Fletcher's Grand Central Hotel was partly covered by insurance; Wilson and Perdue, the butchers, lost their building but saved most of their stock, as did both the Giegerich and the Green brothers' general stores. Byers' Hardware had $10,000 insurance on its stock and some on its building, so did not suffer a heavy loss. However, partly owing to policies being cancelled by the insurance companies due to the firebug, and partly because many carried no insurance on their all-wooden buildings, the loss was exceedingly severe to some of the businessmen.

In a special account of the fire in its Monday morning edition, the *Spokane Review* commented on the pluck and energy of the people who resumed business at once in improvised stores—many of whom were ready to open for business the next day. There were no waterworks at all in a town that now housed 200 little homes. Many of these were tastefully constructed and at that time, Kaslo boasted of being "the neatest wooden town in British Columbia." The fire emphasized the necessity for waterworks, complete with hydrants, and an efficient fire department, but this was not accomplished until two years later.

Before long most of the debris had been cleared away and work started on many new buildings. This time, for some unknown reason, business moved farther up the street and the lower part was never built up solidly again, as it had been before the fire.

By late spring many new places were opened for business and almost all traces of the fire had been removed. People had recovered from the shock of the fire, business was improving, and things seemed to be getting back to normal, when disaster struck again. That winter's snowfall had been unusually heavy; the late spring was cold and wet. Warm weather came suddenly and continued to be much hotter than usual. The streams and creeks were running high, causing the lake to rise to an unprecedented height—estimated at twenty-eight feet above low water mark, rising fifteen inches in twenty-four hours. East of Third Street, the entire city was submerged with the exception of a few buildings on the alleyway between A and B Avenues. Most of the houses in the submerged district were surrounded by water varying from three to ten feet in depth, and could only be reached by boat. The lake had risen to such an extent that the main stream of the Kaslo River overflowed its banks. It rushed almost directly on to a corner of the new provincial building, in which were the assessor's office and the jail. The brewery stood isolated like an island, apparently in deep water, and the new schoolhouse, which had been completed only a short time before, was also surrounded. In many of the buildings the water reached to the top of the windows. As the lake had risen, the large warehouses on the wharf lifted more and more out of position. The Galena Trading Company's store was covered by several feet of water and the floor of the warehouse in the rear was in deeper water. The steamboats had to land far up Front Street, and the water almost reached the present site of the Masonic building.

Sunday, June 3, began unusually warm from early morning, and about ten o'clock it became oppressively hot, continuing so until afternoon. The water of the lake was as smooth as a mill pond and many took advantage of its condition to go boating. Some rowed among the submerged buildings, while others went fishing or just rowed to various points of interest such as the Powder Works or a waterfall in their vicinity. About four o'clock there was a change and it was evident a storm was brewing.

First, a number of hot waves of wind made people wonder what was coming, and men who had experience in tropical climates began swapping yarns, but before they could finish, they had to run for shelter. For almost an hour, such a storm raged as no one there had ever experienced before. Sand, lumber, tin cans, light stoves and everything movable was lifted by the force of the gale. It was impossible to see across the street and all who possibly could sought shelter. The Adams House hotel caught fire but luckily it was soon extinguished. There were two other fire alarms, but no damage was caused by them. On the lake, waves were whipped to a height of five to ten feet by a wind of hurricane force. Many estimated its velocity as between ninety and a hundred miles an hour. On land the air was brownish-black with dust and sand and small stones, which rattled against the buildings like volleys of rifle bullets. Boards, signs, and all things movable were borne along with dangerous speed, making it almost impossible to stand against the fierce onslaught. The immense waves on the lake hit the shore with terribly destructive velocity. The storm expended itself in less than an hour, but the destruction it created was almost indescribable. All the houses below Third Street were swept away, and the Galena Trading Company's store cracked in three places and collapsed. The only things saved were the barrels and cases of liquor found floating up the lake toward Lardeau. Fishing in this vicinity seemed very popular for the next few days. Byers Hardware Store and the Chinese wash houses went together with the floating wharf. Between sixty and seventy houses were broken up, and fifteen or twenty more damaged. The front was blown out of the Great Northern Hotel (319 A Avenue), but no one was hurt by it. The jail went next, along with the Bay View Hotel (317 A Avenue) and several other two-storey buildings.

When the storm struck, the occupants of the many small boats on the lake at the time had to flee to shelter in various directions. Some in larger, well-built boats ran before the storm and managed to keep afloat, but were driven more than five miles up the lake. Others nearer the east shore took refuge there until the storm abated. It was during the height of the storm that the most serious accident occurred. Mr. and Mrs. D.C. McGregor, in a small boat, had been assisting a friend whose house was partly submerged. When they left the house, the full force of the storm struck them and in a moment, the boat was upset. Mr. McGregor managed to seize the boat and also got hold of his wife. In the meantime, the boat was drifting away rapidly across the point and into the bay where it was seen. At considerable personal risk, Constable Chatterton and two other brave men rowed out to them. When they reached the boat, they found Mr. McGregor alive, but unconscious, but Mrs. McGregor had been swept away; her body was never recovered. Mr. McGregor was brought ashore to the boathouse, and both the local doctors had to exert their utmost skill before he was restored to consciousness.

Other people had narrow escapes, but some of these were not without humour. Two Chinese were trying to shove their effects in a boat when the wind blew them out in the lake. Soon their flat-bottomed boat was in imminent danger of capsizing. They became panic-stricken immediately and lost both oars. Their shouts for help were ear-piercing, even above the din of the storm, and their antics invited disaster. When rescuers reached the frightened men, they daren't try to get them to change boats in such a terrific storm, so they commenced to tow them in with a rope which they attached to the end of the boat. This method of rescue did not please the terrified men, who continued their wailing until they suddenly felt the boat touch solid ground. It was only a matter of seconds before they were out of sight "heading for higher ground."

One woman, marooned in the upper storey of her house with several dogs, refused to be rescued until her pets had been taken to safety first. A house belonging to several ladies "of questionable virtue" began to collapse before the occupants started to leave it. While they were saved with no little difficulty, the house went to pieces, destroying the piano and other valuable furniture with which it was lavishly filled.

Two men, who were fishing about halfway between Mirror Lake and Kaslo, saw the storm approaching. They landed their boat on the beach and headed for home. Their boat arrived before they did, landing in a garden on B Avenue, where it remained for several years. Small dogs that were out when the storm struck were blown high into the air, some to disappear without a trace. Many chicken houses, with the entire flock, went floating up the lake. One lady tells of hearing a rooster crowing vigorously above the din of the storm as he perched on a small crate that was being carried away.

Immediately after the storm had subsided, scores of men were out, willingly lending their aid to secure everything that was worth saving. Axes were used to cut through roofs and floors to get at the goods beneath them. It must have been demoralizing to see the many fine goods and furniture dragged from the debris, ruined beyond redemption after a long and arduous journey from the eastern centres. The rain poured down in torrents, accompanied by vivid flashes of lightning and loud crashes of thunder, but the untiring workers didn't quit, working on until darkness prevented further effort.

The town's encounter with disaster was not yet over. For several days, the residents along the banks of the Kaslo River had been fearful of the immense volume of water that was roaring toward the lake, and watchmen were on the lookout both day and night. The bridge crossing the river on Third Street had been strengthened but the water continued to rise until it was lapping against its lower chord. Trees torn up by the roots and borne down by the rapid current were constantly striking it with terrific force. About 2 a.m. Monday, the water was flowing over the floor of the bridge. An immense tree, complete with roots and branches, had lodged against it and it was apparent that the bridge was doomed. Soon, another tree came bounding down and struck the chords fairly in the centre. The heavy braces that secured the ends were twisted from their places, and the two halves, side by side, tore down the stream and drifted far out into the lake. Up the river, a jam had formed during the earlier part of the night. This diverted the river from its accustomed channel and sent it sweeping across the flat upon which were a number of cabins. People who had gone to bed, thinking how lucky they had been to escape the storm, were rudely awakened by the rush of a mighty current past their doors and several inches of water on their floors.

One family was aroused to find themselves surrounded and were saved by the timely assistance of neighbors more nervous and watchful than themselves. The current, thus diverted, was directed against the bank on

Kaslo River in the flood of 1894.
KLHSA no. 988.40.323

which stood the residence of Mayor George Kane, directly south of the church, some ninety feet from its edge. The mayor, awakened by the crash at the bridge, realized that the wearing away of the bank would endanger his own house, hastily conveyed his family to safety and then began the removal of its contents. Within two hours the water was flowing beneath the front of the house. Ropes were passed around it and fastened to buildings in the rear, but were useless. In a few minutes, they snapped like string and the house went over with a crash, being carried down the river in pieces with scarcely two boards remaining together. Soon the house below toppled into the current and was carried away almost whole, until it rested against the outer end of the jam that had accumulated above the John Keen residence.

For a short time it seemed that the Keen house might be saved, but the jam shifted its position and the house was lifted from its foundation, turned half around, and end foremost, sailed down toward the lake until it was stopped by another house that had already changed its position.

Shortly after, two houses on the south side struck against a third, and all three together went floating down the current. The damage continued until Monday night, by which time every house on the south side of the river had been abandoned. Volunteers continued working all day, striving to take everything movable to higher ground. Frequently wading in the icy water, sometimes waist deep, they gave help freely wherever it was needed.

Fortunately, the weather was warm and many made their homes in tents that summer. The Presbyterian Church was thrown open and many of the homeless found shelter there. Others were accommodated in the old school next door. Friends received some, and every hospitable place on the more elevated part of the city was filled. The danger was not yet over, as the lake continued to rise, and the immense volume of the river continued to increase. The buildings at the upper end of D Avenue soon could not resist the pressure. Knapp's Bottling Works building gave way and rested against R.F. Green's residence for a time, then was carried to the other side of the current. Mr. Green's house tilted, was carried from its position and lay nearly on its side. Several others, including the hospital building, were wrecked or deeply embedded in sand and gravel.

On June 9 the water started to recede, having reached a height of 33 feet above low water mark. The total loss, though difficult to estimate, was placed at at least $250,000. Besides losing their homes and all their effects, many lost their land as well—either entirely by erosion or left in such condition as to make it unfit for any further construction.

Kaslo Recovers and Rebuilds

The town presented a sorry sight as the water receded and the inhabitants attempted to restore some sort of order out of the chaos wrought by the flood. Apart from the eighty homes either swept away or beyond repair, many were in a sad state, half filled with sand or gravel, some turned completely around and others tilted at a precarious angle. It was during this reconstruction period that the true pioneer spirit of the early citizens of Kaslo was displayed. Their indominable courage had been evident throughout all these disasters and continued to uphold them during the difficult times that followed. Their resourcefulness was taxed to capacity when they were endeavouring to find homes for the many left without shelter of any kind. There were many instances when their good-neighbourliness took the form of helping to rebuild shattered homes or helping to restore scattered possessions.

A new home was built in a few days for a widow, Mrs. Hughes, with several children, whose son Dick was the first baby born in Kaslo. She had formerly owned a bath house and laundry (operated by the "armstrong" method). The crew was made up of miners and teamsters who were her former customers, supervised by one of the local carpenters, and used lumber salvaged from the wrecked buildings as material.

Many people spent days digging for their possessions in the sand and gravel in the flooded district. One man found a diamond ring while helping to shovel sand from a house, while the children enjoyed themselves immensely digging up anything from spoons to cooking utensils.

The biggest job was to bring the creek under control. After some consultation it was decided to push the creek back much farther south than its former course. This would lessen the danger of subsequent flooding and the town would not be divided in two by the creek as formerly. In the days before heavy machinery, this was a big operation. A breakwater was constructed and many hundreds of sandbags were used, but finally it was completed, forming a permanent bed through which the Kaslo River still runs.

Slowly, new homes began to appear, some in their old location. Many citizens, however, had lost their land as well as their houses, so had to purchase new lots. The previous year, the David Kane family had moved into their new home up the hill on the flat directly west of the townsite. This was known locally as Nob Hill. Now others, fearing a repetition of the flood and looking for cheaper land, also built up there.

Industry in Kaslo

In 1895, an event of great importance occurred. The Kaslo & Slocan Railway (K&S) had been completed from Kaslo to Sandon, with a spur line two miles up to Cody, north of Sandon. This was a narrow-gauge line and the engines were of the wood-burning variety. It was operated by the Kootenay Railway and Navigation Company, of which the Great Northern acquired controlling interest in 1900. Its construction accelerated the recovery from the depression of '93. Business improved as a result of the mines being able to ship their ore so much more quickly and cheaply. The first engine arrived on a scow towed by the tug *Kaslo,* on July 31, causing great excitement among the citizens. By fall, the railway was in operation and passengers and supplies were being carried daily up the line, with loads of ore being brought back on the return journey. A.T. Garland shipped the first carload of ore over the K&S line. The ore was sent to the warehouse at Kaslo.

With the coming of the railroad, a gradual improvement in business followed. The population increased, not by boatloads as in the old "boom" days, but a steady flow of more stable, permanent citizens appeared, who brought their families with them and built nice homes as soon as possible. Kaslo was passing into a new era. While mining was still the main industry, smaller ones began to appear, and the possibilities of the town as a tourist resort became apparent to some of the city fathers.

The Millington Brothers had a brick and tile yard in the southwest portion of the city supplying all the bricks needed in Kaslo and quantities were shipped to various points around the lake. This firm discovered lime rock and built a lime kiln around the point from Kaslo Bay. This also was a success and kept the local building contractors supplied.

The Kaslo Brewing Company (417 Cross Street) employed several men in their plant in the western portion of the city. The sampling plant, owned by the Kootenay Ore Company, continued in operation. It had a sampling capacity of 250 tons daily. It had been built on the terrace plan to enable the ore to pass by gravity through its various processes. The company would either purchase the ore on the day of sampling or resack and ship it to another market. Buchanan's sawmill had a daily capacity of 40,000 feet of lumber, 12,000 lath, and 30,000 shingles. It was operated by steam power and employed as many as seventy men.

The Mirror Lake Ice Company was formed by Charles Bjerkness in 1895. The ice was sawn into blocks by hand and many carloads were shipped during the season, mainly supplying the railroads and steamboat trade. A small cigar factory made about 30,000 cigars a month.

Several new stores were built about this time. After losing both building and stock in the fire, the Green brothers started construction on a new store on the corner of Third Street and A Avenue. They rented a small store until their new one was completed. This building still stands. The second storey, which is now the Masonic Lodge quarters, was not added until later. S. H. Green was now Kaslo postmaster. The post office was in a small building next door, but upon completion of the new store, it was moved into the rear of the new building. Flora Goodwin, who later became Mrs. S. H. Green, worked in the post office. Among other new stores were two fine buildings, side by side, on the north side of Front Street, belonging

Green Brothers Building
KLHSA no. 988.40.273

to Henry Giegerich and Byers Hardware. This building is now known as the Farmers' Institute building.

Other stores sprang up in the city, among them Livers' Drug Store, Eliot's Home Furnishings, Walker & King's Clothing, and Strathearn's Jewellery Store. A customs house occupied part of Colonel O.T. Stone's general brokerage building, until the small provincial building at 413 B Avenue was completed. John D. Keenan had a blacksmith's shop and P. MacGregor had opened a transfer and general delivery business. J. Will Cockle built the Kaslo Hotel in 1896, and the Fletcher brothers the Club Saloon on the site of the Grand Central Hotel, which had been destroyed in the big fire.

The Silver King Hotel (440 Front Strret) was owned by Otto Augustine with his partner Charles Lundberg and the Adams House (407 A Avenue)

The Big 'G'—Byers and Giegerich General Merchandise and Hardware stores.
Photo courtesy of Betty Tate.

by Gus and Theodore Adams.

The St. Pancras Inn, which became the King George Hotel (on the *Moyie* site), was built with American capital to accommodate the rush of '97. For a time, it was managed by Mrs. Davies. Later, it was closed and Charles Caldwell and family resided there. It was taken over by John Reuter and Edward Latham in 1911.

Archibald McCallum had a grocery and dairy produce store on Front Street. He owned a large piece of land by the lake, close to the mouth of the Kaslo River, and had a market garden on the land that later became the ball park. He planted trees, still growing beside the city hall. His daughter, Margaret, married Fred McQueen, later the provincial assessor. She lived on D Avenue for over fifty years from before the time of her marriage until her death in 1952. During her long residence, she showed an interest in anything pertaining to Kaslo's advancement. She won the "Good Citizen" award of the Kaslo Board of Trade for 1952.

Kaslo's first chartered bank was opened on November 27, 1896, when the Bank of British Columbia, whose headquarters were in London, opened a branch in Colonel Stone's office. This bank remained for less than two years. Another British-controlled institution, the Bank of British North America (BBNA), opened in what is now the Langham building in January 1897. Until July of the next year, Kaslo had two banks, but business was insufficient to warrant this and Bank of British Columbia closed. The BBNA moved to the Alexander Block at the corner of Front and Fifth Streets and remained there for many years, until it moved into what is now known as the Kootenaian Building. R. A. Chester was manager of this bank from 1917 until his retirement in 1936, first working for the BBNA in England then in several branches across Canada before coming to Kaslo. When the Bank of Montreal took over the BBNA in 1918, Mr. Chester remained as manager, and continued as such until he retired.

When it was apparent that business was improving and Kaslo had not "bust" as he had predicted, Robert T. Lowery reopened the *Kaslo Claim* office and commenced printing his small weekly paper again. This was purchased by David King in 1896 and renamed the *Kootenaian*, a name that proved a little difficult to spell and to pronounce for the newsboys. Their version of it, shouted on the Kaslo streets, was "Koo-oo-ten-ninny, Koo-oo-ten-ninny, get your Koo-oo-ten-ninny today." For a short time, it was printed as a daily paper, then as a twice-weeky, but it soon returned to its original weekly edition. During the years, it changed hands many times— among the various editors were Hilliard Power, Frank S. Rouleau, James Greer, M. B. MacLaren, Roy Fahrni and Alan Stanley. In April 1898 the *Kaslo Morning News,* a daily paper, made its appearance. For some time previous to this it had operated as a weekly, *The B. C. News.* However, it lasted only a short time.

42

For quite some time, the *Kootenaian* press was run by water power—
a turbine system had been set up to run off the town waterline, using canvas
drive belts that ran the length of the pressroom to build up enough
momentum to turn the press. The paper was put out by the boilerplate
method—press-ready pages were shipped in from Regina to give the paper
more bulk. This gave wider news coverage to Kaslo residents, connecting
the isolated town with the outside world.

The Kaslo Water System

In 1896 the waterworks, a much needed improvement, were installed
in the city and greatly facilitated the work of the Kaslo Fire Department. In
1898 a dam was built in the Kaslo River, which fed a main reservoir at the
northeast corner of A Avenue and Eighth Street. With a capacity of about
40,000 gallons (151,400 litres), this reservoir was in use until around 1980,
when the new water system, fed from Kemp Creek, came on-line and the
Eighth Street reservoir was filled in with sawdust from the old T&H sawmill
site. The 24,000-gallon (90,840 litres) Lardeau Jack reservoir, at the
northwest village limits, gave sporadically troublesome service to those
above Washington Street. This reservoir was fed mainly from Kemp Creek
and the Kaslo River with a periodic casual agreement between the village
and Ted Allen and Jack MacDonald, the owners of the Allen Subdivision
water supply, for overflow from MacDonald Creek when water levels were
low.

The Lardeau Jack reservoir was replaced in 1975 with a 60,000-gallon
(227,100-litre) reservoir, only to be abandoned in 1980-81 when the new
9,000,000-litre Kemp Creek reservoir was completed. Kemp Creek has
been used as a primary water supply since 1936. The move to the Kemp
Creek watershed was precipitated by years of complaints by residents about
the water quality—in the late 1920s and early 1930s tailings from the Cork-
Province and Whitewater mines, which were upstream on the Kaslo River,
were causing a considerable amount of silt in the water. Kaslo residents
wanted an injunction to make the mines to cease or upgrade their operations;
council wanted to tread carefully, fearing a great economic upset in the area
if the mines decided to pull out.

In 1929 council engaged A.L. McCulloch, a former city engineer of
Nelson, to come up with a better water supply system, preferably gravity-
fed, in the Kemp Creek watershed. The report he turned in after making an
extensive survey of the watershed estimated the cost at about $15,000.
Council felt that the mines should pay part of the cost and prepared a bylaw
to this effect, but it was turned down—the public wanted council to get an
injunction to force the mines to end their polluting activities. The will of the
public prevailed—council eventually did get the injunction although the

water system improvements had to wait.

The Kaslo Board of Trade took up the issue in the spring of 1935, passing a resolution to pursue the Kemp Creek development, and Kaslo ratepayers petitioned council to go ahead with the project. The Kemp Creek Waterworks Extension bylaw was finally approved on September 16, 1935, enabling council to go ahead and take an approved loan of $13,000 from the provincial government.

The job was completed in June 1936 for $10,000, using 6,000 feet of British Columbia-made wood-stave piping, which was considerably cheaper than steel pipe. The pipe was hauled up the trail by horse; so was the gravel needed for the concrete work. Cameron Clarke, Charlie Valance, Bob Wallace and Billy English worked on the line for $2.80 a day, with A.L MacPhee as foreman. The wood-stave pipeline was creosoted, wrapped in double burlap and bound with wire. Although the life expectancy of the wooden pipe was limited and it sprang leaks many times in many places, it lasted until it was replaced in October-November of 1992 with 4,000 feet of steel pipe for almost $150,000—prime examples of both quality workmanship and inflation. In 1965, a new dam was built on Kemp Creek, with all the materials going up by helicopter.

John (Jack) Matthews, a long-time village employee who eventually became public works foreman, recalls that while hauling up a five-foot piece of six-inch pipe on a packboard, he met a bear; luckily the bear turned and ran—all he saw was legs and feet going up the trail. Bears aren't the only animals that he encountered—while Mr. Matthews was crossing the Kaslo River on the pipeline one day, he met a cougar; that day the screens were not cleaned.

Improvements have been made periodically since the first system was put in, culminating in 1979-80 when the nine-million-litre reservoir was built and the water mains in town were replaced for a cost of $1.5 million. The new mains established a standard depth of five feet for waterlines; a good thing because in the early years it was common practice to connect to the nearest neighbour's water supply at any depth, causing quite a few problems during freezing weather. These problems are pretty much under control now, with most waterline freezing now occurring under houses with exposed pipes.

The water of Kaslo is cold, clear and good-tasting; but in recent years an organism called *Campylobacter jejuni* has been found in the water. This organism can be introduced to the water by any one of a number of sources—most likely from animal fecal material, and causes flu-like gastro-intestinal symptoms. In 1993 this problem is being dealt with by periodic system flushes with a chlorine disinfectant; additionally, council is examining the pros and cons of installing a permanent chlorination unit in an existing pressure-reducing station. In the home, water can be boiled or chlorinated to ensure safe water until a permanent solution is put in place.

Early Electricity and Telephone

An electric light plant was built by George Alexander before the turn of the century and by Christmas 1896 the citizens rejoiced in this new convenience. In July of this same year, the first public telephone system was installed. It consisted of one line with eight telephones. It was on the call system and included a fire alarm.

The Sternwheelers that Opened the Country

The Kootenay Lake fleet grew as the country opened up. The *City of Ainsworth,* an 84-foot sternwheeler, was built in '92, but sank in November 1898 off Pilot Point with a loss of nine lives. The wreck was located by the Dam Busters scuba diving club on April 7 and 8, 1990, and has since been declared a national historic underwater site.

On November 10, 1893, the *State of Idaho* ran into the rocks at Ainsworth. After the passengers and crew got off safely, she was declared a

The S.S. Spokane *burning in Kaslo Bay as the S.S.* City of Ainsworth *stands by. Photo courtesy of Margaret Jardine.*

45

Above: *The steamships Kokanee, Moyie and Nasookin at Kaslo Beach May 24, 1904. KLHSA no. 988.40.1683*

Left: *The Nasookin under steam. KLHSA no. 988.46. 5.*

*The S.S. Kaslo docks in Kaslo May 24, 1901
KLHS no. 988.40.1536*

complete wreck. She was sold practically on the spot for $350 to George Alexander, who had her towed to Kaslo where she lay partly submerged for many months. She was raised and refitted in 1895, renamed the *Alberta,* and assigned to the Nelson-Kaslo run. The *Spokane* too was short-lived, being destroyed by fire in Kaslo Bay. She was being recommissioned for lake service after serving as a floating wharf when the floods of '94 had washed away the town pier.

In May 1896, the CPR sternwheeler *Kokanee* was launched. On her trial run she covered 12 miles in 40 minutes. In order to compete with such a speedy rival, the Great Northern built the *International* and the old-time boat races on Kootenay Lake were renewed. On November 21, the two steamers raced to decide once and for all which should have the title "the fastest boat on Kootenay Lake." The *Kokanee* won. In 1900, the largest steamer to date was launched at Mirror Lake amid much noise and celebration. She was christened *Kaslo*, and was destined for the run between Kaslo and Kuskonook, which was fast becoming the boom-town of the south end of the lake.

The CPR added the *Moyie* to its fleet in 1898. Later the *Kuskanook* and later the *Nasookin* replaced the *Moyie* on the run from Kootenay Landing to Procter.

There were other ships, large and small, that plied the Kootenay waterways—including the *Argenta*, a small shallow-draft sternwheeler that worked the Duncan Lake and River waterways, and the *Nelson*, the first major ship on Kootenay Lake—and many whose names have been forgotten.

The sternwheelers played an important part in the development of this section of the country. Without them progress would have been much slower. The crowds of passengers enjoying leisurely journeys up and down the lake; the races between the steamers; excursion trips with boats jammed from stem to stern; and huge loads of freight landed right on the beach as well as on wharves are gone forever. However, the old sternwheelers can always be admired so long as the *Moyie*, the last of the fleet, lies in state on the shore of Kaslo Bay. The ship is now being restored by the Kootenay Lake Historical Society in a million-dollar-plus project funded by all levels of government and the volunteer efforts of dedicated members of the community at large. Now, complete with an interpretive centre and guided tours daily during the spring and summer season, the ship will be restored as authentically as possible to the condition she was in during the 1920s, the heyday of luxurious Kootenay Lake steamship travel.

Education in Kaslo

As the population of Kaslo increased, so did the necessity of new educational facilities. The first one-room school was located on the east side

School Class, 1900
KLHSA no. 988.40.407

of the present St. Andrew's United Church, and the second school, built by the provincial government on the south side of the Kaslo River, had been used for only a few months when it was severely damaged by the flood. At the request of parents, the trustees decided to build the new one on much higher ground, as they feared a recurrence of disaster. The trustees requested the Kaslo Townsite Company to grant them suitable land, and the property on the northwest corner of A Avenue and 7th Street was finally agreed upon as being the most suitable. The school was finally built there, mainly from material salvaged from the old one. Stella Kane, a sister of Kaslo pioneer David Kane, continued as teacher until her marriage in December 1896, when she was replaced by James Hislop.

The population continued to increase, and a second teacher, Bella McTaggart, was appointed assistant teacher and plans were formed for building a much larger school. Some property then known as the Church School Reservation, owned by the Municipal Council, was chosen. This fourth school was situated on the south side of the 500 block of C Avenue, just southwest of the present school grounds. Completed by 1896, the building consisted of four rooms and all the modern facilities available. This school served Kaslo's children until 1913, when a large brick school building was constructed for a cost of $31,990 on the northeast corner of the present school grounds.

The brick structure performed quite well for the community—in 1953 a large gymnasium and two classrooms were added beside the building, lengthening the life of the building until 1969, when the present (as of early 1993) building was constructed around the gymnasium. There are plans to build yet another school that will serve the community into the next milennium—and the cost for this school, tentatively set to be built in the northwest section of the present property, is estimated to run close to nine million dollars. The new state-of-the-art facility is scheduled to be completed by the time school starts in fall 1994.

Kaslo has always been fortunate in the men and women who have served and continue to serve on the School Board. These public-spirited citizens have given freely of their time, and were sometimes paid with nothing more than adverse criticism. In keeping with Kaslo's progressive community traditions, Mrs. W. B. Livingstone, the former Melissa Arabella (Minnie) Kane, is believed to have been the first woman school trustee in Canada. She was elected to the board together with G. O. Buchanan and E. F. Stephenson before the turn of the century.

The men at first were rather annoyed at the idea of a woman on the School Board, but soon became accustomed to the idea and saw that it had its merits. Mrs. Livingstone was only the first; Mrs. Frank Chandler, Ruby Shillington, Theresa Saalfeld, and Shelagh Leathwood have all served on the various school boards with dedication and much-appreciated insight to

*J.V. Humphries School picture
circa 1992*

the present.

In 1945, the Cameron Report created Kootenay Lake School District No. 6, including all schools on the east side of the lake from Riondel north and on the west side from Ainsworth north to Gerrard, and west of Kaslo as far as Three Forks. The head office was in Kaslo. One of the biggest problems faced by the district was transportation, due mainly to poor road conditions and too few students spread over a large area. By 1964, School District No.6 boasted a student population of Kaslo 247, North End 79, and Riondel 167 for a total of 493 students, up from 414 students in 1957 and 490 students in 1961.

In 1965, Creston School District No. 5 and Kootenay Lake School District No. 6, after deliberating for two years, decided to amalgamate. The new district was called Creston-Kaslo School District 86; the office would be at Creston and the board made up of representatives from three sections—North (one member for Kaslo, one for Rural), Central (one member for Riondel, one for Rural) and South (two members for Creston, and three for Rural). The amalgamation has proved beneficial to the Kaslo area, as evidenced by the pending construction of the new school.

All the schools once situated on the north arm of the lake have closed except for two. Former schools and their dates are: Ainsworth 1897-61, Argenta 1921-66, Cooper Creek 1920-30, Fish Lake 1914-21, Gerrard 1912-28, Howser 1946-52, Johnsons Landing 1922-54, Lardo 1902-03, Lardeau 1930-52, Meadow Creek 1925-46, Mirror Lake 1909-35, Poplar 1905-07, Retallack 1930-54, Riondel 1915-53, J.C. Cochran (Riondel) 1953-72, Shutty Bench 1913-46, and Three Forks 1897-1932. The only ones remaining open in the Kaslo area are Jewett Elementary School in Meadow Creek, opened in 1948 and J.V. Humphries School (kindergarten-grade 12) in Kaslo.

Churches in Kaslo

Just as schools were deemed necessary for the education and well-being of the children, churches were also important for God-fearing pioneers who were turning wilderness into civilization. It is believed that what is now St. Andrew's United Church was the first formal religious building completed in Kaslo. The newly-completed building was dedicated by the Presbyterians on July 23, 1893, allowing the congregation to move from the small building to the east of the church. The small building (up to then) was used by all denominations on Sundays and as a public school during the week. The new church was pretty much finished on the exterior, but the floor was of rough boards, and the interior lacked any insulation, wall plaster or pews. Nonetheless, the congregation was happy to sit on planks stretched between chairs for about ten years, when the pews were finally purchased

St. Andrew's United Church looking east on B Avenue.

for the princely sum of $400. By 1896, the interior was finished and a bell had been installed. Once the building was completed in most respects, the lot and little school next door was sold for $400, which paid off most of the lumber bills—the rest of the building had been built with volunteer labour.

The original name of the church was Robertson Presbyterian, in honor of Rev. James Robertson, a tall, spare Scot who was then Superintendent of Missions (Presbyterian) for Western Canada and became moderator of the Presbyterian Church in Canada. In 1901, it was renamed St. Andrew's Presbyterian Church.

About a block to the west on C Avenue, the Methodists worked hard on a church and a manse. These were completed, with Rev. W. Lashley Hall as their first minister. Both the Methodist and the Presbyterian churches enjoyed reasonable support until their amalgamation in 1925. Rev. James Calvert was a staunch supporter of the Methodist church, organizing the Navy League Cadets and continuing with this work very successfully. He often took the boys on camping trips and holidays on the lake.

When the Canada-wide amalgamation of Methodists and a large body of the Presbyterians into the United Church was accomplished, the two Kaslo congregations agreed that St. Andrew's was the larger and therefore the more suitable building for the enlarged flock and the church was renamed once again, this time to St. Andrew's United Church.

Ministerial methods of the day would be considered unorthodox now, to say the least. Rev. James Nairn, who held the Presbyterian pulpit in 1896, is remembered for making the rounds of the 30 or so saloons for which Kaslo was famous, urging patrons to attend the evening service because it was cheaper than seeking sport in the bars, and because their heads would be clearer in the morning! Later, in the pre-teen years of this century, Rev. Alan Simpson sought to augment his congregation by making the rounds of stores on Saturday nights and issuing a hearty invitation to all to come to church the next day. Woe befell those who promised and did not attend, however, for the minister was wrathful with them unless they had a very good excuse. These were fire-and-brimstone days, and such actions by clergy were more commonplace then. But in retrospect, it's hard to criticize these methods, for the ministers were earnest in their endeavours to bring new worshippers to their respective churches.

Rev. D. A. Martin, who was at the pulpit in 1894 when Kaslo endured the disasters of fire and flood, put forward a heroic effort; he found accommodation and furnishings for many of the victims, as well as opening the church to those in need during the disasters. The church was one of the few safe havens during Kaslo's trials in 1894.

St. Andrew's was supported in part by members of the Spinners Society and the Ladies Aid, who also supported the Mission Fund with rather substantial donations, by holding fundraising functions and through careful management of their funds.

In 1942, when the Japanese internment program brought between 1100 and 1200 Japanese-Canadians (Nikkei) to Kaslo from coastal areas, Rev. H.J. Armitage was minister. Since a good number of the Nikkei were United Church-goers, St. Andrew's was immediately put at their disposal for regular services in their own language. The internees, in return, supplied labour for rebuilding the church hall kitchen during this time, and the regular St. Andrew's congregation was most appreciative of the help and service that the internees gave so unstintingly.

The Catholic Church was also well-represented in the community right from the start. In March 1893 Oblate Father Julian Bedard wrote to his Superior, Father Jean-Marie Le Jeune in Revelstoke, advising him that 20 lots in total had been purchased in different communities in the Kootenay Lake area. Four of these were in Kaslo, on the present site of J.V. Humphries School, and construction of a small chapel was soon completed under Father

Sacred Heart Church
Photo courtesy G. D. McCuaig

Bedard's guidance.

The first child to be baptised in the chapel was Clarence, son of William White, who arrived in Kaslo in 1892. Clarence lived to be 91, and is buried with his parents in the Kaslo Cemetery. Clarence's wife, Ethel, continues to be an active member of the parish.

The site in upper Kaslo turned out to be unsatisfactory because of its remote and somewhat inconvenient location, so the chapel was torn down and the lots were raffled to provide funds to purchase the land that the present church now stands on, just west of the Post Office. The property was purchased for $500, and the entire building, land included, cost $2,488 to complete, according to church records. Sacred Heart Church was completed in 1902 under the guidance of Father Stephan Côté, who was also responsible for St. Joseph's Church in Sandon, consecrated in 1900. Joseph Stephan Côté was from Montreal. A stocky man described as being strong as a bull, he was a wrestler and got along well with the sometimes-rowdy miners in the camps he served. One Saturday night in Sandon, he consented to a match if his challenger and his backers would agree that if the priest won, the other side would help him build a church. He won, and got his church. Father Côté has been described as an Oblate priest but is not listed as an

55

Oblate in the order's provincial records in Vancouver. He left the area in 1903 and was replaced by Father Nicholas Coccola, OMI, who took charge at Sandon, Kaslo, and other West Kootenay points.

The Corsican-born Father Coccola was also a colourful character. He played a part in bringing in one of the great early mines of the Kootenays—the St. Eugene at Moyie, on the east shore of Moyie Lake. He had come to Canada in 1880, and in 1887 took charge at the St. Eugene Mission, near the present Cranbrook. An Indian named Pierre Ironhead, also known as Indian Pete, brought the missionary a chunk of galena he had found near Moyie Lake. The priest, who had obtained a miner's licence, accompanied by Indian Pete and mining engineer James Cronin, checked the ground and recorded the claims on June 25, 1893, at Fort Steele.

Father Coccola sold his interest to John Finch of Spokane, for $12,000, using the proceeds to build a church at St. Eugene Mission and a house for Indian Pete, who died in 1926 at 80. The priest later left the Kootenays and for 30 years headed the mission at Fort St. James in northwestern B.C. He died in Smithers in 1942 at 88. Messrs. Cronin and Finch sold two-thirds of their interest in 1899 to the Gooderham Blackstock syndicate of Toronto, which in turn sold out in 1906 to a company in Trail that changed its name the next month to Consolidated Mining & Smelting Company of Canada Ltd., known since 1966 as Cominco Ltd. There is evidence that CM&S paid Indian Pete a lifetime pension of $5 a month and supplied him with livestock and implements, although it had no obligation to do so.

Records are somewhat sketchy in the early 1900s but it is known that the first confirmation at Sacred Heart Church was performed in 1907 by Bishop Augustin Dontenwill, OMI of New Westminster. Those confirmed were Edward McKay, Clarence White, Doris Pauline McGovern, Roxanne Magdaleen Bishop and Nora Mary Murphy. From this list it looks as though Mr. White had two firsts in the parish; his baptism and his confirmation.

The Nelson Diocese, which includes Kaslo, was formed in 1936 and the Redemptorist Fathers took charge at that time. Before the formation of the diocese, several secular priests ministered to the Kaslo congregation, including Fathers A.L. McIntyre, J.F. Monaghan, and John Cheevers. Interestingly, Father McIntyre worked as a miner to earn funds for his seminary cost and ordination. These dedicated priests conducted catechism classes as well as and organized summer schools which were taught by nuns—these visits were usually the first contact Kaslo children had with the Sisters. It was also pleasant for the ladies of the community, who opened their homes and supported the Sisters when they were in town for the summer.

Redemporist Father Len McGuire was appointed to the Procter and Kaslo Missions on June 18, 1939; on May 11, 1940 Father Joseph Boyle was appointed to Nelson and given care of Kaslo, Procter, Sandon, Sirdar and

St. Mark's Anglican Church
Photo courtesy of Dan Pasemko

Grey Creek. Other Redemptorist priests who have served Sacred Heart Church are Fathers James Dyer, Robert Cain, Fred Galbraith, Frank Malone, Dominic Langi, Edward Berrigan, Douglas Purschke, Fred Lane and Thomas Finnegan. After Father Langi retired in August 1991, Father John Doherty became Kaslo's first resident priest. Father Doherty administers the Kaslo Missions, which now include Riondel and Procter, and is remembered for his sparkling eyes, lilting Irish accent and inspiring homilies—generally straight from the heart without the benefit of written notes.

The Anglican congregation held services for the first time on Monday, May 30, 1892, with Rev. A. J. Reid officiating. The service was held in the newly-constructed school building next to the site where the Presbyterian Church would be built the following year. A committee was struck to find a suitable location for their own church and on August 19, 1893, a request was made to the townsite directors (forerunners of the Municipal Council) for a site in either Block 18 or 21. Negotiations ensued, and after almost two years agreement was reached for the land the church now sits on. Conditions were attached to the agreement; the land was to be surveyed within six months and a church erected within twelve months from September 1, 1895.

The Church of England congregation set immediately to raising funds and seeking donations of materials; it took less than three months to complete the building well enough to hold the first service in St. Mark's Anglican Church on Sunday, November 10, 1895 with Rev. W.J. Stobart in the pulpit. William James Stobart was a Cambridge graduate of 1864 who had been ordained by the Bishop of London, and was in fact vicar of St. Augustine's in Bermondsey, a South Bank district of London, from 1878 to 1902. He happened to be out in British Columbia for a few weeks and took the service. The donations were generous by the standards of the day— $483.55 was donated in the form of labour, lamps and locks; the total cost of lumber came to $188.32; the walls were plastered for $75, and five dozen chairs were purchased at $5.50 a dozen.

A vicarage was added to the church in the summer of 1899—a gift from a Mr. Tomlinson costing some $800. The same year Rev. Henry Beer arrived. He eventually became Archdeacon of Kootenay, continuing to reside in Kaslo for some 30 years. Two beautiful stained-glass windows were installed in memory of the Archdeacon and his wife, who was also an ardent church worker.

Church records reveal that the first Church of England baptism was that of Henry Arthur Horrocks on December 2, 1893, with Rev. H.S. Akehurst, priest in charge of Nelson from 1893 to 1900, officiating. The first marriage was Nov. 4, 1894; the nuptials were between Pleasant Oakley Hackleman of Kaslo and Margaret Elizabeth Fitzgerald of Chicago. The first funeral at St. Mark's was for William Goodwin on Feb. 12, 1899.

Possibly the most tragic service conducted occurred on July 24, 1910—a joint service for five miners who died in a forest fire at the Lucky Jim Mine. In their memory a beautifully-carved font was donated; the font was still in use in 1993.

A strong missionary practice was favoured by the Kaslo Church of England congregation; all through the First World War, the Depression and the Second World War the congregation sent parcels of food and clothing to the Prairies, the Northern Missions and overseas.

Just as the Kaslo congregation was reaching out to help others, help from afar reached out to Kaslo. In July 1934 the Parish of St. Mary Stafford in the old English county town of Stafford, donated $500 to St. Mark's Church to cover the cost of a missionary boat on Kootenay Lake. In honour of her donor, the boat was christened the *S. Mary Stafford* (the style S. Mary or S. Mark's was common in church usage for St. Mary or St. Mark's). The craft, formerly called the *Forcite*, after a type of high explosive, had been used to carry explosives required in the building of the CPR line from Kootenay Landing to Procter. She was dedicated on June 10, 1935 by the Rt. Rev. W. R. Adams, Bishop of Kootenay, at the Kaslo Boat Club float.

Curiously, a church associated with a famous figure in the history of angling was sending a boat to one of the great trout lakes in British Columbia; the Norman church of St. Mary's in Stafford is associated with

Izaak Walton, author of *The Compleat Angler*, published in 1653; Walton was baptised there in 1593 and did much of his fishing in a river just outside of Stafford. The church there contains a memorial bust of the great advocate of angling but is not his burial place; he was buried in Winchester Cathedral in 1683.

Until the boat was sold eight years later as a result of "...the improving of roads in the vicinity. . . .," the *S. Mary Stafford* carried the resident priest to visit and conduct services in Johnsons Landing, Argenta and the Lardeau Valley, always giving safe passage on the often-tempestuous Kootenay Lake. The motor launch could accommodate up to twenty passengers and had a "staunch hull."

The *S. Mary Stafford* was one of about twenty-five craft given to points around the globe by the English parish and was the second one to be in operation in British Columbia; the other boat served the Queen Charlotte Islands. These boats were intended for general mission work and were to be made available for transportation of the sick and for rescue in time of accident or storm.

St. Mark's continued to hold weekly services in the 1990s with laity conducting 50% of the leadership due to increased congregational duties and needs being fulfilled by fewer clergy. Support and help continues to issue from the Ladies Guild as it did nearly a century earlier, another example of the deep-rooted commitment of St. Mark's congregation.

Other congregations have also grown from humble beginnings to full bloom in Kaslo. The Kaslo Community Church began its life in Kaslo in 1958, when Bill Kerby visited the town and felt he would like to start an Evangelical Chapel like others he had established in Alberta. He gathered a good response from some of the residents, and a location was found on Front Street in the brick building between the Bank of Montreal and the laundromat. In this first location, the church was named the Faith Chapel of Kaslo.

After some time, the congregation purchased their second location; the building on Front Street now occupied by Kaslo Power Equipment. The church continued its quest for the ideal location in 1979, when various properties were investigated. When the Seath family donated two lots on B Avenue to the church, the search was over and the congregation began building their new place of worship. The official opening ceremony was held on April 22, 1984; the name of the church was then changed to its present name of Kaslo Community Church.

Since 1974, the church has been affiliated with Village Missions of Canada, an inter-denominational organization that strives to place Village Missionaries in small towns that do not have a resident pastor. In Kaslo, Pastor Olaf Sorenson currently officiates for the Kaslo Community Church.

The first meeting of Maranatha Christian Fellowship took place in

February 1978 at St. Andrew's United Church Hall with Pastor Dave May presiding. A good turnout of 37 people encouraged the group to continue and to seek a permanent location for their church. A site was purchased across from the arena on Arena Avenue, and building commenced in the spring of 1979.

With volunteer labour, men from the congregation brought logs from the Duncan Valley and took them to Meadow Creek Cedar to be milled. Shakes for the roof were all hand-made in the Lardeau area. By fall 1979, the building was not quite complete; dedication of the new church was held in May 1980. Dave and Teresa May carried on the church's work until 1987, when they moved to Nelson, and Dan and Dianne Walton arrived in Kaslo with their three children.

The Maranatha Christian Fellowship is affiliated with the Bible Fellowship Missionary Society in Surrey, B.C., and continues its work in Kaslo and area, meeting the spiritual and physical needs of the community.

The Jehovah's Witnesses also maintain a Kingdom Hall in Kaslo. They began meeting in 1977 with another group from New Denver, using the Senior Citizens Hall for about ten years. In the summer of 1985, the congregation purchased a small property just off Highway 31 on the south approach to Kaslo. Right around that time, the David Thompson University Centre in Nelson was closed and several portable classrooms became available; the Kaslo members of the Jehovah's Witnesses bought the woodworking shop and made it their Kingdom Hall. The building was completed in 1987, and served a congregation of about thirty in 1993.

Service Clubs and Fraternal Organizations

The history of the Kaslo Freemasons began in 1894. A number of Freemasons had arrived in the mining mecca from all points, and recognizing each other by means known only to them, combined their efforts to obtain a charter for a Masonic Lodge in the pioneer town. Among them was Ebon Ezra Chipman, Past Master of an Ontario Lodge who went on to become Grand Master of British Columbia. Though not a charter member of the Kaslo lodge, he was instrumental in getting the original charter contstituted, and attended all meetings, becoming affiliated with the lodge as soon as it was ready for work. Mr. Chipman also served as City Clerk, until he became Government Agent, a post he held until his retirement in 1913.

The founding membership was diverse—among the signatures on the original petition were five members from the USA, four from the Grand Lodge of Manitoba, four from other lodges in B.C., two from Scotland, and one from Nova Scotia—a true cross-section of Kootenay pioneers of the time. It is interesting to note that excepting Freemasonry, there were no other common threads such as a shared past experience or homeland binding these individuals together.

The Kaslo Lodge #25 was finally constituted on November 4, 1895, with D. C. MacGregor as first master. At first, its members met in the Livingstone store building until 1896 when they secured the upper story of the Green brothers' store at A Avenue and Third Street with a five-year lease. Work commenced immediately to outfit the hall for Lodge purposes, and by March 15, 1897, a report from the building committee listed the cost of making the hall ready at $1139.20; new carpet and other necessary incidentals brought the cost to $1250. The chairs purchased in 1895 for $10.00 a half-dozen were still in use in 1993 and the Masonic wallpaper, added in 1906, still adorns the walls.

In the 1940s during the Japanese internment the bottom floor was converted to a medical clinic for Dr. Shimo Takahara and a dentist Dr. Banno, who installed the hot water heating system. It was during this time

The current Mason's Hall, formerly the Green brothers general store (see page 40). This photo was taken in winter, 1992-93, by Mary Johnson.

that the original drop siding was covered with shingles, probably in an effort to stop the wind from blowing off the lake and through the cracks of the dry siding. A testament to the craftsmanship of the pioneer builders, the wooden frame building is still sound; it was reroofed with metal roofing in 1954 and 1991; a fire escape was added to the west side of the building and major repairs were made to the foundation in 1970. The lower floor is now the banquet hall with seating for about 60 people.

Henry Giegerich served as treasurer of the lodge for twenty-seven years, and in 1938 he donated the building to the Kaslo Lodge #25 and the Kootenay Chapter #3 of the Royal Arch Masons. A prominent citizen in community affairs in Kaslo, Mr. Giegerich was a member of the School Board for twenty years, president of the Victorian Hospital Board for nine years, and president of the Board of Trade for a time. In addition to his retail operations, he had many mining interests. This Kaslo pioneer died in 1940 after a lifetime dedicated to the growth and promotion of the town's best interests.

The Kaslo Lodge produced many successful politicians—Samuel H. Green served as secretary of the lodge for many years, besides holding office as mayor for two terms, and as alderman for nine years in total.

Prominent Mason Robert F. Green, brother of S. H. Green, was also an active politician. Elected as Kaslo's first mayor and then again in '96 and '97, he soon moved on to provincial politics. In 1898, he was elected member of the Legislative Assembly for Kootenay (Slocan), one of the six divisions of Kootenay at that time. Re-elected in 1900 and 1903, he became Minister of Lands and Works in Premier Richard McBride's cabinet. In a 1912 byelection, he was elected a member of the House of Commons at Ottawa by acclamation, was re-elected in 1917, and became a member of the Senate in 1921. He died at Victoria on October 5, 1946.

Several other fraternal organizations were formed during the years that followed, among them being the Imperial Order Daughers of the Empire (IODE). The group was formed in 1918 and was active until 1925, when their dormant phase began. Reorganizing in September 1938, the IODE remained active until 1951. Their main work was raising funds by means of canvassing for the Blind Institute, the Tuberculosis and Cancer fund, and the Winnipeg Relief Fund. Another of their charitable projects was to send a monthly parcel to a family in England. They donated books to the school library, and in a patriotic literary theme, gave prizes for essays written about Canada. They were also responsible for furnishing and maintaining the Dr. Read Memorial Ward in the old Kaslo hospital.

The Fraternal Order of Eagles was also active for a time, although little documentation about this organization has come to light in the research phase of this book.

In 1959 the Kinsmen banded together to do good works for the

The Kaslo Community Hall has been a fish hatchery, a Scout hall, a Rod and Gun club hall and a Kinsmen hall-and it's not done yet. Courtesy of Dan Pasemko

community and have fun. The inaugural meeting was held on March 21, 1959 and saw *Kootenaian* editor Al Stanley installed as the first president. In addition to contributing to cemetery maintenance, the Kinsmen took part in many charitable endeavours such as the aquisition of the first ambulance in Kaslo; building on two separate occasions floats for the bathing beach; remodelling the present Community Hall into a hall suitable for community use; providing many hours of volunteer labour for the demolition of the old hospital and for the construction of the arena; raising funds for the hospital's construction; spearheading and organizing the construction of the Abbey Manor senior citizens home; providing free firewood to seniors and many other good works. Membership in the Kaslo Kinsmen organization was focussed on young adults between 21 and 40; on their inaugural meeting 29 members signed up. Unfortunately, by the early 1980s interest had waned and the club died, leaving behind a multiple legacy of good works.

The Kaslo Kinette Club was formed in 1963, with Joyce Higgins president, Joan Command treasurer, Pat Frie secretary and Betty Porter bulletin editor. The Kinettes worked in harmony with the Kinsmen and initiated a large number of projects on their own, among which was canvassing the town for many different charities. The canvassers became such familiar sights as they knocked on doors that the good-natured inquiry of the occupant was usually, "What's it for this time?"

The energetic group of women worked hard for projects that were good for the community, and made themselves available to assist those in need, such as fire victims who had lost everything. It wasn't all work, however. They were also interested in having fun—sponsoring Christmas family parties, sleigh-riding outings, picnics and informal "come as you are" coffee parties. These parties were set up by two Kinettes who visited other members early in the morning, catching them at their worst. That's how everyone would have to dress for the party.

The Kinettes sponsored a foster child in Hong Kong, paying for his tuition and sending packages for a number of years. On a more local level they were responsible for many long-lasting enhancements, such as the lilac bushes and red maple trees on the boulevard above the swimming beach and a flag for the *Moyie*, just to name a few. Their cleaning crews were worthy of legend—the Kinettes got the contract to clean the newly-completed hospital, including sealing and waxing the floors. It was a three-day task that the group completed just in time and made $400 for their effort. That night the group put on a dance, and everyone was tired; however, that detail did not stop the party.

The Kinsmen and Kinettes were welcome and productive clubs during their time, and lasted until the late 1970s. The clubs were then forced to close because of a lack of interest and age—active members had to be under 40 and enough new members didn't come forward to keep the club going.

Another group of charitable citizens was organized on November 15, 1910. The Kaslo Women's Institute (WI) got to work right away putting a fence around the cemetery. In 1912 the group took first prize for jams and jellies at the Lethbridge fair. These prize-winning jams were probably responsible for setting up a short-lived jam factory by the WI in Kaslo. In keeping with the martial attitudes of the time, the WI was unflaggingly patriotic. Their motto, "for home and country" was exemplified at the outbreak of the First World War when the group raised $50 to provide a hospital cot for the Cleveland Hospital in England, and again in the Second World War when they distributed parcels of food and clothing, sold war bonds and on a more personal note, presented each local boy who enlisted with a pocket knife.

Although their work was based in Kaslo, it was not always evident here; in Vancouver they assisted in the establishment of a Home for Crippled Children. Back home, in 1933 they held a big Fair and Flower Show to commemorate the 40th anniversary of Kaslo's incorporation. These flower shows became an annual event for many years. In 1938 they bought the local skating rink so that young people could continue skating; the icy frolicking was good, clean cheap fun in those days, and for that matter still is.

The WI was farsighted—in the early years of the organization, a building fund was established, and put to good use. In the spring of 1956, the WI felt that the most neglected part of the community was the local senior citizens. To remedy this, the WI promoted the creation of the Senior Citizens Club of Kaslo. With the assistance of City Council, the Kaslo Recreation Association and voluntary donations of funds, furniture and equipment, the WI bought the McCullough building on Fourth Street next to the government building and presented it to the Senior Citizens Club.

The Pat Burns Meat Market with butcher Henry J. Pett, two helpers, Esther Pett (about four years old) and her dog, Prince. Circa 1910. KLHSA no. 989.16.1

The Senior Citizens Club set about equipping the small building with games facilities, and a reading room, and created a social setting in which old friends and new could simply sit down and chat. In 1958, a birthday party was held for the WI and the Seniors of Kaslo, at which the main attraction was the retirement of all debts on the building. The WI eventually disbanded in 1966, after providing the Senior Citizens Club with much assistance by financial donations, providing caretakers and overseeing much of the building's maintenance.

The seniors became quite busy with money-raising projects to finance improvements and renovations as their membership increased. By 1969, there were 79 members at the annual turkey dinner, and by 1992, 119 tickets were sold for the banquet. These large dinners are held at the Legion Hall because the seniors' hall can hold only about 50 people. However, the hall is now complete with an efficient kitchen and adequate bathroom facilities, making it ideal for use by other community groups and organizations when a hall of this size is needed.

In October 1971 the Kaslo Seniors Club became Branch 81 of the Provincial Association of Senior Citizens, and the official charter is dated January 1, 1972. The focus of the association is to provide entertainment and friendship to the older members and to keep them in touch with what is going on in the community, and to inform members as to what the latest legislative acts mean to them as individuals. The seniors still participate in community affairs by donating morale, money, time and effort to causes deemed worthwhile by them. Such causes lately have been the community bus, school bursaries, the Salvation Army, the renovation/restoration of the sternwheeler *Moyie*, hospital drives, and the Kaslo Library.

Indeed, this very book would not be possible without the dedicated support and hard work of Kaslo senior citizens, who have spent countless hours in the Kootenay Lake Historical Society Archives researching and collecting material, writing letters and fundraising in order to see the project through. The Seniors association in Kaslo continues to be active, sponsoring Lawn and Carpet Bowling clubs, Fun and Fitness classes, and holding a weekly open house where everyone is welcome for coffee, dessert, cards and games, or just conversation.

The Kaslo Riding Club Society got started on May 22, 1969, with the goals of promoting riding in all its forms, maintaining a riding facility for the use of its members and educating horse owners in the care and management of their mounts. Ed Davidson was a founding member, and Fay and Herb Thompson and Joyce Davidson joined in 1971. The club held its first May Days gymkhanas just south of the Vimy Park ball field until 1977 when the club obtained land on Arena Avenue. The club built an arena and judging stand there with the help of a government grant and volunteer labour, upgrading it again in 1989 with steel fencing and holding pens with a small

Joyce Davidson just misses the hoop—this time, anyway.
Photo courtesy of Joyce Davidson.

grant and, again, volunteer labour.

The club holds several clinics a year, both Western and English, and Joyce Davidson has become a certified Level One Western Coach. The club also engages Len Cook, a Level Two Western Coach from Oliver, B.C., to be involved with the club's teaching program. Always progressive, the Kaslo club was one of the first riding clubs in B.C. to start its riders on the C.E.F. Western Rider Preparation program. The Kaslo Riding Club Drill Team was active for five years, impressing the crowds with precision manoeuvres and bold red-and-white colours. Riding club members still wear the bright colours during the May Days Parade.

Recently the club has been involved with clearing and maintaining local trails, and in 1993 plans to work on the Silvercup Trail, east of Trout Lake.

In 1992, the May Days Gymkhana became a sanctioned Pacific Rim and Western Heritage show, complete with cash prizes, ribbons and trophies donated by sponsors from Revelstoke, Nelson and South Slocan. The Riding Club has kindled a deep-seated love of horsemanship of all kinds in many members—former member Heather Gilker is furthering her equestrian training in England; and the Thompsons have shared their interest in draft horses with many pedestrians by offering wagon rides during May Days and special events and hayride-style sleigh rides around the airport during the winter season. The club continues to be strong and well-supported, looking forward to introducing new members to better horsemanship, and improving the skills of veteran riders.

The Rainbow Square Dance Club started up in the mid-1950s, taught by Marg Ringheim. The group got together at the Scout Hall on Saturday nights from 8 to 12 and set about learning new songs and dances. Dot Morris recalls "...We started each evening and break with the round dance *Oh Johnny,* as it was a good mixer and got us all going, but, oh did we hate that tune—not to mention the dance—after a while! Another fun dance we did was to the tune of *Red River Valley.* I don't think we ever got through it without laughing so hard we couldn't finish the square."

As the dancers learned more tunes from records, they built up enough confidence to visit other clubs, with the first venture to Fruitvale. "... We soon discovered that the way of square dancing was not to learn a particular dance, but to learn the calls. We struggled, and were pulled, pushed and dragged through the evening. What a letdown! What a lesson!"

After this comeuppance, the club got live callers to hone their skills. The first caller was Doug Cake, followed by Everett Kuhn from Nelson. Mr. Kuhn had a good calling style and was a good teacher—it wasn't long before the Kaslo dancers could hold their own with the other clubs and were travelling all over the Kootenays to take in the dances. Each club had its own banner to hang on the wall when visiting another club. If the banner was "stolen," the only way to get it back was to take a least one square (four couples) to the purloining club's dance and take it back, thus ensuring that all the clubs mixed.

The Kaslo square dancers' antics became legend—they won the much-coveted Idiot's Badge on April 3, 1960. This unique badge could only be won by waking a caller in the night to call a dance. The Kaslo group got theirs by first putting on a dance in town, and after unwinding at the Morris' home, deciding to go for the badge in the wee hours. After rounding up as many dancers as they could, they arrived at Marg Ringheim's home at 5 a.m., politely requesting that she call a dance for the pajama-garbed dancers. The party dispursed from there to get supplies for breakfast, regrouping at Tom and Win Halsey's house across from the drydocked *Moyie*. In honour of the occasion many of the ladies, still in their pajamas, went across the street to invite live-aboard custodian Noel Bacchus to breakfast. Mr. Bacchus thought it was an invasion—but he did accept the invitation.

The club's Ferry Badge was won after a dance in Harrop. The criteria? The dance had to called by a grandmother and danced on a ferry after midnight.

The Kaslo School gym was the scene for a large dance with 24 squares. The Kaslo square dancers had invited the other clubs and the Argenta square dancers and their live orchestra, giving many of the dancers their first opportunity to dance to live music. It was such a hit that the Nelson club invited the Argenta orchestra to one of their dances at the North Shore Hall and of course, the Kaslo square dancers went along too.

The club flourished for quite a few years, but with the advent of television and members moving away, interest waned somewhat. The Kaslo square dancers folded in the mid-1960s when they lost their caller, closing the chapter on a fun-filled social club that spanned ten years. Jack and Dot Morris taught square dancing to an enthusiastic group of teenagers for a number of years after that, eventually quitting the activity when it was discovered that some of the teens were using it as an excuse to get out of the house to frolic elsewhere.

Scouting in Kaslo

The Scouting movement in Kaslo began its intermittent history in 1917, under the leadership of Harry Patterson, Alfred Coombs, Jack Hall and Joe Taylorson. Little information exists until the late 1930s, when it is known that Roy Green and Jack Hendren were holding meetings on the second floor of the Eagles Hall.

There was no Scouting from 1949 until 1953, when Jack Morris re-activated the movement and was leader until Jack Flamank, an RCMP Corporal and professional Scouter, arrived in 1955. Jack Morris then handed

High water in 1958—note the submerged Scout Hall.
KLHSA no. 988.40.326

over the reigns of command to Cpl. Flamank and became assistant Scout Master. Les Stilwell also assisted during these years. Meetings had moved to the old fish hatchery building (later known as the Scout Hall, the Kinsmen Hall and lately the Community Hall) by then.

The hall had a concrete floor, and in the years that followed the groups that used it wanted to put a wood floor down. Funds were scarce but the usual Kaslo pluck and ingenuity came into play once again—a well-placed request to Nelson-based Kootenay Forest Products resulted in the arrival of a load of pre-paid fir flooring; the floor was then installed and sealed in a father/mother/scout workbee. Unfortunately, in 1958, shortly after the new floor was put in, Kootenay Lake rose to near-record levels—rising right into the hall. In order to save the floor, it had to be cut into sections and raised onto sawhorses until the water went down. Until the lake was controlled by the Duncan Dam in the late 1960s, this was always a threat; luckily it did not rise to that level again before the dam was completed.

Scouting flourished for the next few years and in 1961 the troop was proudly represented by Agi Kitagawa, who was awarded the Queen's Scout Badge. After that pinnacle, the movement declined somewhat; and there are no records available until 1967, when the Group Committee of Scouts and Cubs was reactivated. Tom McKinnon, Eric Brown and Bob Wallace took on the leadership duties of the scouts, and Bob Unrau became Cubmaster from 1968 to 1974. These men did a great deal to revive the movement, introducing the troops to camping at Milford Creek, Porcupine Beach and Campbell Bay. Bob Wallace in particular was an outstanding supporter, serving the Kaslo Scouts for 13 years. He was affectionately known as Bobbing Bear around the campfire.

Brownies, Guides and Pathfinders

Brownies and Guides in Kaslo were first organized in October 1939 by Miss Hanna and Miss Illingsworth, and were sponsored by the IODE, calling themselves the 47th IODE Company. Their first enrolment took place in the United Church Hall on December 11, 1939, and activities continued until June 1947; the Shutty Bench Lone Patrol continued until 1949. The lapse continued until 1961, when Irene Wallace, wife of Bob Wallace of the Scouts, became Captain and reactivated the troop.

Captain Wallace, or Running Bear, as she was known to her troop, was devoted to the program. Until ill health forced her to retire in 1969, Mrs. Wallace led the guides through a continuous stream of activities and camping. Running Bear was awarded the Long Service Star in 1963, the Green Tree Badge in 1965, and the Long Service Bar and Chain in 1969. In 1975, Mrs. Wallace was presented with an Honorary Life Membership in Guiding in Canada as a tribute to her long association with the Kaslo Girl

Guides, and was honoured again in 1980, a year before she died, for forty years of service to Guiding. Hers was a truly remarkable contribution to Guiding, and her death was a great loss to the community.

As all things do, Guiding has changed over the years. In 1979-80, the paramilitary designations of Captain and Lieutenant were dropped in favour of Guiders for the leaders, and age groups were altered—Brownies, six to nine years, and Guides, nine to twelve. Pathfinders were introduced for girls aged twelve to fifteen, but a Kaslo unit did not start until 1984 when Elizabeth Van Horn, Kim Davidson, Debbie Seath, and Shannon Budde became the town's first Pathfinders with Kay Knox as Guider. Mrs. Knox has widened her experience considerably since then—in 1990 she accompanied the Beaver Valley Pathfinders to Switzerland and England.

Since then many dedicated leaders have come forward, including Darlene Borley, Darlene Matthews, Judy Hawes, Barbara Bavington and Leah Honkanen, all of whom have provided invaluable help and guidance.

The 75th birthday of Guiding in Canada was celebrated in 1985; the Kaslo tribute included an award-winning May Days Float that featured Bob Unrau and Irene Parker playing the roles of Lord and Lady Baden-Powell, the founders of the movement, accompanied by Guides dressed in uniforms from years gone by.

Brownies, Guides, and Pathfinders have been meeting in the Legion Drill Hall since 1986, when they moved their activities from the Scout Hall. Some of the regular events the girls enjoy are camping, bike hikes, (in which bicycles are taken to Fish Lake and, after a picnic lunch, everyone has fun on the easy downhill ride back to Kaslo), birthday celebrations for Lord and Lady Baden-Powell, torchlight parades on festive occasions like the Christmas Lightup, and fundraising activities, which are happily more for fun than from need.

Winter Sports in Kaslo

The ancient Scottish sport of curling came to Kaslo very early on—it is believed that the first game was played in 1893, with the players using rocks that had been purchased from Scotland by private members. Two sets of these rocks were donated to the Kaslo Board of Trade Ladies Night of April 27, 1950, by C.E. McKinnon of Cranbrook, whose father purchased the rocks while living in Kaslo. It is believed that these are the first curling rocks in B.C. to be imported directly from Scotland. The rocks are in custody of the Kootenay Lake Historical Society Museum, and are currently in storage. One set has been engraved with all the names of the original McKinnon rink and the date of 1893.

Typical of club president G.O. Buchanan, 1895 was a busy year for the new organization. That year the club sent an order to the Smith Arm Co. of

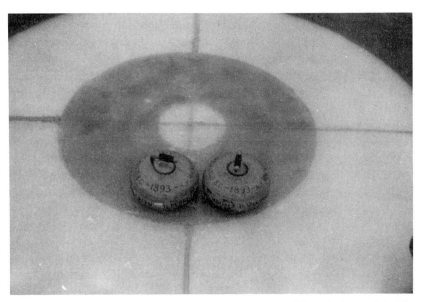

Two of the 1893 stones, pictured on four-foot rings on a Mirror Lake curling sheet.
KLHSA 988.40.707

Winnipeg for sixteen pairs of red hone curling stones. The club presumably used the McKinnon rocks to play its first annual bonspiel on Mirror Lake. The club also visited Nelson, taking their rocks along and playing a pick-up game with an ad hoc team. An application for affiliation with the Manitoba branch of the Royal Caledonian Curling Club (RCCC) was sent off and the RCCC responded by sending a medal which was made a district trophy, won for the first time by Horace D. Buckle at the original Mirror Lake bonspiel.

Rival towns took up the challenge; in the winter of 1896-97 Sandon had a curling club; and at the Rossland Winter Carnival in 1898 Nelson, Rossland, Sandon, Kaslo and Golden formed the Kootenay Curling Association. The Rossland club was formed in November '98 and the Nelson club was formed a month later. The Golden club became affiliated with the RCCC in '94; the Revelstoke club began in November 1900, Greenwood in January 1902, and Trout Lake by 1904; Cranbrook held out until October 1906 to form its club.

Since Kaslo was the instigator of the winter sport in the Kootenays, it was only fitting that Kaslo construct the first curling rink in the area. Using freshly-milled lumber from the Buchanan Mill, this was accomplished in 1896 on the site of the present-day Kaslo Motel and included a skating rink in the centre of the ice with two curling rinks on either side.

The arena lasted a good 40 years, but by the late 1930s, the roof had been taken down or had finally collapsed due to snow, causing an end to curling in Kaslo for a while. However, skating and hockey continued in open

Curling at Mirror Lake. This isn't in the 1890s but it must have looked pretty much like this in those days. This has to be in the pre-arena days. KLHSA no. 988.40.710

air at this location and in at least two others over the next 30 or so years.

In the 1950s the Bluebell Mine in Riondel was in full swing and Cominco, operator of the mine, helped the community build a curling rink there. Interest in the game was good enough for eight or ten avid Kaslo curlers to make the trip to Riondel by boat, embarking from Dr. Besecker's wharf at Woodbury Point. The company boat came across the lake from Riondel to pick them up. The first time the team went to Riondel the home team was told to take it easy on the Kaslo rink, as it had been a number of years since most of them had curled. However, Jack Morris recalls that in that game, played against the Buz Mausley rink, the Kaslo team scored an eight-ender—a perfect end. That game became fairly famous around these parts and Mausley never did live it down.

By the early 1960s, Kaslo curlers, lamenting the lack of local facilities, formed the Rainbow Curling Club in 1962. They arranged to salvage materials from a large building in the abandoned mining town of Retallack, and in June 1963 the Village Council granted permission to erect a two-sheet curling rink in Vimy Park. The proposed building was to be put to other use in summer months, making it accessible to the community. However, a heavy snowfall in the winter of 1963-64 caused the building in Retallack to collapse. Plans to dismantle the building that spring were cancelled, and curling in Kaslo languished again.

In 1966 further discussions with Council took place and public meetings were held; through this process it was determined that a skating

The Isaac rink proudly display an eight-ender—curling's most coveted score—at the Kaslo Curling Club in the 1988-89 season. Members are, from left, Aya Higashi, Irma Freeman, Ernie Johnson and skip Peter Isaac.

rink was the first priority, followed by the need for a curling rink. In 1967, Canada's centennial year, this opinion was amplified when the local centennial committee called for suggestions from the public for an appropriate centennial project—and an arena was the overwhelming choice. A committee was struck to see the project through, consisting of Jack Morris, Bob Howlett, Kurt Thomas, John Morrow, Morley Hyatt, Pat Remple, Cappy Jacura, Shelagh Leathwood, Stan Leathwood, Albert Edwards, and chairman Glen Allen.

The most suitable location was the mill site that T&H Sawmills had recently vacated at the junction of the Back Road and Highway 31. There was room enough to expand on the flat land and once the property was secured a building committee was struck. Once again the energy of the Kaslo volunteer pool was tapped; but all the grants and hours of donated labour and equipment time could not make up the total amount required to fund such a structure.

To fund the Arena from the tax base, a referendum was called for, and failed. Two more referendums were undertaken, and the third one was successful. After one of the failed referendums, $21,000 was borrowed to keep the project on track. The loan was backed by thirty local guarantors, each responsible for $1,000. How's that for community support?

The logical course was to make the facility a Regional Arena, and the only way to make this possible under government legislation was to have

*The 1978 Kaslo Figure Skating club called their 1978 carnival "Movie Magic."
Featured sets and songs from musicals like "Grease," to the crowd's enjoyment .
Photo courtesy of Molly Semenoff.*

Area D of the Regional District of Central Kootenay and the Village of Kaslo form a Recreation Commission. In January 1969, Regional Recreation Commission #2 was approved.

The Curling Club now boasts two temperature-controlled sheets and a well-appointed lounge that seats 110 people. Bonspiels are still a popular event, attracting teams from all over the Kootenays and the Boundary Country. These tournaments are held for all combinations of players; men's, ladies' and mixed teams all compete for trophies, prizes and of course, fun.

In addition to user fees, funding for the arena now comes from both Kaslo and Area D, and controversy has arisen over the distribution of the taxes; certain parts of Area D are objecting to having to pay for a facility that they do not, or at least rarely, use. In 1993 there were rumours of yet another referendum being held to decide how much Area D would contribute to the Arena; the outcome of the referendum would determine the level of funding and manner in which the facility is operated.

All this controversy has not affected the success of the Arena in providing much-needed winter sports facilities; there are healthy programs active for juvenile, junior, intermediate, gentlemen's, oldtimer and women's hockey. A nationally-affiliated figure skating program began in March 1977, and continued sporadically until the late 1980s.

The annual highlight of the figure skating program was the carnival—

the first annual figure skating carnival packed in a capacity crowd of around 250 onlookers, all crowded around the boards and in the bleachers for the show. Clubs from Nelson and Nakusp were also represented, and by all accounts the show was an immense success. The club went on to participate in clinics and to compete in regional competitions held in neighbouring Nelson, Castlegar and Nakusp.

The Kaslo Figure Skating Club produced quite a number of graceful young skaters over the years. The lasting effect of the program is still in evidence when these skaters, now grown up and many of them with children, take to the ice during public skating days.

Moms 'n Tots skating continues to be a popular activity—and the sight of little tykes taking their first shaky strides on ice has created many fond parental memories over the years. Figure Skating in Kaslo is not dead, merely at rest—hopes are high that a new program will be in place by the winter of 1993-94.

During the 40 years or so that the original covered ice rink operated (1896 - 1936), quite a number of successful hockey teams that came out of Kaslo—second to none in the province. In a letter to C. Roy Fahrni, editor of the *Kootenaian* in January 1948, Tom Allen of Kaslo chronicles the accomplishments and members of the *Kaslo Falcons*. ". . .They first organized in 1921, disbanding spring of 1924. The team was composed of: Len Garland, goal; Harry Hewat and Bill Zwicky, defense; Raymond Butler,

Hockey as it was played in 1940 in Kaslo.
Photo courtesy of Mary Johnson.

centre; Don Calvert, right wing; Russell Tinkess, left wing; Bill Rouleau and Harry Timms, utility men; Gus Carney, coach; Tom Wilson, manager. Hockey was in high gear during that period, and young and old alike discussed hockey with great enthusiasm. *Nelson Wanderers* gave *Falcons* their stiffest battles, but in all the games I believe *Falcons* came out on top. *Nelson Cubs* also put up some smart games against the *Falcons*; New Denver couldn't get a look in, and Nakusp was taken into camp to the tune of 21-1. . . ." Allen notes that the game was not the same in the twenties as it was in 1948. ". . .Rules were quite different then: a forward pass would be considered an offside, and the blue lines were not even thought of then, but the type of hockey was fast and team play was pretty to watch. . . ."

Allen's letter indicates that in the winter of 1935-36, he and Art Bennett managed the covered arena; and that previous to that, when City Council intended to condemn the structure, the Kaslo Hockey Club came forward and promised to make the repairs. For their efforts, they were rewarded with the responsibility of running the arena, turning over between $500 and $600 in one season. ". . .we had nine games with outside teams, winning six, losing three. We did what we could to help the younger boys at their hockey, and no girl or boy was turned away for not having sufficient funds. . . ."

At the time of his January 1948 letter, it appears Allen was concerned that the open-air arena that the Kaslo Recreation Association was operating on the south side of the Kaslo River (where the village equipment yard is now situated) would be closed. Some things never seem to change—controversy still looms over the continued well-being of the arena, although the location of the facility has changed. In the end, the open-air arena was closed, due to difficulty in keeping any kind of ice in good enough condition. Kaslo skaters eventually moved out to Mirror Lake, which has a reasonably safe ice cover when the weather is good and cold.

For about three years in the mid-1960s, George Baker, Jack Flemank, an RCMP corporal, and Jack Morris flooded the unused lawn bowling grounds to make a skating surface. The men worked in shifts through the night, flooding the rink so there would be ice for daytime skating. Jack Morris recalls that there were several apple trees there they would spray with water, creating ice sculptures that would glisten beautifully under the lights left there from the lawn bowling days.

By 1975, the present arena was completed, ushering in a new "ice age" in Kaslo. The hockey side of the new facility had a regulation-size ice surface, spectator bleachers, players' benches, two dressing rooms and an upstairs viewing room—and skaters galore. Hockey in the first few years saw all sizes, shapes and calibres of players, with equipment as varied as the players. Lack of state-of-the-art equipment did not hamper the neophyte league—all you needed was skates and a stick to play in those days, much as it was in earlier years.

As time marched on, minor hockey became well organized with a team in each category: Peanuts, Atoms, Peewees, Bantams and Midgets. Although Kaslo's smaller teams usually competed at a slight disadvantage against teams from Nelson, Nakusp, and other larger towns, their pride and spirit made for great games, if not a great number of victories. Bonds formed through small-town team play would never be broken, as evidenced by "six-pack" pick-up games during Christmas holidays, when old friends and adversaries take to the ice for a few friendly games.

By the end of the 1970s several teams had come and gone in a men's hockey league—the *Highways,* the *Ghosts,* and the *Kaslo Hotels* had all fallen by the wayside. Finally, remnants of the *Ghosts*, who boasted no two players wearing the same jerseys, were successful in obtaining sponsorship from T&H, the local sawmill. The team was called the *T&H Burners* and their first game, against New Denver, was a come-from-behind 8-7 victory. Although a dynasty was not created, the *Burner* legacy lives on; the team is still active, competing in other Kootenay towns, enjoying the occasional victory and hosting an annual hockey tournament. Interestingly, the present *Burners* feature the first and only full-time female goaltender, Karma Halleran, playing Gentlemen's Hockey in the Kootenays.

What happens to old *Burners?* They move on to the *Kaslo Oldtimers Hockey Club.* Formed in 1982, the club is focussed on players over 35, and boasts of having the second-oldest active hockey player in Canada on their roster—Tudor Rutherglen, who was 75 years young in 1992, plays left wing for the team. The *Oldtimers* hosted their first tournament in 1983, and have continued the event annually, inviting teams they have played against from the east and west Kootenays and eastern Washington state. This offers a lot of practice for their goaltender—yes, the *Oldtimers* also make use of the considerable talents of Karma Halleran; another compliment to her skills.

Ladies' Hockey has been active in Kaslo since even before the completion of the Kaslo and District Arena. A spirited group of women got together and formed the first of many fun hockey clubs. The *Dynamic Dolley's* were an eager bunch; so eager that the team had water transported up to the uncompleted building to make ice so they could play as soon as possible. With coaches Dennis Johnston and Bob Reimer, the *Dolley's* played teams from Nelson and Trail. The Trail team was *the* women's hockey hotbed at this time and while the *Dolley's* didn't win, the Kaslo team hung in there and had lots of fun.

Soon after the Arena was completed, a girls' hockey team was formed. The *Kootenettes* worked on their skills for about a year and a half before they set up a game against the *Dolley's*. It was, in some cases, mother against daughter. The game was a competitive one; it brought out the primal urges in both sides. There are reports that some of the *Kootenettes* were quite "put out" when the *Dolley's* would stop the game to help them up after a collision.

The *Kootenettes* continued for about eight years; eventually interest waned and veteran players were no longer replaced by new players. Ladies' hockey in Kaslo languished for about two years before Kaslo Lodge owners Dave and Daphne Seath sponsored a team. The newly formed *Kaslo Girls Hockey Team* played other Ladies' teams from Nakusp and Nelson for a few years, with the ability of some of the players being noticed by other teams. The Nelson team was bold enough to try a Ladies' Hockey Tournament in Kamloops, but to augment their roster they invited Kaslo players Jane Seath and Karen Semenoff to join them. Competition was stiff; teams from all over B.C. were there and the overall skill level of the teams was very high. Nonetheless Kaslo goalie Karen Semenoff came away with a Most Valuable Player trophy for one game.

This taste of highly competitive play stuck with a few of the ladies—hockey just for fun just wasn't fulfilling their competitive desires. After five years of playing teams from Nelson, Nakusp, Creston and Spokane with coaches Murray Pearson and Glen McRae the girl's team took on Pete Vass as coach.

With a new coach, a new team direction came to pass. The new focus for the team was to become a competitive team, paying off in 1989 when Lil Olson, Ruth Thomson, Karma Halleran and Sheri Gentles were invited to join the Trail team to go to the B.C. Winter Games in Penticton. Again, the experience fuelled their desires to play more competitive hockey and toward this end women from Kaslo, Nelson and Nakusp decided to join forces to finally ice a competitive club. After considerable deliberation, a new name was chosen of accurately reflect the atheletes and the *Kootenay Lakers SR "AA"* Women's hockey team was born.

The team has fared well—guided by coaches Pete Vass, Glen McRae and Jack Staples and manager Donna Stroup they have garnered a berth at the B.C. Winter Games two years in a row; narrowly missing the medals each time. These experiences have cemented their competitive spirit, and now a girls' team has been iced to indoctrinate new players. There are still hopes to begin a ladies' hockey dynasty based in Kaslo and why not?

Golf

In the spring of 1922, a group of prominent citizens had garnered enough private financial support to form a company in order to start a golf club. Twenty-one subscribers had offered $100 each "with more to come . . . ." The target was 250 shares at $100, but fewer than 70 subscribers were ever found. Among this group were Mayor James Anderson and *Kootenaian* publisher Frank Rouleau, and on September 7, 1922, a provisional executive was appointed with Mr. Anderson as president.

The city of Kaslo held approximately 20 acres of level benchland on the south side of the Kaslo River, but public support was needed to cancel the land's park reserve status. The executive went to work at canvassing taxpayers, and the fact that the mayor of the town and the publisher of *The Kootenaian* were spearheading the effort likely did no harm. In an open letter to his readers, Mr. Rouleau pointed out the attraction of a golf course to summer visitors and ". . . other benefits accruing to the villages from currently useless land. . . ," drawing attention to the golf courses that existed at Cranbrook, Balfour, Nelson, Trail, and Rossland. He advocated early public support for a proposed bylaw so that work could commence in the spring of 1923.

Bylaw 198 was not actually passed in council until October 1, 1923, but its effective date was December 31, 1922. The lease was for 10 years, rent $1 a year, with an option to buy for $1250. By the fall of 1922 the provisional directors were sure they had enough support to have the first fairways surveyed by a Mr. Dunn and were going ahead with the incorporation of a company, using the Nelson golf club's incorporation papers as a guide for their application.

The first four fairways were finished by November 1923, with three other temporary ones. Temporary greens had been built so that the 50-foot-square permanent greens did not have to be used until the following season.

In March 1924 the directors decided to fence the property and to erect what they termed a shelter building behind the first green. In April of that year, they decided to go ahead with the installation of a water system, believing that ". . . success of the venture depends largely on water supply for growth and maintenance of greens. . . "

The course was officially opened on July 9, 1924. Membership dues for the opening season were $15 for men and $10 for ladies, and green fees were $1. It seems that the original intent was to tee off near the pavilion and play the first hole due north, to the present ninth green, or somewhere in that vicinity. However, an old score card indicates that the first fairway was the current second.

The land originally available was only about 20 acres; it did not include the 7.4 acres known as Holmes' Orchard. Exactly when this piece was added to this course is uncertain—it could not have been before October 1928, when the orchard reverted to the city for non-payment of taxes. In 1925, club records show ". . .the matter of acquiring Holmes' orchard at $300 plus taxes was discussed. . . ," and in 1932 Mr. Anderson wrote to the club from the coast, stating ". . .my impression was the club paid Col. Holmes so much cash for a quit claim deed . . .but where the city comes in, I don't exactly recollect. . . ." This part of the course, known as "the dog's leg," is quite steep and is a popular toboggan run in winter.

By September 1924, ". . .five fairways were in playing shape. . . ," and on the weekend of October 18-19, the club's first tournament was played.

The winners were: match play, men's, Frank Rouleau; ladies', Mrs. Anderson. On August 6, 1925, it was reported that ". . .the balance of the fairways was complete. . . ." Sand and oil greens were still evidently in use, but there was at least one grass green.

Kaslo's first hole in one was achieved on June 12, 1925, by Bob Smith, a golf professional from Calgary. It wasn't until April 1928 that the first hole in one by a member was recorded by R. H. Graves on what is the present third hole.

In August 1925 Col. H.H. Armstead, an American engineer with mining properties near Kaslo, presented the club's first trophies, ". . .two handsome sterling silver cups, one each for men and women. . . ." The tournament was 18-hole match play for men, and nine holes for women. The first winners were E. H. Latham and Mrs. J. Hamilton.

By September 1925, the full nine holes seem to have been in play—and this would have been without Holmes' Orchard. In April 1926, Mr. Anderson donated a trophy to be competed for annually at the opening of the course by teams from the surrounding area.

October 1927 saw the introduction of medal play and no improvement of lie to be permitted—a hardship for some players. That year the club closed with a cash balance of $100. ". . .thanks to the thrifty supervision by its Scots president. . . ."

By June 1930 there were 45 members, and in 1932 dues, which had been raised, were lowered "owing to the hard times." The fees went back to: men $15; ladies $10; juniors $3; these rates persisted until 1937.

Club records from March 1941 to March 1963 are missing and those for the period 1963-1967 are not very informative. The Rainbow Open tournament began in 1948, and there is a reference to a grass green (number six) being readied for the 1954 competition. In 1958, the clubhouse site was moved to its present location, and the present sequence of play probably dates from then.

The sand greens required special grooming after play. A cocomat on a long handle was dragged around the green to level it and fill in the footprints. During tournaments students worked the mats and were used a ball spotters.

By July 1970, at least two greens—one and four—were still sand and it wasn't until 1974 that the "possibility of starting grass tee-offs" was discussed. These seem to have been completed by 1978 or 1979, as was the putting green.

July 1993 marked the 69th anniversary of the course's opening. The course remains a unique challenge, with straight hitting being the first requisite with a subsequent battle when the greens are reached.

The Kaslo Golfer's Lament

(with apologies to Edgar A. Guest)

Little ball upon the tee,

What will be your history?
Lying there so clean and bright
Will you travel left or right?
How to solve that ancient riddle—
How to hit you down the middle.

Such ambition I have nursed
To break a seven at the first
Or to hit a proper drive
Off the tee at number five
And when at last my drive is straight
I hit the pine on number eight.

Little ball upon the tee
Please oh please don't go o.b.
Let's forget this day of sorrow—
Perhaps a bogey round tomorrow?

N.B. Matthews   April 1992

Tennis

Sports of all kinds have always played an important role in the social fabric of the town. As early as 1899, the sports facilities of the town were being touted in a Board of Trade publication, *Health and Wealth—Kaslo, the Lucerne of North America,* which advertises "...On all sides throughout the city and suburbs evidences of permanent places of recreation are in evidence... On top of the plateau overlooking the main portion of the city and lake are the base ball grounds. Not far distant therefrom, but in a more isolated spot, is the rifle range used by the Kaslo shooting association and the Kaslo rifle club. Two excellent clay courts for the lovers of lawn tennis are also provided, and a thoroughly equipped gymnasium will soon be one of the attractions. . . ."

The original clay courts were on the west side of Kane Street, close to the Kaslo River, but by the late 1920s Jack Strachan, the owner of the land, decided he needed his land to grow vegetables. New clay courts were constructed by volunteers at Vimy Park on the flat area where the maypole is now situated. Then as now, that area was used for the maypole dance and other May Days festivities. However, by the 1950s use of the courts had declined severely, so the town fathers decided to tear up the courts and seed them over with grass.

Henry Giegerich had built a veritable mansion up on Nob Hill in 1900; part of the charm of the place was its grass tennis courts. It is very likely the courts were in use by the early 1900s. These were probably more for social than seriously competitive reasons, and eventually were even used for a short time for lawn bowling. After the Giegerich family sold the property, the courts fell into disuse.

It wasn't until 1976 that the Kaslo Tennis Club became reactivated, its members focussing their efforts on constructing a tennis court once again in Vimy Park. These efforts proved fruitless, and the club dwindled to three members—Margaret Dallyn, Tom Humphries, and Pat Haegedorn. Not to be thwarted, these avid players arranged with the Kaslo and District Arena Committee to use the concrete-floored arena for tennis in the summers of 1980 and '81. Volunteers painted lines on the floor and two old nets were repaired and used. Pauline and Gordon Carlson provided the caretaking, and fees were $2 an hour plus a key deposit.

In 1983 the Kinsmen Club decided to pitch in and build a tennis facility that would last. The land, just south of the arena, was leased from the Village of Kaslo and sale of the logs helped offset some of the levelling and paving expenses. Donations of labour and machinery kept costs down—but when the courts were ready there was a debt of $17,500 remaining. The tennis club had reorganized itself into the Kaslo and District Tennis Club, with Margaret Dallyn as president, and agreed to assume the debt. Dennis Jensen, an untiring worker in the development of recreational sports in the area, helped the club a great deal at that time in its efforts to pay the debt.

The club was successful in paying it off, and in addition to the usual fundraising events, membership fees and grants, several community-minded citizens took out charter memberships—and then never played a game on the courts. The club even raised close to $8,000 to upgrade the surface with an acrylic coating. Keith Raby and Charlie Allen provided volunteer assistance to the pavers in this case, again keeping the cost within reason.

In 1993, the club appears to be in as good shape as its playing surface is—and according to club treasurer Tom Coonce, the club is financially able to resurface the courts when the need arises. A healthy membership of about 30, which includes families, couples and singles, is ensuring the club's success—and the courts are second to none in the Kootenays, a fact that keeps visiting players and coaches coming back for more than great scenery.

Lawn and Carpet Bowling

The Giegerich tennis courts became the town's first bowling green in 1938. At the instigation of St. Andrew's United Church minister J. Fielding Shaw, the club met for the first time on March 5 of that year. The first consideration was a playing surface, and Henry Giegerich was approached in this regard. He agreed, and the club lost no time in electing its first executive: Henry Giegerich, honorary president; J. F. Shaw, president; G. Willington, vice-president; Frank S. Rouleau, secretary-treasurer; G. W.

*George and Cecil Morton discussing strategy during the preparation of the Lawn
Bowling grounds between the Kaslo Hotel and the Blue Ridge Motel on Front Street.*

Lawn bowlers enjoy one of the first games on the newly-created greens in 1984

Tinkess, Al MacPhee, and Henry Larsen, grounds committee; E.C. Cherry and George Baker Sr., membership committee.

After one year on the Giegerich courts, the club moved its activities to Front Street between the present Blue Ridge motel and the Mariner Inn hotel, where it is situated today. The city council agreed to let the club use the property, even agreeing to level the ground for it. An order for 16 pairs of secondhand bowls (bowling balls) was sent to Vancouver, and the club paid between $4 and $6 a set of four. Membership fees for men were $5 for the season, ladies' fees were $2, and game fees were set at 25 cents per game. The men and ladies had separate leagues. The first mower was purchased for $32.50, less 5%, as quoted by Mr. Giegerich.

By 1940 lighting was in place, but by 1954 interest had waned. Despite the best efforts of club president Jack Morris, the club became inactive and the bowls were put into storage. The nice, flat bowling grounds ended up as a parking lot.

In 1972 a group of Kaslo senior citizens started a carpet bowling club with a grant from *New Horizons,* a federal program designed to help senior citizens work together for their own or their community's benefit. The grant enabled them to buy four carpets and sets of bowls, and with the Legion providing support and facilities, a healthy indoor carpet bowling league developed.

Interest for outdoor lawn bowling was once again revived in 1980, and a group of carpet bowlers leased the old bowling grounds. Under the expert leadership of brothers George and Cecil Morton, club members got to work screening several loads of topsoil and adding sand and sawdust to it, making an excellent base for the grass bowling lanes. By 1982 the bowlers were back in action again, with some 37 members.

The bowls were taken out of storage and a few members ordered new ones. Popularity for the gentle sport grew, and lawn bowling in Kaslo is now enjoyed every year by both local and visiting players. The highlight is the Bank of Montreal annual tournament, where trophies donated by the bank are vied for in the season's wrap-up. Cecil Morton still maintains the grounds in exemplary condition, and the club's goal is to continue to provide recreation and pleasure for all ages for many years to come.

Badminton

Badminton was played in Kaslo, but little information has come to light in the course of researching this book. What has come up is interesting, though. In the 1940s and early '50s the game moved around town quit a bit—it was played in the Eagle's Hall, the Legion Drill Hall, the vacant Methodist church and on the third floor in the City Hall. The players must have been enthusiastic to overcome the shortcomings of the various venues—in the City Hall location, the floor space was too small for the legal lines, so the back line was marked about three feet up the back wall. This made for a very fast game. The Drill Hall also made for a fast game—short courts, combined with the low ceiling kept the game very interesting. Accordingly, during these years it was a non-competitive school sport.

When the new school gym was built in the early '50s it could accommodate three full-size courts, and interest intensified in the sport. A community Badminton Club was formed around 1955, becoming quite popular. Community rivalries sprang up, and players from Ainsworth, Balfour, Procter and Nelson regularly came on Tuesday and Sunday nights, braving legendary Kootenay winter weather at times to compete. Some of the better players competed in B.C. Open tournaments, held in Nelson on occasion, with some teams making it to the semi-finals, but by the late 1970s interest in badminton as a competitive sport had pretty much dropped off.

Fishing

Fishing has always been one of the main recreational activities of local residents—and one of the main attractions for tourists who take to the lake year after year looking for the elusive big one. Giant Gerrard rainbow trout are the biggest, hardest-fighting prize; the next favoured game fish is the bull trout (Dolly Varden), which is technically a char. Kootenay Lake also has a history of being a good source of kokanee (landlocked sockeye salmon).

Some of the catches in the old days are legendary—Ole Johnson describes how he and his son caught one of the biggest rainbows: ". . . .Here it was that Alvin, my son, and I caught one of the largest rainbow—a 32 1/4-pounder in 1968. It was caught on one of my own hand-carved yellow cedar plugs. We had put out one of these mysterious phantoms on 300 feet of wire line and a three-ounce sinker on the leader approximately 30 feet from the lure. The whole world seemed to explode before our eyes. At fourteen years old, Alvin was already a seasoned fisherman, and was lightning-swift when it comes to answering to bend of the rod and scream of the reel. This one pulled off 300 feet of wire line three times before we could even get a glimpse of a dorsal fin. Then, about 50 feet from the boat, he churned the water in a close circle exposing his back. 'Did you see the size of his fin, Dad?' 'Yes,' I replied—it looked like a Japanese fan. After about 45 minutes. . .he finally relented and let me net 'Kahoona.' We decided to cut the hook out and bail water on him—he kept breathing through his top gill quite freely so when the water rose in the bilge he closed the top gill and breathed from the bottom gill for survival. We got back to the marina as quickly as possible for a weigh-in and picture before letting him go. It was 45 minutes before he splayed out his fins, erected his body and swam under the dock and then out into deeper water. . . ." The Johnsons were practising catch-and-release long before it became fashionable—indicative of true sportsmen.

Not as many big ones have been caught in the 1980s and '90s, due to several factors. The most important factor is the construction in the 1960s and 70s of the Duncan and Libby dams, which now control the flow of water into the Kootenay Lake system. In addition to supplying hydro power, the dams control flooding; unfortunately, a side-effect of the dams is that life-nourishing nutrients become trapped in both the Duncan and the Libby storage areas. The lack of these nutrients, now unable to move down into Kootenay Lake, has caused a decline in the algae and zooplankton that feed the kokanee, which in turn feed the larger fish. Ironically, the purity of Kootenay Lake now threatens some of its marine inhabitants.

The regulated flow of the lake has also affected the giant sturgeon that were once more prevalant in the system upstream of Kootenay Lake. Their reproductive cycle is triggered by naturally-occurring spring high water periods, and now that the Libby Dam no longer permits these natural fluxes of water levels, the number of sturgeon has dropped dramatically.

Measures have been taken to improve the situation; in the summer of 1992 the Fish and Wildlife Branch of the B.C. Ministry of Environment, Lands and Parks began a carefully-monitored five-year experimental fertilization program to try to enhance the growth of algae and zooplankton in the North Arm of Kootenay Lake. Preliminary results appear promising—according to biologist Jay Hammond, the experiment has increased algae and zooplankton in the North Arm.

Fish biologists —and anglers—hope these measures will be enough to ensure a productive supply of fish for generations to come. At least we can

Regatta goers Roy Green on top of car, George Greenwood, Bill Henrdren, Gordon Bowker, Kay Butler Elder, Minona Rouleau, Jack Riddell, Murray Elder, Walter Hendricks and Fran Rouleau. KLHSA no. 988,40.1727.

Bathing In Kaslo; not too many motorboats in this photo.
KLHSA no. 488.40.392

admit that mistakes have been made in the past, and we now have the will and technology to try to keep Kootenay Lake in good shape for generations to come.

Boating

Ever since the first natives arrived in Kaslo in their sturgeon-nosed canoes, boats and boating have been an important factor in the growth of the town. The early pioneers didn't have much in the way of fancy boats, but they looked after what they had. Tender loving care was lavished on most of the small craft owners cleaned and painted them every year or every other year for good reason—frigid Kootenay Lake is no place for a leaky boat.

A greater variety of boats came into use as the century progressed, some of them powered. It was a need to shelter these expensive boats that brought a group of launch owners together at the home of avid boater and Methodist minister James Calvert on January 19, 1914. Present at the initial meeting were Dr. Calvert, J.F. Robillard, W.E. Zwicky, Stanley Menhinick, Alfred Taylorson, David Kane and A.T. Garland. A committee was struck to look into securing a suitable location, driving piles and putting in a walkway. In late April the Kaslo Boat Club decided to incorporate under the Benevolent Societies Act; Dr. Calvert was chosen as commodore of the club, an honor he held until his death in 1927. David Kane was the club's new captain; A.J. Curle was mate. W.E. Zwicky and O. Strathearn were also on the first board of governors. Senator R.F. Green was contacted to procure suitable foreshore privileges in the present location, and William English was contracted to drive the pilings and build the floating walkway.

In 1923 the Kaslo Boat Club, realizing the potential of Kaslo as a summer resort, decided to stage a regatta for the enjoyment of the summer visitors as well as the townfolk. The first regatta was not unduly pretentious but improvements and refinements were made in the following years, leading to the first big water carnival in 1928. By then outboard motors had become popular, and the races that took place were thrilling. The fastest boats around came to race, including Lewis Gilbert's famous *Lady Bird,* the fastest boat in western Canada from 1933 to '49 with a speed of 68 miles per hour. Two-day water carnivals became popular, and before the Depression of the thirties really hit the Kootenays, it was the biggest event of its kind in the Interior of the province.

The grand regattas are no longer held, although the club began sponsoring the newly-revised "Bang and Go Back" May Days race in 1990 and plans to continue promoting safe boating practices.

It wasn't until fall 1980 that the Kaslo Bay Marine Club came into being, born from need of moorage. By then all existing moorage space at the Kaslo Boat Club was taken and the Jones Boys Marina across the bay was full—the only way a boater could find moorage was if someone died or

The Kaslo Boat Club (foreground right) and Marine Club (at far left).
Photo courtesy of G.D. McCuaig

moved out of town. Expanding the Boat Club facilities was viewed as too expensive a proposition; the water is quite deep and the club members already had their own moorage—understandably, they were not interested in taking on the expense of leasing and building new facilities.

When a federally-controlled offshore lot became available for lease, a public meeting was called to see if there was enough interest to form a new club willing to take on the task. There was—and in short order a name was chosen, the society incorporated under the act, and a lease was signed for the property adjacent to the Kaslo Boat Club. Everything was ready to go but just before construction started in 1982 the provincial government stepped in with a stop-work order, claiming that the federal government had no juristiction over the property and the lease was therefore null and void.

Long negotiations were undertaken, it came to light that Marathon Realty (the real estate branch of CPR) actually owned the land that the access road was on, putting everyone in a trespass situation; and topping it all off the B.C. government was insisting that no lease be given to anyone until a fire-damaged portion of the existing wharf was either repaired or removed. In 1983 the Village of Kaslo council jumped into the fray after several unsuccessful attempts to reach a solution. Council called a meeting of all the interested parties, and it worked—some progress was made with the round-table approach. It still took until May 1987 before all the details were worked out and the lease, which would cover both boat clubs as joint tenants, was executed.

The Kaslo Bay Marine Club has built up its facilities since then and has managed to retire its debt, allowing the 52 members to look forward to years of enjoyment of their hard-won facilities.

Certain Kaslo Buildings, Beings and Events

In 1895 Kaslo was honoured by a visit from the Governor-General of Canada, Lord Aberdeen, and his wife, who were touring Canada. The streets were decorated with trees, flags and streamers. A huge crowd gathered to see the boat arrive with the vice-regal party. After an inspection by Lord Aberdeen, school was dismissed for the day. The Governor-General also granted the children an additional day's holiday to be taken "when they liked."

In describing this visit, Stella Kane, the teacher, said ". . .Jimmy Carney, son of Augustus Carney, government timber inspector, sang very sweetly for the visitors. This pleased them all immensely but not nearly as much as an extra day's holiday pleased the children. . . "

At the death of Queen Victoria in 1901 the community of Kaslo staged an impressive memorial funeral service, preceded by a long parade consisting of the city council and all the citizens of note in Kaslo at the time.

Quite a number of homes had been built up on Nob Hill besides the Kane home by the late 1890s. The people living there had to use the wagon road, which was rough and winding, or a trail up the bank. A trestle bridge over the railway track was built in 1898, giving the name Bridge Hill to the short—but steep—grade. Gust Carlson was awarded the contract, and William English excavated the cut at the top of the bridge. James Speirs had a subcontract for hauling timbers for the bridge. Mr. Speirs worked at G.O. Buchanan's sawmill before the bridge contract, later clearing three acres of virgin forest and working up a fine fruit farm in the western part of town. In addition to his farming interests, he also served as alderman for eleven years.

Bridge Hill, now commonly known as the Post Office Hill, is steep and slippery in winter even now. This is evidenced quite often when fully-loaded logging trucks, turning west (up the hill) from Highway 31 to Highway 31A, become stuck; these are often helped up the hill with a tow from friendly Bel Maintenence sanding or plow trucks.

Paving has replaced the bridgework that covered the hill, and the grade has been filled in across the old K&S railway bed, but when the bridgework was in place there was a height of thirty feet from ground to bridge. A fatal accident occurred there on October 31, 1936, when a car driven by Mrs. Papworth plunged over the side to the ground. She was accompanied by her

A view from upper Kaslo. Notice the trestle bridge descending the hill.
KLHSA no. 990.5.6

husband, Mayor W. Vilder Papworth, and W.P. Rudkin, the CPR station agent. The exact cause of the accident is not known, but the conditions were stormy; the car was travelling up the hill when it went over the south side of the bridge. Alice Augustine heard the noise of the crash and told her brothers Paul and Otto, who ran to the scene. Tommy Beck also heard the racing motor and after investigating, phoned for Dr. D. J. Barclay.

The car had struck the ground upside down; the three injured people were taken to the hospital, but Mayor Papworth died in a few minutes without regaining consciousness. Mr. Rudkin suffered a broken leg and wrist along with cuts and bruises. Mrs. Papworth was the least injured, suffering only broken ribs, bruises and shock because of her somewhat protected position behind the steering wheel; the injuries Mr. Papworth sustained included a badly crushed chest, a skull fracture and a broken neck, any one of which was sufficient to cause death.

Funeral services were held on the following Wednesday, with Rev. J.F. Shaw of St. Andrew's United Church and Rev. T.W. Reed of Rossland officiating. Among the many mourners were Nelson's Mayor J.P. Morgan, Alderman A.G. Ritchie and City Clerk W.E. Wasson; pallbearers were Ronald Hewat, S. A. Hunter, A.T. Garland, H.S. Whellams, Walter Hendricks and A.S. Exter.

An interesting footnote to this is that present-day Kaslo resident Margaret Jardine was invited to ride up the hill in the Papworth car, but at

The parade commemorating the death of Queen Victoria, 1901.
KLHSA no. 988.40.192

the last minute, she spotted her husband Andy coming to pick her up. She declined, avoiding a brush with death.

The building that still serves Kaslo as a City Hall was built in 1898. D. J. McLachlan of Sandon received the contract as his bid of $9,977. After 95 years, the City Hall is still in good condition and now houses the Kaslo Public Library in the basement; the Kaslo Volunteer Fire Department, a cinder-block building, is attached to the northern side of the building. There have been discussions about the removal of the fire department building and its replacement with a park and parking facilities, but as of this writing, no final decisions had been made.

In the early 1950s, a proposal was made to have a more modern building erected in its place but Kaslo's future direction toward a heritage theme was assured when popular opinion dictated that the hall was a landmark and should not be destroyed. Largely due to the efforts of Roy Green, the building was repaired, has since received several paint jobs, and renovations are planned to restore the third floor of the building.

In the 1980s the council chambers were moved to the south side of the building's main floor, which had been vacated when the library moved into the basement. In 1988 the building was designated a national historic site and a plaque was dedicated to it on the southeast corner of the property. This wooden city hall is one of only two wooden frame municipal government buildings still in use in Canada; under the careful stewardship of heritage-conscious village councils, it should continue in use for many years to come.

The Drill Hall was constructed in 1901 by the Dominion government for the Rocky Mountain Rangers, known as the RMR. The land was donated by the town, but the plans and financing came from Ottawa. The RMR had been formed from five independent militia companies, one of the Kaslo Rifle Company, established on July 1, 1898. The other companies were in Kamloops, Revelstoke, Rossland and Nelson. The RMR included members of the pioneer families of Kaslo, among them David Kane and Alfred Coombs. In the Boer War of 1899-1901, three Kaslo members of the RMR—W. H. Moodie, G. H. Wilkins and Alfred Coombs—volunteered for duty in South Africa.

In the First World War, many men from the region joined the 54th (Kootenay) Battalion, which went to England in November 1915 and on to France in August, 1916. The 54th served with distinction under the command of Lt.-Col. Arnold H.G. Kemball, a veteran of the Indian Army who had settled at Shutty Bench. Col. Kemball was killed at Vimy Ridge in 1917. After the war, the Great War Veterans' Association was formed to further the interests of veterans; it operated until November 17, 1926, when the British Empire Service League, affiliated with the Canadian Legion, issued a charter to establish Branch 74 of the Canadian Legion in Kaslo. (The Legion changed its name to Royal Canadian Legion in December, 1960.)

The Kaslo Cadet Corps, circa 1921. Mr. Brown is teacher and leader.
KLHSA no. 988.40.538

From the 1920s to 1935 the Drill Hall was leased from the Department of Defence, but in 1935 the government asked for tenders to tear down the hall, citing the belief that the hall could not be operated by private enterprise in a town as small as Kaslo. Objections from the town were heard and the Legion stepped in to save the building from demolition. Walter Hendricks, Jack Riddell and Roy Kreuger were appointed to the daunting task of dealing with the government. Miles of red tape and many difficulties had to be overcome; but the three persevered and finally the transfer of title was made.

Over the ensuing years, Branch 74 has evolved into a community service organization while at the same time upholding the aims and goals of the Royal Canadian Legion. Actively involved in community affairs, the Kaslo Legion Branch financially assists youth organizations, school programs and bursaries, senior citizen activities, Christmas hampers and the Victorian Hospital of Kaslo. These are among an endless list of charitable undertakings. One of these, begun in 1982, is the care and maintenance of the Kaslo Cemetery—Legion members have worked tirelessly on this project since then. In 1988 a memorial stone was erected at the cemetery in memory of all the veterans buried there.

Every Legion branch has a Ladies Auxiliary and Branch 74 has been doubly blessed through the years with a dedicated and supportive auxiliary. Their charter was granted on August 1, 1933, with members Pearl Abey, Kate Abey, Kate Billings, Hetty Carney, Gladys Driver, Edna Horner, Nancy Lect, Ellen McGibbon, Sophia Moulton, Anne Mayze, Dorothy Palmer, Louise Tinkess, Nellie Seamark, Elsie Smith, and Margaret Whittaker in attendance. As of this writing, Pearl Abey is still a member of both the auxiliary and branch. Over their 60-year history the Ladies Auxiliary have worked hard and given generously to charities in Kaslo and beyond.

One of their first endeavours was to sponsor a dental clinic, and during the Second World War they contributed to the war effort by gathering various items for overseas parcels, sending a little bit of home to the armed forces in Britain and Europe. One outstanding worker for the auxiliary was the late Edna Horner, who was a devoted member for over 50 years. Mrs. Horner was eventually honoured by Dominion Command for her service. Her specialty was knitting socks and laprobes—hundreds over the years—for distribution to veterans in hospitals.

The Drill Hall was and is still used by all manner of groups for all manner of reasons; Cadet meetings, Legion functions, large public gatherings and dances. There is even a 20-yard shooting range in the basement, suitable for rim-fire rifles or handguns. Although the gun range hasn't seen use since the early 1980s, at one time there was a healthy membership. An article in the May 16, 1963, edition of the *Kootenaian* reports that the new Legion Gun Club was organized under RCMP Constable Paul Grudniski. The club got off to a good start with a membership of 70 people, consisting mostly ". . . of young children but there are 11 married women who are turning out. . . ." These ladies impressed the constable—the article also reports " . . .The women are, even though I hate to admit it, our best shots," murmured the range officer Paul Grudniski. . . ." The other range officers were Norm Stranberg, Sam Nofield, and Bill Seafoot, whose duties included supervising and instructing the groups, which gathered six nights a week.

The enthusiastic shooters registered their club with the Dominion Marksman Group and at the time of the article twenty members had already earned their bronze pins (10 targets scoring 80 or better); eight members were working for their silver pins (10 targets scoring 93 or better); and some were working on their gold pins (10 targets scoring 95 or better).

There is only a remote possibility that the indoor shooting range will be reactivated now, due to recent renovations and construction that have made the range all but inaccessible and hard to insure without extensive (and expensive) upgrading to the Drill Hall structure and substructure.

Before the turn of the century, the Green brothers were operating two stores, having rented the Blue Ridge Hotel as their second place of business. In 1902, the stores of Henry Giegerich, the Green brothers and H. Byers were amalgamated under the name of Byers, Giegerich, Green and Company. This was soon dubbed the Big G by local residents; it was taken over entirely by Henry Giegerich in 1924; eventually the building was taken over by the Farmers' Institute, which name stuck, even through the years the Women's Institute owned it; it was sold in 1982 to what is now Kaslo Building Supply Ltd.

A notable feature of the building was a two-foot earthen floor between the basement and the ground floor; it is unclear whether the dirt insulation was to protect store stock from fire or to provide a safe place to store explosives. The dirt was removed when the building recently underwent a substantial restoration from the foundation up.

Now known as the Farmers' Institute building, it is at the northeast corner of Front and Fourth Streets, and is still prominent in downtown Kaslo. It now houses many businesses: Osprey Cycle and Fitness, the Your Arts Desire Craft Store, Carrie's Stationery, the offices of Dr. Philip Olsen, MD, and Mountain Crafts Westminster Wind Chimes Factory. The building features textbook examples of tin cupolas on the roof; they have been used as "living samples" for restoration experts in recent workshops.

Dave Kane became postmaster in 1900, succeeding S. H. Green who had established the post office in a small building on Front Street. Kane moved it across the street and continued as postmaster until his death in 1937. He also conducted an insurance business and was interested in civic affairs, serving as mayor for one term; he was an alderman on the first City Council and for nine yearly terms in total. In addition, he served on the School Board for years, and also held offices as police magistrate and judge

The wooden-framed Victorian Hospital of Kaslo.
KLHSA 988.40.266

for the juvenile court. His widow, May Millington, moved to Calgary.

The years from 1896 to 1900 were Kaslo's most prosperous era. It had become the leading city of the Kootenays and its citizens were proud of its facilities, industries and scenic beauty. It was often called "the City of Energy." The mines were producing profitably and this prosperity was enhanced by the granting of the lead bounty. In 1898 G. O. Buchanan was sent to Ottawa to represent the Kaslo Board of Trade and other interested citizens concerning a duty on lead imports. This facilitated the granting of the bounty, and Buchanan was made Inspector of Lead Bounty.

John Keen was appointed Mining Recorder, Assessor and Collector in 1897. At one time he owned the townsite of Poplar, beyond the north end of Kootenay Lake, and had many mining interests in that area. During the First World War, he was elected as Liberal member of the Legislature for the Kaslo-Slocan riding, later becoming Speaker of the House and Clerk of the Legislative Assembly. During their entire residence in Kaslo, both Mr. and Mrs. Keen were indefatigable workers for the welfare of the town.

Hospital History

The Victorian Order of Nurses Hospital was built in Kaslo in 1903, mainly due to the efforts of Mrs. Keen and her brother W. J. Twiss. On the occasion of Lady Aberdeen's visit to Kaslo in 1895 with her husband, the

Governor-General, Mrs. Keen became friendly with her, and the necessity of a good hospital in Kaslo was discussed. Lady Aberdeen was the founder of the Victorian Order of Nurses, a fact that no doubt was helpful when the VON agreed that if the citizens of Kaslo and district would donate $1,000 and procure a suitable site, the Order would grant the sum of $1,500 for the purpose of establishing a hospital. Mrs. Keen and Mr. Twiss headed the canvassing committee and with many generous donations, together with a $400 grant from the City Council, the necessary amount was soon procured. The site, up on the hill directly opposite the Giegerich residence, was donated by the Kaslo-Kootenay Land Company, and a contract was let to James Speirs for grading and stumping the lots.

In a characteristic display of Kaslo's independence, that first hospital was built entirely with funds raised from the VON and the community. An excerpt from the *Kootenaian* of July 30, 1903, reads ". . . Considering the depression times we have been passing through, the erection of a $5,000 hospital free from Government aid is a matter for congratulations, especially so when it's practically paid for. . ." Donations came in cash from ten of the mining companies and in items from numerous households—china, pillows, chairs, tables and the like.

On October 12, 1903, the hospital was formally declared open. It was the first VON hospital in Canada. The first nurses were Miss Ford serving as matron and Miss Campbell as nurse; the matron was paid $41.66 a week and the nurse earned $30 a week—very good wages for the time. Both were from Revelstoke and members of the Victorian Order. Dr. Gilbert Hartin was the first resident physician and surgeon; he remained in Kaslo until 1907, when he moved his practice to Nelson. In 1896 Dr. Hartin had also built the first hospital in Kaslo located on A Avenue between Third and Fourth Streets.

The first patient to be admitted to the Victorian Hospital of Kaslo was Edward Kennedy on October 19, 1903; the first of four cases in the two and a half months remaining in that year. The first baby born in the hospital was Edna, daughter of Mr. and Mrs. George Lingaard. Edna was presented with a silver cup by the ladies of the hospital committee and was the first of five babies that year.

Throughout the years the doctors have contributed a great deal to the hospital, and with the help of capable staff have performed operations that are almost legendary today.

Early in 1922, a boat accident claimed the life of Dr. George Carruthers Read. Well-loved by the community, Dr. Read began his service in 1912. The Dr. Read Memorial Ward was established in his memory as was an X-ray machine. Dr. D.J. Barclay was appointed as the hospital physician in April 1992 to replace Dr. Read, whose death had occurred while he was on his way to treat a patient across the lake at Riondel.

The following years brought difficulties and problems, financial and otherwise, but they were faced always with courage and ingenuity; the hospital board of directors, augmented by the Ladies Auxiliary, managed to overcome these problems until August 1963, when the hospital had to close due to being unable to find a doctor. Dr. L. D. Besecker, a retired American-born doctor, came to the aid of the community, taking up practice from 1964 to 1968.

Dr. Besecker came to Kootenay Lake on vacation in 1936, fell in love with the area and migrated here in 1940. He purchased Woodbury Point, just north of Ainsworth, and began working on his property until he was called to service in the US Army in the Second World War. Upon returning from the war he hoped to establish a sanitarium on his peaceful property, but was unable (or more likely unwilling) to meet Canadian medical criteria for such a facility. Instead, he was granted a temporary licence to practise medicine, which he did until the arrival of two doctors when he again retired. The good doctor came out of retirement in 1964 to help the community keep the hospital open, and again in June 1973, when he served until his successor Dr. Paul Trotman arrived in July 1974.

Kaslo will always be in the debt of Dr. Besecker, who loved fishing. And he didn't let fishing interfere with his work (or vice versa)—when he was on the lake, and a call or an emergency came in, a white flag was run up from his downtown office signalling him to come in off the lake.

Even as the directors were desperately trying to find a doctor to keep the hospital open in 1963-64, they were also looking ahead toward replacing the 60-year-old building. In February 1964 they received approval in principle from the provincial Minister of Health of the day, Eric Martin, to build a ten-bed hospital. Provisional to construction of the new facility was an integrated administration and co-operation system with the Kootenay Lake District Hospital in Nelson; this became operational in May 1967. The new hospital was finally opened of October 16, 1971, after a long bureaucratic battle. Corey Ross Jacobs, son of Opal and Bruce Jacobs, was the first baby born in the new hospital, arriving on November 23, 1971.

Every area needs a hospital; every hospital needs an ambulance. Before 1953, water taxis operated by Fire Chief Roy Green Sr. and later by Fred Jones, were used to transport the sick or injured from all points north on Kootenay Lake. The job must have been a good money-maker—Fred Jones built a house strictly from the proceeds of his water taxi.

When the mines were operating, miners in need would be met and carried by any vehicle available. Land transportation of patients was handled mostly by volunteers from the Fire Department. No set vehicle was used—anyone who had an appropriate vehicle like a van or station wagon was eligible to be the ambulance driver. Volunteers would be on standby to transport anyone in need of pre-hospital care, leaving their phone number at the hospital. One of the sayings in those days was if you owned a station wagon, you now drove the ambulance. Always community-minded, Jack Morris and Bob Jones made themselves available for this work quite often.

With financial aid from the Kinsmen Club, the Village of Kaslo and the Fire Department, in 1966 an ambulance van was purchased and housed in the fire hall. The Kinette Club purchased a stretcher for the patient's comfort and supplies were furnished by the village. The entire effort was completely volunteer-driven, and many people gave willingly of their time with no compensation for their trouble. People like Bob Jones, Roy Green Sr., Jack Morris, Pat Rempel, Bruce Tate and John Surina were among those volunteers, and their commitment sparked interest in the younger crowd; Roy Green Jr. and Dennis Tyers started even before they were of age. Mr. Tyers started in 1963 and is still active; his sons Andy and Jeff are also actively involved in the Provincial Emergency Preparedness program.

On July 1, 1974, the B.C. government implemented a complete review of pre-hospital health care being provided throughout the province. A new agency of the Ministry of Health—the Emergency Health Service Commission—was formed to give direction to Canada's first provincially-funded and operated pre-hospital emergency medical system. The result is that now all vehicles, equipment and supplies are supplied by the province and staff is trained to provincial standards in the latest techniques of care. It is the responsibility of the community to provide enough manpower to staff the vehicle 24 hours a day; a duty that Unit Chief Mrs. Jackie Greer has overseen since 1978, when Pat Rempel retired from the post.

The ambulance has been temporarily housed in the Kaslo Automotive building across the street from the fire hall, but plans to build a new station near the hospital are underway with a probable completion date in summer 1993. The new station is expected to serve the community well into the next century.

Kaslo Community Bus

The Community Bus concept was initiated as a result of a single-car accident involving a group of teen-aged hockey players returning from a game in Creston in winter of 1975-76. There were a few broken bones but luckily no serious injuries.

A community bus seemed to be the ideal solution. Stan Leathwood, father of one of the injured boys, brought the matter to the Village Council with the support of Alderman Garfield Belanger, and council agreed to support the project. A committee was struck, consisting of Gar Belanger as chairman, and Herb Thompson, Tom McKinnon, Jack Humphries, Isabel Wassick, Mary Johnson, and Stan Leathwood as members. Consequently, the Community Services Society was created and registered under the

Societies Act to see the project through.

The committee discussed several methods of fundraising and decided to act decisively—they asked every organization they could think of for a donation. The response was good—typical for Kaslo—and along with private donations, the committee raised approximately $8,000 in the community. In the spring of 1978, with the assistance of a Go B.C. grant, they bought a twelve passenger bus, which served until usage increased. It was then replaced by a twenty-two passenger bus.

The format and operation of the bus was simple: Wednesdays were set aside exclusively for seniors, and youth organizations or sport groups could rent the bus for a kilometre-plus gas charge if they supplied a qualified driver. The community-funded bus was also available for private individuals and groups. In later years a small subsidy was set up to help defray costs to youth groups.

Special mention must be made of Al Lund, Terry Kusyk and Ron DeForest, senior citizens who took on the maintenance and operation, scheduling, rentals and records on behalf of the society. These dedicated people parked the bus on their property and, in addition to the upkeep and operation, volunteered to drive. Their contributions helped make the bus service the success it was. Gar Belanger, the first committee chairman, spent much of his free time driving the bus for the seniors. Joe Scarbo was chairman of the transportation committee when B.C. Transit extended its service to Kaslo. An indefatigable advocate, Mr. Scarbo not only worked toward the maintenance and adminstration of the bus, but was also involved in developing the B.C. Transit agreement.

Many people have contributed to the operation of the community bus, all on a volunteer basis. Thanks to the initiative and hard work of these community-minded people, public transportation is available to Kaslo residents to Nelson on a regular basis and throughout town twice a week.

Fruit Growing in Kaslo

As more permanent residents moved into Kaslo it didn't take long for their thoughts to turn toward industries other than mining and logging. Soon after the turn of the century as it became evident that the soil was very suitable for fruit growing, particularly Gravenstein apples, and later Bing and Lambert cherries. Men cleared acres of virgin forest, and soon small farms dotted the surrounding area,with several in the city limits as well.

By 1908, Kaslo fruit was famous all over the province. It was equal to any produced in the Annapolis Valley in Nova Scotia, which at that time was claimed to be the best in the world. J. Will Cockle was the Kaslo pioneer of this industry, and it was due to his foresight and enthusiasm that the Kaslo Fruit Growers' Association was formed and the new industry made such progress. For many years the cherry industry prospered, bringing added

You are invited to

The First Canadian
Cherry Fair

KASLO, - - B. C.
July 31st, 1912

An invitation to the First Canadian Cherry Fair. Courtesy of Margaret Jardine.

income, not only to farmers with their large orchards, but to many house-holders as well. Cockle, born in England in 1853, had arrived in the Kootenays in 1884; with his brother Rex he later established a boatbuilding business in Kaslo. He was in the hotel business in Kaslo for several years, but had always been interested in fruit growing. His farm, on the road leading out to Shutty Bench, became one of the best in the neighbourhood. He eventually sold the Kaslo Hotel, which he operated with W.V. Papworth, to dedicate the rest of his life to fruit growing with outstanding success. His son Leonard became a doctor after serving in the First World War, and practised in Trail for many years.

By 1906, on Will Cockle's suggestion, the first Annual Fruit Fair was held, sponsored by the Fruit Growers' Association, of which he was president and A. J. Curle was secretary. The fair was a great success and the Fruit Growers' Association sponsored it for five years. Subsequently, it was sponsored by the Women's Institute. Exhibits were shown from all the surrounding districts, including Creston, and the Kaslo fair was the outstanding event of its kind in the Interior. A beautiful Challenge Cup was competed for by fruit growers' associations all over the district. During the next few years, Kaslo Gravenstein apples and Bing cherries became world famous. Exhibits were shown in various exhibitions and fruit shows, meeting with outstanding success. Kaslo apples won first prize at the Canadian National Exhibition and at the Fruit Exhibition in Chicago in 1912. When fifty-six boxes from various growers, including James Speirs, Will Cockle and Otto Augustine, were packed carefully and sent to the Royal Horticultural Society's Colonial Fruit Show, they carried off the society's highest award in competition with fruit from all over the world. Kaslo cherries were no less famous, winning the first prize in London in 1909 and again at Wembley in August 1924.

The first Canadian Cherry Fair was held in Kaslo in 1912, and was very successful. By now, cherries had become more popular with the growers than apples, as the financial returns were considerably better. Everyone with even one lot or two lots planted one or several cherry trees, depending on the size of their land. Cherry orchards became numerous throughout the district.

In August 1924 a Cherry Carnival was held in the Drill Hall, when 500 cases were on display. Some of the cherries were so large they resembled small plums, and the spectators agreed it was an unforgettable sight. Some of this fruit was shipped to England, and received the highest award at the Fruit Exhibition.

In 1932 the city fathers had cherry trees planted on the boulevards and along the streets instead of shade trees. This was an excellent idea, and tourists marvelled at the luscious cherries to be had for free.

Unfortunately, cherry growing as an industry is now a thing of the past. A tree disease, tentatively diagnosed as an unknown virus, struck the orchards. The fruit did not mature, but remained small and red. Called Little Cherry, this disease has blighted the orchards to a great extent. A few trees still produce fair-sized fruit but for the most part pears and apples have been planted instead of cherries.

A new fruit growing district, directly north of Kaslo, was named Shutty Bench after the Shutty family who arrived there around the turn of the century. They were Slovaks, and had emigrated to Canada from a part of the Austro-Hungarian Empire that later became Czechoslovakia and in 1993 became the independent nation of Slovakia. (In early documents, Shutty Bench and Shutty Creek were shown as Schuletty.)

This district produced many tons of cherries in the prime fruit-growing days; today the area has developed into a kind of suburb to Kaslo. Several vegetable farms exist there now along with a few hobby farms and resorts— and quite a few private residences too, which provide a quiet place to live for those who seek it in the hectic days of modern life.

As an industry, fruit growing in Kaslo and area is now pretty much defunct except on a local level; fruit and vegetable growers find a market for their goods almost exclusively in the Kootenay Lake region. The Okanagan Valley and lower Fraser Valley have taken over as the pre-eminent fruit and vegetable areas in the province—Kaslo and the Kootenays are now primarily residential, with forestry and tourism providing the bulk of employment. Mining is still an active consideration now, though not nearly the great driving force it once was here.

The first locomotive arriving at Kaslo.
KLHSA no. 990.31.6

The K & S Narrow-Gauge Railway

The battle that was fought for the right to be the distribution and service centre of the Kootenay-Slocan mining district was finally won by Kaslo, thanks to the completion of the Kaslo & Slocan Railway. The project was initiated by Alexander Ewen, John Hendry and Daniel James Munn, three Vancouver-New Westminster entrepreneurs who had acquired land, timber and mining interests in the West Kootenay before 1890. These men were associated with the New Westminster Southern Railway, which began service in 1891 between Brownsville (opposite New Westminster on the south bank of the Fraser River) to Blaine, so they knew something about the railway construction business.

On April 23, 1892, they secured a charter from the B.C. Legislature to build a railway link from Kaslo to Sandon, a distance of 32 miles. They were to receive a subsidy of 10,240 acres of Crown land for each mile of railroad constructed, with the expectation that the land's value would increase once the line was complete and its sale would recoup the consortium's investment.

The financial panic of 1893 delayed financing of the project, but the trio eventually persuaded James J. Hill, president of the Great Northern Railway (GNR) to advance them enough money in 1895 to keep their contractors, Foley Bros. & Guthrie, going on with the work. A heavy price was paid, however—in order to repay the GNR the $916,000 it had advanced them, Ewen, Hendry and Munn had to turn over most of the stock they had received as payment for their services. This made GNR the major shareholder in the Kaslo & Slocan Railway.

The K&S, as it was known from the very beginning, ran through the most prominent silver-lead-zinc mining district in the province at the time, and its favour was courted by large U.S. railways for tonnage. According to a newspaper report of the time, "...It sassed, bucked and licked the great big Canadian Pacific to a fare-you-well. Oldtimers still recall with glee when the little line, with a stout cable and snatch block, snaked into smithereens the brand-new depot building of the big company, erected on ground claimed by the K&S at Sandon. ...."

The little wood-burning engines climbed the steep grades daily, returning with heavy loads of ore to be loaded onto the barges at Kaslo wharf. It is claimed that its one and only coach was formerly Brigham Young's private car. The coach did a fine business with passenger rates at seven cents a mile, and a Klondike scale on foreign traffic. The roadbed was rough, winding and steep, hugging the sides of the mountains, crossing torrential streams and dodging snowslides. Oldtimers used to say that if the stumps got too large, the K&S line ran round them. It skirted Payne Bluff; 1080 feet of straight drop with a "grasshopper" trestle, and the travellers used to swear McGuigan bridge was built of telegraph poles. However, it was the lifeline of the Kootenay-Slocan mining industry, and without it, Kaslo and its surrounding district would have had a much tougher go of it.

In 1900 it was taken over wholly by its major shareholder, the GNR. By then the mining industry in the Kootenays was in the grip of a deep recession; the Boer War was dampening the enthusiasm of British investors; and the Klondike Gold Rush had become the focus of many if not all those prospectors and labourers who were free to follow their fortune to the big strike.

In spite of this turndown, the Kootenay Railway & Navigation Company, a GNR subsidiary that had been formed to run the K&S and to expand railway lines in the area, still saw fit to institute a phenomenal service; a trip from Spokane to Sandon in a mere twelve hours. This was made possible in November 1900 when a fast express train was put in service between Bonners Ferry and Kuskonook, at the southeast end of Kootenay Lake, connecting with the speedy sternwheeler *Kaslo* for Kaslo and for Nelson via the steamboat transfer point at Pilot Bay. From Kaslo passengers transferred to the K&S and *voilà*—the 1900 equivalent of rapid transit.

Unfortunately, Sandon had been gutted by fire on May 3, 1900, and was still recovering and rebuilding. Kaslo itself was no longer a booming settlement, and fewer and fewer passengers were making the trip on the steamer *Kaslo*. The summer of 1901 brought no upswing in traffic and so the Spokane express was cancelled. The *Kaslo* was assigned to the Nelson-Kaslo run, formerly the *International's* run, and the *International* was put into relief service.

Traffic remained light throughout the first decade of the 20th century; despite this the GNR continued to bankroll the heavy operating costs. The roadbed of the K&S was a triumph of creative engineering, but was prohibitively expensive to maintain. Each winter saw huge slides wiping out large sections of track between Sandon and Bear Lake, necessitating costly trestle and track rebuilding year after year.

The chief business of the line was hauling zinc ore from producing mines in the Kaslo River valley to the sampling works in Kaslo Bay; the refined product would then be hand-bagged and loaded onto a sternwheeler or a barge for transport to Troup Junction at Five Mile Point on the south shore of Kootenay Lake's West Arm. There the product would once again be hand-loaded, this time onto standard-gauge railcars for shipment via Spokane to smelters in Iola, Kansas, and Bartlesville, Oklahoma, where abundant supplies of cheap coal provided economical smelting. This method of shipping was quite costly, and the brunt of it was borne by the shippers.

As that first decade wore on, the GNR continued to operate and maintain the K&S, although improvements or expansion of the service were not undertaken because the parent company was unconvinced that the volume of traffic could warrant the expense. Still, the GNR refurbished the

International in 1906 so she was fit to be the regular vessel on the Kootenay Lake steamer run. That refit apparently did not extend to the ship's boiler; in 1908 it was condemned and the vessel withdrawn from service while management pondered what course of action to take—to patch the boiler, or to replace it with a new or used one. In the meantime, the *Kaslo* was put back in service, although her hull was in poor condition and her operating costs were higher.

The *Kaslo's* somewhat tender condition resulted in frequent interruptions of service while she underwent repairs at the CPR shipyard in Nelson. During the bitter winter of 1908-09 the *Kaslo* was often kept in port for days at a time while the tug *Hercules* was chartered to provide a skeleton service, thereby reducing operating costs. To make matters worse, the heavy snowfall that winter caused slides in February that wiped out key sections of K&S track between Bear Lake and Sandon. The GNR executives had just about had enough; they were reluctant to rebuild the line, and from then on rail service terminated at McGuigan station.

Things kept going downhill; on a stormy May 27, 1910 the *Kaslo* struck a submerged piling as she eased out of the wharf at Ainsworth, causing a fatal breach in her stern. She put in to shore at nearby Munn Creek, where the passengers and crew disembarked. The stricken ship was later patched and towed to the Mirror Lake shipyard, where she was hauled up on the ways and left to rot for the next six years while the company struggled to dispose of her.

A new boiler was finally to be ordered for the *International*, but in July 1910 a devastating forest fire wiped out all the trestles and culverts on the K&S line west of Sproule's, a station 14 miles west of Kaslo. Rudimentary weekly service was maintained between Kaslo and Sproule's until December 24, 1910, when the following notice was posted: ". . .account of illness of engineer, impossible to operate train on K&S until further notice. Public will be advised re trains later. P. H. Walsh, Supt."

Mr. Walsh never did come forth with any further information, and the new boiler for the *International* never arrived—the GNR had finally called it quits. The *International* was finally sold to Gus Matthews of Riondel and beached in Galena Bay, just south of Riondel. Over and above its capital investment, the GNR subsidiary, the Kootenay Railway & Navigation Company, incurred more than $850,000 in operating losses to provide service on the K&S line throughout the first decade of this century. Not only did the GNR have to endure this considerable loss, but the company also had to take considerable flak for abandoning its support for the mining industry in the Kaslo area.

The Kaslo Board of Trade didn't take the abandonment lying down. A telegram to the GNR's head office in St. Paul, Minnesota, was ignored until a second telegram was sent demanding an answer. When it came it was most unsatisfactory, stating ". . . the matter is under consideration." Some of the

The S.S.Moyie as she pulls out for her final voyage to Nelson.
Photo courtesy of Margaret Jardine.

mines, including the Utica, had closed until better transportation could be provided.

When several weeks passed without any further information, the Board of Trade appealed to Premier Richard McBride and the Legislature at Victoria for assistance. They asked that the GNR be forced to make public its intentions or, by act of legislature if necessary, its charter should be cancelled. The board met with excellent co-operation from the government, which looked into the matter at once. The Premier was assured by GNR officials that the line would be reopened to Sandon and repair work would start at once. Meagre repairs were started but were soon abandoned. The Board of Trade struck a permanent committee to deal with the railway matters: James Anderson, John Keen, W. E. Zwicky, G. O. Buchanan and John Retallack. These men worked many long, hard hours in a seemingly useless effort as time went on and the GNR had done nothing further.

At a meeting of the Associated Boards of Trade of Southern British Columbia, of which G.O. Buchanan was president, a resolution was sent to the Legislature asking that if the GNR did not give a positive guarantee of immediate repair and promise efficient operation, the charter be cancelled immediately. The argument was that the company had received a land grant of 212,763 acres and had been exempted from taxation for several years, but was not fulfilling the terms of its charter; therefore, it should be cancelled.

In January 1911 a public meeting was called by Mayor F.E. Archer to discuss the whole situation. John Retallack was sent to Victoria to bring the matter before the Cabinet. Neil Mackay, the local MLA, R. F. Green, and Premier McBride worked unceasingly to get satisfaction from the GNR officials. Finally, on April 21, 1911 word came that they had agreed to dispose of the K&S right-of-way and rolling stock for $25,000.

Previous efforts had been made to interest the CPR in the little line, but to no avail. It now became apparent that a local syndicate would have to be formed to take up the option. A public meeting was called and $19,000 was guaranteed before it opened. A second $25,000 had to be raised for operating expenses, but liberal aid was received from the government which proposed to guarantee the bonds of a new company to the extent of $200,000 free of interest for three years, then with four per cent interest, the government taking first mortgage on the line as security. Also, the government was to take over the roadbed and reimburse the owners to the extent of the purchase price if, at the end of three years, the company found they it could not operate the line to advantage.

John Retallack made another trip to the Coast, and plans were made for reconstructing the line. The line would be put in shape to McGuigan as soon as possible. Work on the line to Sandon would be undertaken later if conditions warranted it. The members of the local syndicate greeted these plans with enthusiasm and the future looked brighter than it had for many months.

However, matters remained at a standstill for some time as the GNR delayed turning over the roadbed and rolling stock until the papers were drawn up and signed. Further delays were caused by the news that the CPR was extending its line six miles from Three Forks to Bear Lake. This caused

Kaslo well-wishers seen from the deck of the departing S.S. Moyie on her final voyage.
Photo courtesy of Margaret Jardine.

a great deal of apprehension as it meant ore from the Whitewater and the Lucky Jim would be sent over this route, and would make it impossible for the K&S to operate. Henry Giegerich and James Anderson were sent by the City Council to interview Sir Thomas Shaughnessy, president of the CPR, in Montreal and point out to him that the building of this spur would ruin the K&S Railway and cause the mines from Bear Lake to Kaslo to be without transportation facilities other than the old wagon road (a road that had been repaired but was of little use to the mine operators in comparison with the railway).

Sir Thomas received them courteously and offered to place the matter before the CPR board as soon as possible. However, the CPR officials felt it was in the best interests of their railway to build the spur, but offered to assist the K&S as much as possible—for instance, CPR barges would be furnished to handle the ore from Kaslo, thus saving the syndicate a large expenditure.

Repairs were to be completed to Sproule's by the fall of 1911, and from there to McGuigan in the spring. Almost everyone in Kaslo had an interest in the K&S by this time. The City Council had contributed $5,000 toward the operating fund and also granted freedom from taxation and free water. As matters progressed, countless difficulties arose; these were met with characteristic Kaslo resourcefulness and pluck.

As a result of B.C. government negotiations with the CPR, a telegram was received from Neil Mackay, MLA, in February 1912 stating that the company had agreed to take over the line, reconstruct it to standard gauge as far as Sandon, and "... thereafter continuously maintain and operate same as part of its system in British Columbia. . . ." For this, the McBride government made a grant of $100,000 to the CPR. This news caused great rejoicing, as it had long been hoped that the big company could be induced to take over the line. When work was completed, the CPR would operate a standard-gauge line from Kaslo to Nakusp, with a branch up to Sandon.

Premier McBride paid a visit to Kaslo shortly after this announcement, and was given a splendid reception. With him were the Attorney-General, the Premier's private secretary and several other officials, and newspapermen. A salute was given as the boat rounded the point, and a large number of citizens were at the wharf to greet the party. Mayor A.T. Garland was chairman at the luncheon given at the King George Hotel and it was ". . . conducted on a scale of magnificence never before attempted in Kaslo. . . ." The Premier was assured of the gratitude felt by the citizens of Kaslo for the work done in negotiating with both companies.

As the CPR started work at once installing the standard-gauge line, the affairs of the local railway syndicate were wound up. All subscriptions were refunded and a dividend of 10 per cent was declared, with the possibility of a smaller dividend later. This delighted the shareholders, who had given the money almost as a donation to a cause in which they were vitally interested.

It was brought out at the meeting that Messrs. Giegerich, Anderson, Retallack and Oliver T. Stone had contributed their services without charge throughout the entire proceedings — also that Neil Mackay had given the syndicate free legal advice besides his work as a member of the legislature.

The new railway opened on July 1, 1914, with a free excursion trip from Kaslo to Nakusp. This was on the suggestion of G. J. Bury, vice-president of the CPR, when he visited Kaslo in June. He was much impressed with the determination and resourcefulness displayed by the citizens in their struggle to retain the railroad. Alderman James Speirs ". . . had a prancing team hitched to a buggy down at the wharf and took Mr. Bury and the Mayor for a spanking drive through the city as far as MacDonald's Addition . . . ."

A large number of residents of Kaslo and the surrounding district took advantage of the excursion trip. They were interested to see something that most of them knew—that the CPR had not followed the old line around Payne Bluff, but had chosen one not nearly so spectacular but much safer. The people of Nakusp joined with the Kasloites in making the eventful day a memorable one. All commented on the excellent manner in which the trip was managed by the CPR officials.

Jack Cadden was engineer on the first trip after the July 1 excursion, J. (Scotty) Bird was brakeman and Tom Mooney conductor. Mr. Cadden remained as engineer until his retirement, and Harry Beck was roadmaster for almost thirty years. Tom Horner was section foreman for twenty-seven years until his retirement. Among other long-time local railwaymen were Alex Sutherland, Ed Clark, Bill Foote and Bill Reeves.

The CPR continued to operate the line until 1955 when torrential rains caused several hundred yards of track to be washed out at Three Forks. The line had been used to transport freight only for several years so it was considered impractical to rebuild it. This ended rail service west from Kaslo, and most of the roadbed was then used to reconstruct the Kaslo-New Denver Highway 31A.

Barge service to Kaslo continued until 1978, primarily because the Bluebell Mine in Riondel along with other provisional stops on the North Arm of the lake made the run profitable. Boxcars were loaded by hand in Kaslo Bay by sawmill employees. After the service was discontinued, the CPR station was abandoned; the ways lay neglected and the once-solid wharf began to rot. The station was dismantled in the early 1980s.

Kaslo Shipyard Company

The ways (the tracks that allow the railcars to move on and off the barges) did not stay empty for too long. In the spring of 1969, Richard Smith and his family moved to Kaslo from Calgary with intentions of establishing

DeeDee Smith christens the M.V. Cameronian, the third of the Kaslo Ship Yard Fleet. Photo courtesy of KSY.

a shipyard to build holiday charter vessels. Dick Smith, like many before him, had become smitten with the unique, powerful beauty of the lake while vacationing from his job as a chief draftsman for a large Calgary company. After years of preparatory work, the Greenock-trained Mr. Smith, his children Toby, Lorna, and Barbara, and his wife, Dee-Dee, finally moved to Mirror Lake to pursue his dream.

Lacking major financing, the Smiths began building their first ship, the MV *Cacambo*, using the back of the Farmers Institute building as their workshop and the rocky beach below as a shipyard. The ship took shape only by virtue of the Smiths' ingenuity, stamina, and implacable enthusiasm for the project. When money became scarce, Mr. Smith returned to a drafting position in Calgary during the winter while the family remained in Kaslo.

Daughter Lorna recalls the launch of the ship ". . .If daily life was exhilarating, the launching of that first ship was pure magic. It was a vibrantly sunny day in June 1970. The MV *Cacambo* sat high upon her perch of keel blocks, shuddering to be born. My sister, Barbara, and I smeared thick black oil on the two logs which sloped from the keel blocks, down the beach and into the lake. Mom and our brother, Toby, climbed aboard the ship and stood on her upper deck, smiling precariously. Dad and Alfie Jensen hammered her keel blocks away, slowly inching her 12 tonnes toward life. Suddenly, her great, smooth hull met the greased logs and in a breeze of colour she flew down her launch and met the water with a glorious splash. She was then, finally and very profoundly, alive. . . ."

The launch of the 40-foot *Cacambo* marked the inauguration of the

114

Kaslo Shipyard Company, and was the first of four (as of 1993) steel-hulled craft to be built by the company. Her modifed twin sister, *Candide*, was launched two years later in May 1972 and the *Cameronian*, a smaller (35 feet, eight tonnes) ship based on a North Sea fishing design, was launched in July 1980. The 50-foot, 21 tonne *Ariadne,* the flagship of the fleet, was built on the abandoned CPR ways, just west of where the other three vessels were constructed in Kaslo Bay. These craft were designed with functionality and stability as the prime requisites; they were built to handle any weather the tempestuous Kootenay Lake could throw at them in relative safety.

Also on the once-abandoned ways, the Kaslo Shipyard Company built a 100-foot, twin-screw passenger yacht for owner Vern Helleckson, which had not yet been commissioned by early 1993. Previously, in July 1990, the company completed a total refit of the City of Nelson's *Osprey V,* a one-time cable ferry that was motorized by the Ministry of Forests to move heavy equipment to inaccessible areas on Kootenay Lake. Nelson had acquired the ship in 1987 and found out that if the city was to insure it, it needed to be completely refitted as a new ship.

That was an interesting job for the Kaslo shipbuilder—in addition to the actual refit, Mr. Smith had to provide blueprints of the craft to the Coast Guard, creating them completely from scratch because the original ones had been lost. This entailed crawling around the bowels of the vessel with a tape measure, an unpleasant but necessary task. When the job was completed, an article appeared in the *Nelson Daily News* on July 19, 1990, entitled "Kaslo Shipyards launches Nelson's navy."

The merry fleet of the *Cacambo*, *Candide*, *Cameronian* and *Ariadne* is on the lake regularly during all seasons. Their sturdy construction and

A general view of Kaslo, sometime after 1913, when the government building was completed. Note the additions on the Langham building at left. KLHSA no. 988.40.490

115

stable designs have provided many delightful voyages for weekend skippers and crews. From their home base, the "Admiralty," Dick and Dee-Dee Smith track the movements of their little navy by two-way radios that can reach to both ends of the lake.

The Langham; its role as a Nikkei Internment Centre

The three-story Langham building was constructed in 1896 when the boomtown frenzy was in full swing. As soon as the first floor was close to being finished, the Bank of British North America (BBNA) opened for business; the rest of the first floor was used mainly for businesses like mining company and livery offices, but the upper floors were rumoured to have been bases of operation for ladies of easy virtue.

As the boom times eased themselves across the threshold of the twentieth century and into the inevitable recession, the BBNA pulled out and a long succession of short-term and long-term tenants took up residence in the Langham. There was a wide variety of tenancies—the Slocan Bottling Works, the Hewbard & Waltz Lumbering Office, the Goodenough Stables (a freight and livery company), and a myriad of promoters and general offices. Upstairs, the rooms and apartments were available to let by the week or month.

By the 1930s, the large, uninsulated building was underutilized—at times totally abandoned. Early in that decade Jack Riddell, a master carpenter, moved his shop and lumber storeroom into the Langham, and remained until the early 1940s.

After the entry of Japan into the Second World War, the Canadian government came up with a relocation policy for Japanese Canadians. Kaslo was among the communities chosen to isolate the Nikkei (people of Japanese origin) from the strategically sensitive Coast. When the first contingent of evacuees arrived aboard the sternwheeler *Nasookin* in the spring of 1942, the town must have looked pretty bleak; most of the downtown buildings and some of the private residences were vacant and in a sorry state of disrepair—sad reminders of boom days that never returned.

By the end of '42, almost 1,100 evacuees had arrived in Kaslo by boat and bus, outnumbering the residents by at least twofold. Most of the able-bodied men had been sent to build roads at various locations "in the Rockies," breaking up families indiscriminately. Conditions were generally so poor in the internment areas that what men there were set immediately to making available accommodations at least bearable, if not comfortable for their fellow internees.

Things were not quite as bad in Kaslo as they were at some places in the Slocan Valley, where the lodgings first consisted of discarded army tents, some of which leaked. These were followed by hastily-constructed

18-bȳ-24-foot cabins built of green lumber, intended to house two families to a cabin. The internees sent to Kaslo were housed in abandoned houses and the Langham—one family per room, filling the place with 78 people. The cracked windows and broken plaster did not keep the weather out.

To make matters even worse, the winter of 1942-43 was said to one of the most severe winters in 40 years. Snow was piled up to the windows of most houses and pedestrian pathways had walls of snow nearly five feet high. The roads to Nelson and New Denver were blocked by slides, and the wind was so fierce that the sternwheeler *Moyie* couldn't make it north to Kaslo. The town was completely cut off; it was almost two weeks before the wind died down enough for the ship to make it all the way to Kaslo with a load of precious supplies.

More able-bodied Nikkei men had been sent to Kaslo and the other centres from the road camps in order to help make the buildings habitable. They also built public bath houses and got firewood for the cookstoves. The interiors of the buildings or rooms were patched with newspaper and paste to stop the wind from coming through. The severe winter must have seemed excessively cruel given the circumstances, for the Nikkei came from the Coast where the weather was generally mild.

Surprisingly, the internees did not complain loudly about their situation or the government that placed them there. Instead they made every effort to make life easier for each other, sparing themselves unneccessary trouble. They began to organize; churches, clubs, the Red Cross, music lessons, sewing, cooking, and sports. The sports were varied—baseball, basketball, badminton, gymnastics, softball and kendo were popular, and the local boys were not excluded if they wanted to join in. The ladies continued to knit and sew for the Red Cross—working for the war effort the way other good Canadians should.

After seeing to their shelter, education for the children became the first concern of the adults. The Nikkei children were not allowed to enroll in the Kaslo School, so a kindergarten was started in the United Church. In the summer of '42, elementary classes were held in the park, on the beach, or at the ball field; there were no books or blackboards, and the students sat around their teacher on boards, boxes, logs or rocks on the beach. Those first teachers were untrained high school graduates and a few university students whose education had been interrupted by the war.

The fall of '42 prompted a move indoors to whatever spaces could be found throughout the town. By winter of that year all the children—over 200—were taking classes in the Legion Hall. There were no partitions, possibly making it the first multi-grade classroom of its size in British Columbia.

The B.C. Security Commission, which co-ordinated the movements and administered to the needs of the internees, leased the vacant Giegerich

This float was in the 1953 Jubilee Parade on August 15.
KLHSA 988.40.98.

building (now known as the Farmers' Institute building) for the next school year. Temporary walls were put up; outdated, discarded textbooks and old desks were donated, and the school year got into full swing.

Ayako (Aya) Higashi taught in this school. After the war years Mrs. Higashi stayed in Kaslo and taught at the Kaslo School for thirty years, but during her internment here, this energetic young woman kept very busy. In addition to her regular classroom assignments, she sponsored two boys' basketball clubs, taught sewing to teen-age girls, camp cooking to boys, as well as gymnastics. At night she taught Grade 11 and 12 English, and on the weekends she sang in the choir and taught Sunday School. Somehow she also found time to help with the Junior Choir, and on occasion would accompany elderly Nikkei to the commission to act as interpreter. She was an avid tennis player, usually finding time for this activity early in the morning.

Bilingual church services were held at the United Church, which had opened its doors wholeheartedly to the internees. The services were conducted by the Japanese minister in the afternoon and prayers and hymns were repeated or sung simultaneously in Japanese and English. The sermons also were given in both languages, so that their message could be understood by all.

It is interesting to note that even though the Nikkei saw their families torn apart, their businesses and homes confiscated and were uprooted, relocated, and put under constant surveillance by the RCMP, they never rebelled. Instead, they became absolutely model citizens. Mrs. Higashi

The Langham Cultural Centre as she appeared in 1985. The building received a new paint job during the summer of 1992. KLHSA 988.40.282

recalls, ". . .I was fortunate to have a father with deep understanding who reminded me that I was a Canadian and Canada was my country. It was not Canada, my country, that had disowned me. It was only the men in the government and those who were given the authority to deal with the present situation who were dictating the course of history in which we were entrapped. Have faith, he urged. Eventually right would prevail. In the meanwhile, be the best Canadian possible. Separate the men in authority from the country of your birth. Because of my father's wise counselling, I was able to keep faith throughout the years of travesty, and continue to believe in Canada and love her with all my being. . . ."

The restrictions under which they lived were quite severe—each person was issued an "Enemy Alien Identification Card," but after protests the cards were re-issued in three colours to distinguish between Canadian-born, Naturalized and Nationals. The cards were to be carried on their persons at all times. Phone calls were to be made in English only—telephone operators were instructed to disconnect any calls if the callers spoke any Japanese, and radios were banned.

Just before the mass relocation, three Japanese-language newspapers were forced to cease publication in Vancouver. Only *The New Canadian* was allowed to continue because of its consistent advocacy and emphasis on loyal Canadian citizenship. Publisher and editor-in-chief Thomas Kunito Shoyama and his colleagues, editor Takaichi (T.U.) Umezuki, Harry Kondo, Roy Ito, Harold Mayeda and Junji Ikeno, relocated to Kaslo and began to publish the paper there, using C. Roy Fahrni's *Kootenaian* press and equipment on the Kaslo paper's off days. *The New Canadian* became a bilingual paper, distributed across the country, and was the only source of information for the Japanese-Canadian community.

The editorials that Mr. Shoyama and Mr. Umezuki wrote fought incessantly against cases of official racism. In addition to providing entertainment and a means of communication between friends, they also sought to sustain the morale of their readers by pointing the directions in which the bewildered Nikkei and Nisei (Canadian-born Japanese) might move. Through his strong editorship and optimistic outlook, Mr. Shoyama became an important community leader, known and respected throughout Canada. In 1945, he enlisted in the Canadian Army—the federal government had rescinded the Japanese-Canadian enlistment ban because British forces needed interpreters in the Far East.

Mr. Shoyama was born in Kamloops and was a 1938 graduate of the University of British Columbia. After his military service, he held a senior post in the Saskatchewan public service, moving on to become a senior economist with the Economic Council of Canada in Ottawa; during the Trudeau years, he held two federal deputy ministerships—with the Department of Energy, Mines and Resources, and with the Department of Finance—

under three finance ministers. In 1978, he was named an Officer of the Order of Canada. Currently, he is a visiting professor in Public Administration at the University of Victoria, a post he has held since 1980.

Throughout the war years, families were relocated out of the province as their "numbers" came up—they were sent to work on beet farms in Alberta, in homes as domestics, or as foundry workers or loggers in Ontario. By 1946, most of the internees had dispersed from Kaslo, but it wasn't until 1949 that the Nikkei and Nisei were granted total freedom and had their Canadian citizenship reinstated. Finally, they were free to go where ever they wished, even back to the Coast—if they could afford it.

One of the outstanding internees who remained in Kaslo was Tomio Baba, whose Coast boatbuilding business was expropriated upon his relocation to Kaslo. Mr. Baba stayed on, eventually purchasing the Langham in the early 50s and re-establishing his boatbuilding business there. He crafted three fifty-foot fishing boats in his Langham shop, and by the late 50s and early 60s his woodworking skills were in great demand for house, boat and cabinetry building.

The Langham was a hive of activity in these days; and to add to the happy mayhem Noreen Halleran was giving music lessons in what is now the northwest gallery. This breath of life for the Langham lasted until the early 70s when Mr. Baba sold the Langham to Walter Schmidt, a Cape Cod resident who saw the building's potential but could not afford even basic maintenance. The fact that Mr. Schmidt lived 3,000 miles away in Massachusetts didn't help either. The Langham deteriorated and by 1974 had become earmarked by the village council as a derelict building fit only for burning.

Fortunately a forward-thinking young restaurant owner, Michael Guthrie, had a more creative vision and was able to find enough like-minded and energetic people to form the Langham Cultural Society and buy the building. The society's vision was to save the building, restoring it from the foundation to the shake roof and transforming it into a community arts and performing centre. The daunting task took years of dedication from tradesmen, organizers, fundraisers, local businesses and Kaslo's legendary core of stalwart volunteers, but the effort paid off. In 1977, the building was awarded the Heritage Canada Award for the best restoration project in the country.

The Langham Cultural Society developed the building into an arts centre, which houses two galleries, a gift shop and a soft-seat theatre with a capacity of eighty on the first floor. The second and third floors contain a darkroom and one-and two-room studio/offices. The society has recently received funding to create an archival display/re-creation of a typical internee apartment and to establish a rock and native plant garden in the back yard. In addition, the society sponsors an annual multi-discipline summer

Michael and Dare Guthrie's Village Green Café, now Rudolph's Bakery.
This photo was taken in the mid-1970s, when the café was
'the' alternative nerve centre. Photo courtesy of G.D. McCuaig

arts school, calling it the Kaslo-on-the-Lake Summer School of the Arts. This well-attended event highlights the beauty and serenity of Kaslo and area to instructors and students.

Recent History

To bring this book truly up to date, the tumultuous times beginning in the mid-1960s through to the '80s must be included. During this time, the first waves of American conscientious objectors, or draft dodgers, arrived in the Kootenay area. Lured by the remoteness of the area and spouting popular idioms like Timothy Leary's "tune in, turn on and drop out," many came to the Slocan Valley and other parts of the Kootenays seeking an alternative way of life.

They found it—and were soon imitated, followed and joined by young Canadians fleeing heavily urbanized parts of Ontario. In defiance of the

This happened a lot in those days—alternative types discussing what the alternatives were just outside the Village Green Café. Photo courtesy of G.D. McCuaig.

industrial-military complex they were rebelling against, they developed skills in gentle crafts such as weaving, macramé, leatherwork, carving, pottery and other types of artistic endeavour to sell to support themselves. Some of them lived wherever they could find a place—in abandoned shacks and chicken coops, or squatted on abandoned farms—sometimes with and sometimes without the permission of the owners.

Land prices were quite affordable then, compared to prices in 1993, and a number of the new arrivals actually bought houses or land in or around Kaslo to realize their "back to the land" dreams to build themselves a homestead, complete with a log cabin, chickens and a dog. As time went on, these people have been successful in developing an interest and awareness in contemporary arts for many in the community. A particular example of this legacy is the Langham Cultural Centre, an accomplishment spearheaded and largely carried out by those who favoured the alternative lifestyle.

Change never comes easy, and there was friction between the "rednecks and the hippies" for some time—but eventually time and circumstance weeded out both the feelings and the people that didn't really belong here. Throughout the 1980s, many left—probably because, for them, the advantages of living in a rural village couldn't compare to the bright lights, culture and educational opportunities available in the city.

Now, in the early 1990s, a new wave of so-called urban refugees is arriving. These are people who, for the most part, are seeking the quality of life that only a picturesque community like Kaslo can offer. In some

123

instances, they have sold their property in urban centres for a large profit, allowing them to purchase property in rural areas like Kaslo for a reasonable if not small amount of money.

Technology now allows professionals to work away from the ivory towers of the city by the use of facsimile machines, modem-equipped computers and telephone technology that is improving every day. Soon, through the use of fibre optics and cellular communication devices, isolated places like Kaslo may well become bedroom communities to cities hundreds or even thousands of miles away.

A town 100 years old is a very young town by world standards. That Kaslo will survive is not the issue any more, even though the forestry and mining industries that were once so prominent are now waning. These industries are feeling pressure because of environmental issues and the increasing competitiveness of the global economy. What is the issue in Kaslo is the direction and quality of future developments in the town.

Careful stewardship, loving care and intelligent, sustainable development will ensure that future generations can enjoy the beauty, peace and opportunities that only a community like Kaslo can offer.

••••••••••••••••••••••••••••

Families of Kaslo

The following stories, recollections and family histories have been contributed by members of the community. Their submissions have been edited for clarity, style and veracity where possible, while keeping the message of the various authors intact.

David Abbey

I was born George David Abbey on February 14, 1925, at the Victorian Hospital of Kaslo and attended Kaslo School for grades one and two; grade three was attended at Mirror Lake. For grades four and five I bussed to Kaslo. My grade one teacher was Miss Smith, who married our principal, Mr. J. Fraser. In 1936, my family moved to Nelson where I attended Hume School, Trafalgar Junior High and L.V. Rogers High School. While in Nelson I was active with the Boy Scouts. During this time, some of our weekends and most of our holidays were spent at Mirror Lake.

In 1943 I joined the RCMP and took training in Regina, Saskatchewan, and Rockcliffe, adjoining Ottawa. Upon graduation I was stationed in Quebec, Edmonton, and Calgary, and at High River and Gleichen, Alberta. I purchased my discharge in 1947, and returned to Nelson, driving the mail bus to Kaslo for my father. In 1949 I bought the bus line from my father and operated it until 1952 when I sold it to Stu Fyfe.

In 1952 I moved to Calgary and worked for Assiniboia Engineering. I returned to Nelson and married Eve Stan, RN on July 1, 1952. We then lived in Calgary and I worked for Assiniboia until 1955.

In 1955 Eve and I went into the equipment rental business, which we operated until 1980 when we sold it. Much of our time was then spent at Mirror Lake.

We moved back to Mirror Lake in 1983 and remodelled the family log house. After moving back to the Kootenays Eve and I served six years on the Kootenay Lake Historical Society (1984 - 90). Since moving here we have spent our winters in Arizona.

We have two daughters, born in 1956 and 1960; both live and work in Calgary.

We are currently active with the Kaslo Cemetery committee, Mirror Lake water users and the Kaslo Masonic Lodge #25 as well as taking a continuing interest in the Kootenay Lake Historical Society.

Douglas Abbey

Norman Douglas Abbey was born September 12, 1927, at Victorian Hospital of Kaslo. He lived in Kaslo and attendedschool part of one year. The balance of his school was taken at Mirror Lake, and for grades two and three he bussed to Kaslo. His grade one teacher was Margaret (Queenie) McQueen. The family moved to Nelson, and Douglas finished his elementary and secondary education there before getting his BA from UBC; he received his MD from the University to Toronto in 1953, furthured by studies in anaesthesia at New Westminster and pediatrics in England at Joyce Green Hospital in London. He was the government doctor in Fort Smith, NWT, and had a private practice in Hay River, NWT It was there he married Beatrice Purdy, matron of the Hay River hospital, in 1958. They had three children, Robert, Mark and Heather.

He went on to be a medical missionary to Lesotho in southern Africa from 1962 to 1972, although he returned to practise in Kaslo for six months in 1967. When he returned to Canada he practised at Merritt, B.C., until his death July 8, 1986. His hobbies were hiking, photography, drawing and painting.

Mr. & Mrs. Atagi

Kiyomatsu Atagi ventured to the New World in the 1890s as a teenager to study English and economics in Boston, arranged through a missionary. He was a man with a vision and daring, far before his time.

His boat touched port in Victoria, then proceeded to Seattle as scheduled. There, all his plans came undone when he was kidnapped and forced to go with the labourers, or coolies (coolie means bitter labour), who had come to work on one of the northern transcontinental railways in the United States. They were virtual slaves, working long hours and then locked in boxcars and compounds after the day's work was finished. They suffered greatly, forced to work in the terrible heat of summer and fierce cold of winter. There was no contact with the outside world. In all probability the families of the men had given them up for lost. Especially for Mr. Atagi's family, it must have been great mental torture—he was not only brilliant but also their youngest son, who had a dream for the future. And they had let him go.

The account of the life experienced by Mr. Atagi during the five or six years before his group arrived within sight of Chicago could fill a book. There he escaped from the gang when, being the youngest and with some knowledge of English, he was released to go to a nearby town to purchase some food staples. He made his way back to the Pacific coast, working on ranches and wherever else he could find employment. He stayed a couple of winters in Nevada and Colorado hunting mountain lions for bounty and pelt. He told of the badlands, the "painted desert," the rocky buttes which turned an incredible pink, rose and purple hue in the sunset, the petrified forest, the rattlesnakes and tumbleweed—all unheard of to those who lived on the coast. He recounted stories of cattle drives, the drovers roaring into Pocatello in a cloud of dust, carousing and shooting up the saloons on payday, only to return quietly and broke when the money ran out. He went into California's redwood forests and was pained to see the stately and aromatic giants devastated by man and fire as the land was being opened up to accommodate the influx of homesteaders.

At last, a decade later from when he first set foot on the continent, he succeeded in making his way back to the coast. In Vancouver (at that time only a shanty town among the trees extending from the waterfront to present-day Hastings Street; beyond that the Indians lived in what is now downtown Vancouver and all around False Creek),he was surprised and delighted to discover that his older brothers had established themselves at the mouth of the Fraser River and were operating a thriving boatbuilding business and a store.

While attending school in Vancouver, he helped his brothers in the office and in the trade of boatbuilding. In 1903 he became a naturalized British subject. His desire for knowledge and understanding was insatiable. To his last day he read books on philosophy, new discoveries in science and medicine, space programs and current events.

In the second decade of this century he returned several times to Japan to visit his widowed mother. The first time he met a girl, Kane Hayashi, treasured daughter of a country gentleman, who lived near his aunt's home.

126

On his second visit he discovered that she had blossomed into a beautiful 18-year-old. Traditionally, meetings, marriage contract, and other arrangements had to be made through two sets of go-betweens, the heads of the families and parents. The proper protocol was observed, and on his third visit they were married. Despite tears and pleadings from her parents, Kane bid farewell to her family and friends and left her comfortable, protected life for an unknown country with her handsome new husband. Immigration laws required a Canadian marriage, and so they remarried in Victoria before Mr. Atagi took his bride to his home in Vancouver.

The pioneer life for Kane must have been very difficult. She was gentle and quiet, accomplished on the koto (a classical musical instrument like a horizontal harp) and in flower arrangement. A finishing-school graduate, she was unaccustomed to the rough trappings and rigours of pioneer life here. However, according to her husband, relatives and friends, she never voiced a word of complaint but learned to cook, sew and keep a home—and enjoyed it.

After a few years, and the birth of their first child, Kimi, Mr. Atagi struck out up the coast to set up his own boatbuilding business. He located at Quathiaski Cove on Quadra Island across from Campbell River. When his boatworks became well-established and he was appointed foreman of marine carpentry at Anderson Canning Company, he moved his family—now including a daughter Ayako and a son Yutaka—to the Cove. The Atagis had made many friends. They could not ask for more from life. Then, in 1941, this idyllic life ended. (This is another story.)They were sent to Kaslo—Mrs. Atagi, Aya and Yute. Kimi was marooned in Japan, caught at the wrong time in history, unable to return to Canada. Mr. Atagi was relocated to Crowsnest, far from his family, to work on the railroad. No communication. Censorship imposed.

After the war they chose to stay in Kaslo, leading a peaceful life, contented among their family and circle of friends. They enjoyed their beautiful flower garden and pets (Persian cat and a cocker spaniel). As they aged gracefully together, devoted husband and wife and loving parents, they faced each day happily, thankful for every day spared to them, each day a gift.

They lived by their motto, Mr. Atagi's haiku which roughly translates:
> *Welcome each day with joy:*
> *Living*   *Glad*

The Conrows

Thornton and Sara Conrow first drove to Kaslo in September 1952. They were en route from California to visit Sara's sister's family in Argenta. They arrived in Kaslo in time for the Wednesday morning 11 o'clock sailing of the *Moyie*. They disembarked at Lardeau as only the Saturday sailing stopped in Argenta. It was evening before Bob Boyd and his son, Bill, came to get the Conrows in the Boyds' small boat. The residents of Argenta built a huge bonfire on the beach to guide them across the lake. Before leaving Kaslo, the Conrows had arranged with Fred Jones to meet them at the Argenta wharf early Friday morning with his water taxi.

They returned to the area with their three children, Roger, Teresa, and Connie, to visit in the early summers of 1960 and 1962. In 1962 Sara was interviewed for teaching in the Argenta School. She met with Superintendent Watson and the members of School Board 6 in Theresa Saalfeld's living room. The Conrows bought the Sawszuks' log cabin in Argenta before returning home. Back in California things did not move as quickly as the Conrows had hoped. Sara resigned her teaching position, and California neighbors, the Weber family, bought and moved into the log cabin in Argenta.

Two years later, in 1964, the Conrows moved to Argenta. Roger started grade four in the log cabin school in Meadow Creek. Teresa and Connie were in grades three and one in the Argenta Primary School. Thornton was a draftsman at the Duncan Dam then under construction. Sara learned to keep house with wood instead of electricity in Roy and Jane Lake's cabin on the Argenta Flats. The whole family was enamoured of the area.

Sara taught for a year at the Argenta Friends' School. She was the principal's relief teacher and substituted at the Jewett School in Meadow Creek. In 1966 she finished out the school year for George Weber, who had moved to the South Pacific. Sara continued teaching in the area. In 1967 she asked to be transferred to Kaslo because their children would be attending the Kaslo School. She taught in Kaslo until her retirement in 1989.

Thornton injured his back in 1966. Later he did occasional drafting jobs in the area. In Kaslo he served on several boards, including the Langham, the Victorian Hospital, and the Homemakers.

In 1974 the Conrows moved to Mirror Lake and a smaller home. Roger had moved to a job in Prince George. Teresa was attending Argenta Friends' School. She later received her degree from a Friends' college in Indiana. Connie aslo graduated from Argenta Friends' School.

As of 1992 Thornton lives in the Okanagan. Roger is in Vancouver. Theresa and Connie live with their families in California. Sara is the only one still in the Kaslo area.

The Davidsons

The Tim (Clarence Burton) Davidson family arrived in Kaslo in the fall of 1949, coming from their farm at Lost Lake in the Bluffton area of central Alberta. Opal, the youngest of the six children, was born in Kaslo in the spring. The family took up residence at 232 B Avenue and lived there for 28 years.

Tim worked at several area mines as a welder-mechanic until his death in 1961. Pearl worked for the Kaslo Meat Market, the Post Office and Overwaitea for more than 20 years.

In 1977, Pearl remarried and moved to Nelson's North Shore. After she was widowed a second time in 1986, she moved into Nelson, where she still lives. Although her house and yard keep her busy, in 1991 she officially accepted retirement by taking up golf.

The eldest child, Ed, has remained in the Kaslo area. He worked for T&H Sawmills for 13 years and now works as a contract welder for Meadow Creek Cedar Ltd. Ed has one daughter, Kim, from his first marriage, who will be returning to university this fall. Ed is now married to Joyce Siebert, formerly of Calgary, and they live on a farm just outside the village limits. Joyce is active in the Riding Club and is also the SPCA agent for Kaslo.

Ron married Sandra Lane of Ainsworth Hot Springs, where they have made their home. They have three children; Cynthia, a word processor, Bill, a pipefitter/welder currently in Castlegar, and Rob, an assayer in the Lower Mainland. Ron's working career has been with the Pipefitters Union and he has worked throughout B.C. The family own and operate the Lakeside Motel and Campground on Kootenay Lake.

Mary married Dennis Hutcheson and lives in Kamloops. Dennis is the Kamloops regional protection officer for the B.C. Ministry of Forests. They have two children, Shannon and Scott, both attending university. Mary is a certified professional electrologist and has worked with her sister Pixie since 1983.

Bernice has two children, Sandra and Ritchie. She married Larry Diede of Calgary, where they live. Larry is parts manager for Auto Marine Electric, formerly Hutton's Automotive. Bernice worked in the school system while her children were young and is an avid bingo player. Ritchie is still in High School and Sandra is married with one child, Nichole.

Pixie (Jean) married Barry Fifer of Vernon. Barry is the general manager of Okanagan North Growers. Pixie is a certified professional electrologist and has operated her own business since 1977. They live beside Kalamalka Lake near Vernon and have recently purchased a lot in Wood-bury Village for a summer home. Both are avid golfers and come back to the area often.

Opal, Tim and Pearl's youngest child, married Bruce Jacobs of Kaslo. They have two boys, Colin and Corey, losing Allan as an infant. Colin and Corey subcontract for Bruce Jacobs Contracting Ltd., a logging contractor. Opal in her time away from the family business indulges her love of travel by organizing family trips to many exotic locations. They have all remained in the Kaslo area and make their home at Shutty Bench.

The R.W. Douglas Family

The Douglas family moved to Kaslo in 1967, when Bob accepted the position of vice-principal at Kaslo Elementary-Secondary School (later renamed J.V. Humphries School). Bob and Barb raised a family of four; Bryan, a highways worker and all-round handyman; Laura, a teacher at Jewett School; Catherine, a hairdresser; and David, who is working towards a Bachelor of Arts degree in music at UBC.

Bob grew up in Rossland, where he never learned to ski but, true to his Scottish heritage, did learn to play the bagpipes. Barb grew up in the Stampede City of Calgary, where she spent her youth wishing for a horse. The two met when Bob was working his way through university. The first time Bob saw Barb, she was impersonating the Queen for the pipe band that was rehearsing for Her Majesty's impending visit in 1959.

Bob has always been deeply involved in community affairs. His long list of community service includes being a life member of the Kinsmen Club, a coach and referee for Minor Hockey, a long-standing member of the Hospital and Historical Society boards and a director and at times president of the Riding Club. In addition he has been involved in the Kootenay Lake Teachers Association and as geographical representative to the B.C. Teachers Federation.

A dream came true for Barb in 1980 when she became the proud owner of an aging Half-Arabian mare named Gypsy Rule. A year later a brown-eyed blond horse named Bonnie Rebel won Bob's heart and although these horses have been replaced over the years, the Douglases have spent many happy hours with their animals. They hope to continue their passion for horses and their involvement with the Riding Club and are sharing this interest with their grandchildren.

Bob has taught two generations of Kaslo kids, including his own. Three of their four offspring have settled in their hometown of Kaslo and Bob and Barb are Grammy and Grampy to six grandchildren.

Bill and Doris Drayton

William Vincent Drayton was born in Toronto in 1912 and Doris Christine Nelson was born in Moose Jaw in 1913. The couple met and married in Vancouver in 1944. In 1946, they moved to Kaslo where they purchased The Lodge, renting rooms and serving meals. Their daughter Joanne was a year old when they came to Kaslo, and Penny was born in 1947.

Bill built cabins at The Lodge and did many more construction jobs in the area, including two houses, the Bank of Montreal building and the Golf Clubhouse. He became an alderman in 1948, holding that office for five years; was elected Mayor of Kaslo in 1954 and again in the 1960s for a total of ten years. In 1964 he was appointed a judge of Small Debts Court and Family and Children's Court; in 1969 the post was altered to judge of the Provincial Court of British Columbia. He retired after eleven years. During these years he also served terms as president of the Kaslo Board of Trade and president of the Kaslo Golf Club.

Doris was a substitute teacher for many years and an active member in the Kaslo Library, the United Church Service Club and the Hospital Auxiliary. The couple's hobbies throughout the years have included squaredancing, bridge, fishing, curling, golf and gardening.

Joanne died in 1972, leaving her husband, Mel Buerge, and three children, Lissa, Kevin and Melanie. There are now two great-grandchildren as well, Shara and Seron.

Penny has been head nurse in the maternity ward of Kelowna General Hospital for the past fifteen years.

In 1976, Bill and Doris moved up to 8th Street, where Bill still pursues his gardening interests

Franz Eimer

Franz Eimer was born in 1916 near Moyie, B.C., at the Greenbay Ranch, situated at the head of Moyie Lake. (For most of his life he had been known as Franz and did not know himself that his correct name was Francis.) His father leased the land at Greenbay Ranch and ran cows and other livestock on it.

Franz first came to the West Kootenays in 1937. His partner at that time was Paul Stevens. The men came as horse packers and found work in that occupation, often transporting their horses by sternwheeler.

Franz also worked in the Whitewater mining mill and it was here that he met Eva. They married in October of 1939. They had two children, both girls, but the marriage didn't last and they parted after only five years. Most of Franz's life was that of a bachelor.

Franz led an interesting life and at times worked for the Forest Service clearing rivers or supervising fire crews. His feet certainly covered many many miles in the Kootenays and for most of his life he ran a trapline every winter.

Until his poor health forced him to sell and move into town, Franz lived in a log house he built on a nine-acre farm about seven miles north of Kaslo. Franz had many a good story to tell, but to hear them now you must rely on those he shared them with. Franz Eimer died June 2, 1992.

The Gilker Family

In the spring of 1933, R.C. Gilker arrived in Kaslo from Prince Rupert to take over the duties of Provincial Policeman for Kaslo and area. He later took over the policing of the City of Kaslo, which then employed its own police.

Constable Gilker was accompanied by his wife, Stella, two sons, and two daughters, Margaret, now living in Surrey, and June, who married John (Jack) Dryden in Kaslo in 1941. Jack was killed in 1944 over Germany; a plaque in St. Andrew's United Church honours his memory. Two older Gilker children remained in Prince Rupert. Bob followed the family to Kaslo in the fall of 1933 and got a job with Henry Whellams to drive the mail and passenger bus to and from Nelson. The road in those days was very narrow and dusty, with only one-way traffic at the worst spots, making the trip to Nelson a long and arduous one. Folks along the route depended on Bob to do errands for them in Nelson but always with some sort of reward in the form of cigerettes or other gifts.

In 1936 Bob married Anne Scott of Nelson and they had four children, Roberta, Janice, Gary and Colleen.

The teens of the forties and fifties spent a good deal of time in sports and school activities. Their spending money was earned by doing chores, and what little they had (in comparison to today's teenagers) usually was spent in Larry Potter's coffee shop. Larry always had time for the young people and one big attraction for the kids was the huge ten-cent ice cream cones he served.

Bob owned and operated the "66" Transfer business in the 1940s, hauling and delivering coal and freight that was brought into Kaslo by barge. After selling the transfer business the family moved to Trail where Bob was employed by CM&S (now Cominco Ltd.). In 1952 the Gilkers returned to Kaslo, the place they loved best. Bob enjoyed being involved in community affairs and especially taking part in the local drama club. Anne kept busy with the family and part-time employment. They still live in Kaslo, as does their eldest daughter, Roberta Garrett, and three of their grandchildren and six great-grandchildren. Of the other three of their children, Janice lives in Nakusp, Gary in Campbell River and Colleen in Vancouver.

The Kennett Family

Charles and Daisy Kennett moved from New Denver to Kaslo in February 1948 with their girls, Dorothy, Colleen, Evelyn and Linda. Charlie and Daisy divorced in the early 1950s and he remarried, this time to Mabel Bennett. Charlie was employed as foreman in the Department of Highways in Kaslo until 1964 when he was transferred to Nakusp. He and Mabel retired there in 1978.

The girls all attended school in Kaslo. Dorothy Harris now lives in Merritt and has had three boys, Blaine, Brent and Vann.

Colleen never left Kaslo, and makes her home here with her husband, Ron Hewat. Colleen runs the Treasure Chest, a clothing store on Front Street, and Ron operates a trucking company in the area. They have three boys, Len, Rick and Ken and a daughter, Ronda Tate.

Evelyn left Kaslo in the early '50s and now lives in Kamloops with her husband, Dan Pochay. They have two boys, Tim and Kevin, and one daughter Michelle.

Linda left Kaslo in 1959, moving to Ontario. In September 1990 she moved back to Kaslo. She has one daughter, Suzan and a son, Stephen, both residents of Kitchener, Ontario.

The Kozun Family

Bill and Beryl came here because of Beryl's grandparents, John and Lillian MacPherson. The MacPhersons came to Kaslo in 1894, and Beryl's father Cassel MacPherson was born in Kaslo. Beryl's mother Edna, came to Kaslo in 1925 from Creston, B.C., and lived here all her life until her death in 1988. Beryl and her two brothers, Allan and Ralph, were born and educated in Kaslo.

Bill came to Kaslo from Selkirk, Manitoba, to work in the mines in 1951. He and Beryl were married in Kaslo in 1953. After the mines shut down in 1958 he went to work for a few years with the Department of Highways. Later, when the Columbia River Treaty dams were being built, Bill went to the Duncan Dam and all of the other construction jobs created by the treaty. He retired in 1988 and still lives in Kaslo.

Beryl worked at the Victorian Hospital of Kaslo from 1959 to 1974, then took a six-year break and built the Kozy Burger and operated it until it was sold and renamed the Mountain King. She then went back to work at the hospital and is still there.

Beryl and Bill's two daughters were born and raised in Kaslo. Wendy married a local boy, Don Edwards, and they have two daughters, Dianna and Anita. Cindy married Alan Tarr, the son of another long-time area family, Court and Lena Tarr. They have two children, Tyler and Ashley.

The Miller Family

Norman and Mary Miller moved to Kaslo in 1951 with their three children—twin sons Lance and Leigh and daughter Elaine. He had worked for the CPR from 1930 and was to be Kaslo's last CPR agent. The days of the telegraph and rail transport was coming to an end. The roads were impassable that December so quite appropriately the family moved by train. Norman remained in that job until 1967 when the CPR closed the station, at which time he purchased the Kootenay Lake Hardware Store, which he operated until he retired in 1975. He found time in those years to serve on the hospital board and on the Village Council. He was coroner for many years. He was killed in a motorcycle accident September 4, 1984, at the age of 71.

Mary was a teacher and taught in many one- and two-room schools in the area—at Ainsworth, Retallack, Passmore, Crescent Valley, Meadow Creek and finally Kaslo. She loved books and worked long hours in both the school and public libraries. She loved gardening, music, travel and golf. She was an active member of her church and bridge club. Leukemia took her life in 1973 when she was 60. Lance, Leigh and Elaine graduated from Kaslo School. Lance joined the U.S. Air Force and served in Korea, Vietnam, Japan and Germany before his retirement in 1988. He now lives in Nuagua, Missouri. Leigh worked for Inland Gas, laying gas line all over the province, and now lives in Salmon Arm. Both brothers had two sons. Elaine received her nurse's training at the Vancouver General Hospital, married a Kaslo boy and raised her three girls in Kaslo while she worked at the hospital.

The R.C. Morton Family

The Morton family moved from Sandon and Retallack to Kaslo in August 1934. The oldest son, George, had come to Kaslo in 1931 to complete high school. Cecil, the second oldest, also came to work in Kaslo about the same time. He worked for Dunc McCuaig on the Lofsted ranch for three years, his pay—room and board, no cash. When he learned that the remainder of the family would be moving to Kaslo in 1934, he cut 20 cords of wood—this was all gone by June. That was a very cold winter. Cecil and Bill Tonkin worked night shift at the three-mile water intake "punching" anchor ice. He would get home after midnight and relieve his mother stoking the fires. His father was working at the Yankee Girl mine in Ymir at this time. There was no money for post-secondary education, so the boys sought work wherever they could. George was employed in a local mill and Cecil went to work cutting poles 35 miles from Howser up the Duncan River. The rate of pay was one cent per pole peeled in the bush and one dollar per 1000 board foot for the butt logs. Frank, Arthur and Mary earned what they could during the summer holidays, picking cherries, mowing lawns, delivering the Vancouver *Province* and, as they got older, took on other jobs—Frank working at the Overwaitea store, Arthur as freight hand for Kaslo Motor Transport and Mary as telephone operator. The younger Mortons had their fun too—sports became their social outlet, with competitive games between Kaslo, New Denver, Nakusp and Nelson. They enjoyed music, under the direction of George Drennan. The instruments were owned by the city. Several May Days celebrations included the participation of the band in the parade—either marching or riding on the back of a flat-deck truck. All five

Mortons played in the city band.

With the outbreak of the Second World War, the family gradually left Kaslo, Cecil had joined his father at Ymir before joining the Merchant Marine. George was married and had one son; they moved in 1942 to Vancouver, where George was employed by Vancouver Engineering making corvette boilers. Frank joined the RCAF, Art the RCA and Mary the RCAF (WD). George and family returned to Kaslo in 1944 to take over the Gus Adams cherry orchard.

When the Little Cherry disease devastated the cherries in this area, he removed all the diseased trees and replanted the orchard in Bartlett pears. They continued to live in Kaslo until George passed away and his wife, Hannah, left after a few years to be near their sons in Port Hardy.

Cecil returned after the war and resumed work in mining, working for some 22 years at the Bluebell mine in Riondel. The men from Kaslo and Ainsworth who worked there commuted daily by car and boat, embarking from Woodbury. Except for five years at Yellowknife, he and his wife have always lived in Kaslo. Their two children attended school in Kaslo and were active members of the school band. Vivian has pursued a career in cooking and Brian in the entertainment field. Frank and Art didn't return to Kaslo after the war—Frank went to UBC, graduating in horticulture, and found employment with B.C. Tree Fruits. He was district horticulturist in Kelowna for about 20 years, before being transferred to Victoria.

Arthur followed his vocation in architectural drafting, and worked for many years in Nelson before accepting a position with the University of Victoria. Mary entered nursing in Ontario after her wartime service, returning to B.C. in 1949 to New Denver where she nursed at the Slocan Community Hospital for three years. She returned to Kaslo in 1953 with her husband and young daughter. Three more children were born and raised in Kaslo. Two have returned to work in the area after their post secondary education; the other two are teachers, in Battleford, Saskatchewan, and Calgary, respectively.

Their eldest daughter Darlene, husband Ben Borley and family took up residence in Kaslo in 1978. The Borleys' eldest daughter, Dalouie, graduated from J.V. Humphries school in 1991—the first of the third generation of a Kaslo Morton family to do so (Mary Morton graduated in 1942, her daughter Darlene in 1969, and granddaughter Dalouie Borley in 1991).

The Mack Murphy Family

Mack came to Canada from Shanigolden, Ireland, and met his future wife, Vera Moulton, at Willow Point on the West Arm of Kootenay Lake. They were married in 1931 and lived up at Howser and Gerrard in the Lardeau Valley for a few years before moving to Kaslo in 1937. They raised a family of six—five still living and all of them residing in British Columbia. Mack belonged to the Masonic Lodge and Vera was a member of the Rebekah Lodge.

Mack worked hard and played hard; he loved life. He worked in mining and logging, and was an electrician, a school janitor and a rock driller on the Duncan Dam. He became a shift boss and eventually caretaker of the Cork Province mine. At one time he loaded poles at the pole yard where the Esso bulk station in Kaslo is now; in those days poles were loaded by horse power—forward and back.

He was quite a baseball player—sometimes employing slightly unorthodox rugby tricks when fielding a ground ball. Mack enjoyed hunting but didn't have the patience for fishing except when he could harpoon a char trying to jump the falls at the Duncan Dam.

Vera was a dressmaker, baker, gardener and teacher although she never worked away from home; she was always a mother first. A long-time member of St. Mark's Church, she was also an avid reader who enjoyed the Kaslo Library.

Like most other families growing up in Kaslo, the Murphys spent much of their time on school activities and sports. When summer came the cherry crop provided a little extra income; up at 4 a.m. to pick until about 10 a.m. and spend the rest of the free time at the beach.

Wilfred (Bill) Seafoot

Wilfred Seafoot moved to Kaslo in early 1957, leaving his family in Rossland to relocate here after he had established work. Bill had logged in the Grand Forks/Christina Lake area when the natural gas line was built in the 1950s. Finding work with T & H Sawmills Ltd., Bill worked with a D4 Cat (an old grey mare). He had two partners, Fred Steiner and Gerald (Jiggs) Seafoot, his nephew.

Irene and the children—Bev, Linda, Bonnie, Craig and Keith—travelled for two summers to spend time with their father, and Gordie was born in Rossland in 1958 just before they moved permanently to Kaslo. The kids' first memory of Kaslo was the four-hour drive from Rossland along a road that had grass growing down the middle. They would spend the summers at the beach, along with Shelagh Leathwood and Mary Wood and their children.

Bill, Fred and Jiggs formed Kaslo Skid Contractors Ltd. in 1963. They developed their logging technique to include a D6 cat, and landed a contract with Kootenay Forest Products Ltd., working in Deception Creek in 1967. Bill bought out Fred Steiner in 1964 and Jiggs in 1972. He continued to log in the Duncan River area, employing many men and increasing the company equipment to include a skidder, log loader, three more Cats and two trucks. Bill retired from logging in 1989, after Irene died of cancer.

Bill and Irene were involved with Legion Branch 74 for over 32 years in various ways, serving as presidents of the branch and the Ladies Auxiliary respectively, and washing dishes for the banquets and bar. Bill was also involved in the baseball clubs, from Minor Baseball to Senior Men's Baseball. Linda remembers her father playing ball with the Oldtimers in New Denver with Lefty Turner, Einar Linn and Ole Johnson. Bill developed a charley horse and couldn't finish the game; his leg was black and blue.

Bev married and had two children, Karen and Brett. She moved to Elko in 1972 to work for a pulp company. She is now a certified log grader working in Mackenzie for Fletcher Challenge Canada (formerly B.C. Forest Products) and has become grandmother to a little girl. Karen is in Mackenzie and Brett is in Vancouver, working in a manufacturing company.

Linda lives in Powell River with her four boys and is the office manager for one of the largest construction companies on the Sunshine Coast. Ron is at Simon Fraser University, and Gary is working for the construction company. David and Leroy are enjoying school and the extra-curricular activities that Powell River has to offer.

Bonnie is married to Rick Zinck and living in Boutiliers Point, Nova Scotia. Her children, Jason, Ryan and Pamela, are all attending university in Nova Scotia. Pam is taking computer programming, Ryan is taking a forestry course and Jason has completed a second year.

Craig is a member of the RCMP stationed in Fort McMurray, Alta. He is married to Mary Ann Gordon and has two boys, Billy and Kevin. Billy has completed school and hopes to join the RCMP; Kevin is completing his last year of school.

Keith is living in Nakusp, working in the logging industry. He has had a logging company, using the new high-lead technique. His boys, Allan, Mark and Kelly, are still in school.

Gordie is living in Kaslo, working in the logging industry. He has two children, Tanya and Sheldon.

Bob Swanson

I first came to Kaslo in 1953 when they put the road through to Lardeau, working for the Deptartment of Public Works, which became the Department of Highways in 1955. My first impression—what a beautiful spot! Beautiful lake. The winters not too severe. I settled in Kaslo in 1968, working for the DOH until 1973, when illness forced me to take an early retirement at the age of 57. I continued living in Kaslo and soon joined the Senior Citizens Association and became active in the Royal Canadian Legion.

In 1975 I married Betty Bjneland in Nakusp and we both decided to live in Kaslo. It's a very special place with such friendly people, a beautiful golf course, skating rink, curling, lawn bowling, and carpet bowling. I'm still an active member of the Legion. After living here for 20 years, I still think it is a beautiful place to live.

The Bud Garrett Family

Norman (Bud) Garrett was born in Kaslo, the youngest child of Clarence and Gertie. He grew up in Retallack and moved to Trail in his teens, later returning to Retallack. As a youth he earned his spending money picking and selling huckleberries by the hundred-pound pail to the Overwaitea store in Kaslo. He also made sandwiches in the cookhouse for the miners, and learned to drive an ore truck down the mountain road before he was of legal age. Bud was quite a tease and enjoyed pulling pranks on others. His mom tells about the time he didn't change his clothes after school, and somehow ripped his new pants. Afraid to go home, he went to Paddy the cook at the mine for help, and old Paddy proceeded to sew up the rip, which pleased Bud, as now his mom would never know. But she found out, as the old boy had sewn the pants to his long underwear.

There were few cars in camp, so when the young people wanted to go swimming they would walk to Bear Lake, or to Zincton to see a show. In the winter the camp was quite isolated except for the train going through to Kaslo twice a week, so supplies had to be purchased in the fall to last until spring. As a young man Bud was working on a Cat, when somehow he caught fire. His leg was severely burned, and he was in hospital for a time. He worked in the mine concentrators at Retallack and then Zincton until they closed, and worked at the King mine for two years. He always returned to Kaslo on his days off, and eventually came back to work for Kaslo Motors. He married Roberta Gilker, eldest daughter of Bob and Anne.

Roberta was born in Nelson and grew up in Kaslo, Trail and Castlegar. Except for the years in Trail when Bud worked for McGauley Ready Mix, Bud and Roberta have made their home in Kaslo, raising a family of five children: Gordon, Debra (Reimer), Mark, Diane and Pamela (Walker). Bud has worked for T&H Sawmills as a logging truck driver, owned his own trucking business, and as foreman for the village. Roberta was employed by B.C. Telephone Co. for six years and was the Sears agent for fourteen years; for the past five years she has been behind the Sears counter at Cornucopia. Bud is a former member of the Kinsmen Club, Volunteer Fire Department and Curling Club. Roberta is a former member of the Kinette Club, Rebekahs, United Church Service Club and the LA to the Guides, Brownies, Scouts and Cubs. They are grandparents to eight and enjoy spending time with the grandchildren. Roberta says of her family's home, "Over the years there have been many changes in Kaslo, but we feel it is still the best place there is to live and raise a family."

Cliff and Judy McGillivray

Cliff and Judy McGillivray (née McIntyre) moved from Calgary to Kaslo in 1981 in semi-retirement. Cliff worked for ferries on the run from Balfour to Kootenay Bay until his retirement in 1988. Judy worked for the Bank of Montreal in Kaslo and is then part-time for West Kootenay Power. Cliff is an avid Legionnaire and is interested in model railroading. They have five children and eight grandchildren.

The Carpenter Family

Claude and May Carpenter and family arrived from Viceroy, in the south of Saskatchewan, in September 1946 after buying the old Morphet ranch on Shutty Bench. Claude worked at radio repairs and as an electrician at various mines including the Cork Province, Utica Mines and Yale Lead & Zinc. When the mines started closing down Claude tried his hand at lease mining but when this didn't work out he obtained his Electrician's B ticket and worked as a general electrical contractor on houses and small industrial jobs. However, his main interest was mining and prospecting and he spent much of his spare time up in the mountains. May delivered mail from Kaslo to Retallack for four or five years in the late fifties and early sixties. Both were active Legion members.

In 1975 Claude and May sold the place on Shutty Bench and retired to a house trailer in Kaslo until Claude died in 1984. May then moved into Abbey Manor. Their children Helen, Ted, Donna and Joan all attended school in Kaslo. Helen married Gerald Cummings, but was widowed; she then married Barney Johnson and lived in Kimberley until she died in 1982. Ted is a mining engineer living in Williams Lake with his wife, Yvonne. Donna became a nurse, married George Alberton and lives in Kimberley. Joan married Merril Carlson and lives in Armstrong. May has 13 grandchildren, 23 great-grandchildren and 2 great-great-grandchildren.

The Cowan Family

Lt.-Col. and Mrs. James deButts Cowan arrived on Shutty Bench on April 1, 1929, with their three children. They raised Great Danes and farmed all their lives, until Col. Cowan died in 1962 and Mrs. Cowan in 1965. They were both avid horse people, a taste that the colonel acquired during his years as an Imperial Army cavalry officer. Mrs. Cowan had spent the 1914-18 war years driving ambulance for the Red Cross.

Their son, Robert, attended Kaslo school until he joined the Royal Navy, in which he served till 1945. Robert, also known as Robin, now lives in Spruce Grove, Alberta.

The elder daughter, Robina Haegedorn, lives on her parents' place on Shutty Bench. She attended school on Shutty Bench before furthering her education with the Department of Education correspondence school as did her younger sister, Alison.

Robina has three children: Sheila, a teacher who lives in Victoria; Pat, a veterinarian, and Janet, who works in Red Deer where she hopes to become a nurse.

Alison and her husband, Keith Carnegie, have five children: John is married with two children and drives buses for B.C. Transit in Vancouver; Doug and his wife, Linda, have three children, and he works for the Royal Bank in Smithers; Carolyn and her husband, Dave Courtemanche, live in Delta and have two children; Bruce works for B.C. Gas in Penticton; and Kathy and husband Ken Belrose have one child and reside here in Kaslo.

The Cowans emigrated from England to Crawford Bay in 1928 and the next year bought a ranch on Shutty Bench which had been owned by Lt.-Col. Arnold Kemball, killed at Vimy Ridge as commanding officer of the 54th (Kootenay) Battalion. The Cowans brought some registered Great Danes—gunmetal-coloured Danes known as blues—to establish the bloodline in Canada. They would later travel to dog shows across western Canada and into the United States and won numerous show awards. Their puppies were exported worldwide.

The Kemball place had been rented by Henry Howell Armstead, an American mining engineer who had served with the U.S. Army Corps of Engineers in the Firts World War. With his brother, D.M. Armstead, he had mining interests in the Kaslo and Trout Lake areas. He optioned the Cromwell property near Ferguson and for a time controlled Utica Mines Ltd. which held the Utica mine near Kaslo, and the Kootenay Belle and Crown Point properties. He spent some of his time in the 1920s around Kaslo and Shutty Bench.

Many of the family's neighbours were from what is now Slovakia, having followed Andrew Shutty, who had purchased most of the land for $1 an acre and in turn resold it for $5 an acre. The settlers cleared their own land by hand and planted fruit trees such as cherries, plums and apples and put in large vegetable gardens. The fruit was picked and packed on site, then delivered to a shed in Kaslo, from which it was shipped to a co-operative in Nelson. Until the Little Cherry disease ruined the cherry industry in the area, this income financed quite a few university educations. Haying for livestock was done by scythe, hand raking and hauling by horse wagon or rack.

From 1913 to 1946, Shutty Bench had a one-room, one-teacher school for about 20 pupils ranging from grade one to grade eight. After that, students either continued with correspondence or walked, cycled or rode horseback up to six miles to Kaslo High School. The road between Kaslo and the Cowan property, which was the north end of the existing development, was very narrow and often blocked by slides. There were only a few cars on the road at that time; even that often meant backing to find a wider place to pass.

Robina Haegedorn continues to live on the lakeside section of the Cowan property and her sister, Alison Carnegie, lives a few miles south on Shutty Bench. Robina married her late husband, Wilhelm (Bill), who had emigrated in 1952 from Germany, where he had been a farm manager before serving in an army parachute division. He arrived in the area to work in a mine at Ainsworth, and continued with his farming interests. Before returning to Shutty Bench after their marriage, the Haegedorns lived in Rossland, Saltspring Island and Renata, on Lower Arrow Lake, where B.C. Hydro acquired their property during clearing for the reservoir for the Hugh Keenleyside Dam. They continued breeding the renowned Cowan Rungmook Great Danes after receiving Champion Sheba as a wedding gift in 1955.

Bill and Robina's children have often returned to spend time on Shutty Bench since completing their schooling in Kaslo. Pat and Nicola, with their daughter, Rebecca, returned recently from Quesnel. Pat plans to establish a vet practice on the Bench.

Marge Ringheim

I was a member of the Kaslo school staff from 1945 to 1969. That was when the younger Japanese internee children attended elementary school in an empty store downtown, and were taught by Japanese teachers, while the older pupils were enrolled in the High School. This arrangement continued until the end of the war, but as the families were relocated the enrolment dropped until there were not enough pupils to keep the Elementary School open. In September, 40 Japanese students were sent to the Elementary School. This necessitated an extra teacher so I was hired for a year, and stayed for twenty-five.

I had the grades three and four class, 26 of whom were Japanese children; they were excellent pupils. Not having taught for 17 years, I found it difficult to adjust to a class of 35 at first. However, things went well and we had a good year. One of our most rewarding projects was writing the original *Early History of Kaslo*. The children interviewed the pioneers and learned a great deal from them. They found it interesting and learned a lot of respect for people they hardly knew before. We had 28-page booklets, including a few pictures, printed; 500 copies sold quickly and we made enough profit to buy a music system for the school.

Kaslo's Diamond Jubilee was celebrated in 1953. I rewrote the *Early History* and extended it with the help of an excellent committee. We had 5,000 copies printed, and they sold quickly. Later I brought them up to date and another 5000 copies were sold—many on the sternwheeler *Moyie* when it became a museum.

Kaslo School staff and students assisted in various public activities. The May Queen voting, ceremonies and maypole dancing were produced by them for many years. Voting was by High School students for one of their members. Those in the maypole dancing were from the primary grades.

When the new school building was completed the Students' Council organized a unique "Goodbye, Old School" ceremony. All the children from grades 1 to 12 participated and each one brought a piece of ribbon. These were tied together and extended around the entire building. During a suitable program the ribbon was cut by the Students' Council president. It was sort of an inverted opening ceremony and was really impressive.

The Kaslo School—now J.V. Humphries School—is probably one of only a few schools where twelve grades are taught in one complex. Actually, there are definite advantages to this type of school. As pupils progress from Elementary to Secondary little change is needed, such as changing schools or districts. As well, they know every teacher as they progress. The position of principal is a difficult task but that has advantages, also. I taught under Brian Thompson, Greg Dickson, Don Kaye and Jack Humphries, and they all handled the task well. The two schools often combined in various activities. Many of these were under the direction of the well-organized Students' Councils. This resulted in an excellent introduction to High School activities for the younger children.

The Christmas concerts, the Drama Class productions, the assemblies are a few of the enjoyable memories of my twenty-five years in Kaslo School.

The Semenoff Family

Paul and Molly Semenoff and their four children, Karen, Leona, Russell and Gail, moved to Kaslo from Ymir in June of 1971. Originally Paul was from Grand Forks and Molly was from Puerto Rico Creek, just north of Ymir. Paul came to Kaslo to work with the Chernoff Brothers Sawmill, a portable mill specializing in selective logging of white pine and cedar for plywood manufacture. He was a sawyer and foreman for this company until 1983 when he and Molly purchased a building on Front Street and established a health food store that they called Cornucopia.

Ironically, the first house the Semenoffs rented in Kaslo is now owned by their oldest daughter, Karen, and her husband, George McCuaig, originally of Nelson. The McCuaigs have a daughter, Kayda, and a son, Tavish. They own Semco/Kootenaian Press, a home-based printing and publishing company that prints the monthly publication *The North Arm Voice*.

Leona, the Semenoffs' second daughter, married Fred Wood of Kaslo. They now live in Houston, B.C. with their two boys, Lindsey and Collin. Leona works at a drugstore and Fred is a shift foreman for Houston Forest

Products.

Russell, their son, married Heather Olsen of Kaslo and they live in upper Kaslo with their daughter, Danica. Russell is employed in the logging industry.

The youngest daughter, Gail, married Alexander (Lex) Jones of Kaslo and they live in lower Kaslo with their daughter, Casey, and son, Chad. The Jones' are employed with Jones Boys Boats, based at Woodbury.

Paul and Molly now live in the home they built in 1972 at 547 C Avenue. Molly served as Alderman for a term and a half. She worked with the Guides and Brownies and was a Commissioner for three years. She has also served as president of the Figure Skating Club. She now sits on the executive of the Chamber of Commerce which both she and Paul are active members.

The Settle Family

The opportunity of work brought Edwin (Ted) and Maurine Settle (née Bowles) to Kaslo in January 1960 from Enderby, where Ted had worked in a sawmill. They had four children; Wendy, born in 1960, Glen in 1961, John, in 1964, and Richard, in 1965. From his arrival in Kaslo until the mill shut down in 1983, Ted worked for T&H Sawmills. He then purchased a heel boom and went into business for himself. Meanwhile, after spending fifteen years at home raising their children, Maurine went to work at Shop-Easy, where she spent twelve years until 1987. In September of 1989 Ted joined with his sons Glen and John to form a logging contracting company under the name of Settle Holdings Ltd.

Ted and Maurine's children have all left home now. Wendy lives in Silverton with her husband, Blair Nelson, and their three children, Kyle, Wesley and Brittani. Glen married Sharon Seafoot (née Aasen) in 1986, and, along with Sharon's children Tania and Sheldon, they have three sons, Brent, Kirk and Cameron, and live in Kaslo. John married Cindy Brown in 1987 and they have two children, Aaron and Kimberlie. They also live in Kaslo. Richard lives in Nanaimo and has worked at the Ladysmith sawmill of Canadian Pacific Forest Products since 1987.

Ted and Maurine remain very close to their family and if their spare time isn't spent with their children and grandchildren, they can be found on the golf course or travelling in their motorhome.

Don Sicotte

The first time I came to Kaslo was in 1944 to visit my aunt, Rita Fontaine, the B.C. telephone operator. The office was in a house two or three down from the post office. She married Bob McGregor, an RCMP guard out at Fletcher bluffs.

I worked on the *Moyie* in the early fifties for two or three years and got to know some Kaslo people: Tom Hetherington, who used to travel around with his movies; Fred Aydon; Bob Jones; Cecil Morton and Ole Johnson, who used to travel to Riondel every day to work at the Bluebell mine.

I hauled logs from Mount Buchanan, Murphy Creek and Powder Creek for Timberland (Wilf and Claire Higgins) for a few years. We dumped the logs in Kaslo Bay, where the booms were made up. Some of those on the crew were Bill Pomponio, Ken Frie, Ernie Aasen, Frank Bodard, Bob Isaacs, Ziggy Baschzok and Dale Johnson. Fred Aydon owned the Imperial Oil gas station in those days; Frank Carney delivered diesel fuel and other things to logging outfits; Mac Laybourne repaired trucks and tires. Logging in general was quite different then. Skidding was done with Cat tractors; log loading was done with heel booms with tongs and the logs were scaled right there by hand, 20 to 30 minutes per load. Every log had to be timber-stamped on each end. The trucks were gasoline powered; on the downhill sections, water was piped to the brakes to keep them cool. This system made great clouds of steam when a truck was coming down the grades.

I worked for Timberland until they sold out around 1970, then went to work for the B.C. Forest Service. We were building the road from Riondel to Powder Creek on the east side of the lake, and Glen Allen was the forest ranger then. I worked for the Forestry until 1985, building roads, campgrounds and bridges all over the Nelson region, then I bought a grader and became self-employed.

In 1963 we moved to Kaslo from Sunshine Bay, where the Sicotte family had lived since 1944, bringing my wife, Jean, and children David, Cheryl and Craig to the North Arm. Glen was born in 1965 and all the kids went through school here. David went to Selkirk in the forestry program and now has his own logging truck; Cheryl married and lives at Howser; Craig went to the University of Victoria, then UBC Law school, graduating in 1991; Glen is working locally.

The Turner Family

John H. Turner arrived in Kaslo in 1947 to visit an army buddy, Art Bennett. When Art found him a job mining, he stayed. He played baseball in his free time, earning the nickname Lefty for his skills as a left-handed pitcher.

In 1948, Lefty married Florence MacNicol, formerly of Johnsons Landing. Flo had a small photography business for many years, then in 1960 she went to work in the Kaslo Post Ofice, where she remained until her retirement in 1983.

Flo and Lefty had three boys, Pat, Jim and Terry. Jim married Ilsa Thomas of Kaslo before his death in 1971.

Pat married Norma Wallace of Nelson in 1972. They have lived in Kaslo since 1975 and have two daughters, Jennifer and Penny, both in high school.

Terry married Wanda Visnoski of Meadow Creek in 1986. They have two small children, Jason and Amanda, and live in Kaslo.

Pat and Terry both have their own trucking businesses, subcontracting for Meadow Creek Cedar.

Lefty died in 1983 and Flo in 1988.

The Edwards Family

Irene came to Kaslo in the summer of 1945 from Trail, with her parents, Vera and Ben Frie, and two brothers and a sister. After finishing school she became a telephone operator.

Albert came to Kaslo in the spring of 1947 from Gem, Alberta, a small community north of Bassano on the CPR main line. He was employed at various jobs in the Kaslo area.

After their marriage in July 1950 they lived in Zincton, where Albert worked in the mine's mill until it closed in 1953. They then moved back to Kaslo and Albert was with the B.C. Department of Highways for 28 years until his retirement. He was active in social events with fellow employees.

Albert was treasurer of the Boy Scouts for several years, and was on the Hospital Board during planning and building of the new hospital. Irene was employed at the school for several years.

They have five children: Don of Meadow Creek, Glenn of Kaslo, Joy Fletcher of Surrey, Leah Honkanen of Shutty Bench and Connie Hum of Nelson.

Albert and Irene Edwards have lived at their present home since 1960 and enjoy family activities, gardening, woodworking, travelling and camping.

The Frie Family

Ben and Vera Frie lived for many years in Trail where Ben worked at the Cominco plant. They had four children: Irene, Denis, Ken and Verna. In 1945 the family moved to Kaslo, where Ben continued to work in small mines in the area.

Denis grew up to be an engineer and operates a business out of the Kelowna area. Ken worked in the bush as a faller, chokerman, and a bucker on landings. He spent some years in local mine mills as a flotation operator and was involved with the Duncan Dam project. He also spent thirteen years in the Forest Service, mostly as a truck driver. Irene is married to Albert Edwards and continues to live in Kaslo. Verna trained as a psychiatric nurse after moving to the Vancouver area and lives in Surrey with her family.

Two sides of the world combined with the meeting of Ken Frie and an Australian nurse named Patricia Hoad who had arrived in Kaslo in July of 1961. She was entranced with the natural beauty of snow-capped mountains and sparkling lake and enjoyed the friendliness and individuality of the residents. Pat quickly found work at the Victorian Hospital of Kaslo where she has continued to work over the years. Ken and Pat were married in October of 1962 and chose what had been the site of the old Halleran residence as the land on which they would subsequently build their home.

Out of what at the time had been an overgrown tangle of bush, Ken, an avid gardener, has created a park-like acre of peace and beauty. A waterfall, fashioned by him, spills down Lardeau Jack Creek through the property. He leaves his signature of his love of trees and flowers inscribed on his land. His main aim was to build something beautiful for his wife to look at each day from her kitchen, no doubt believing that the scenic view would inspire great culinary feats.

Over the years, Pat and Ken have been active in Kinsmen and Kinettes and later were much involved with the Figure Skating Club.

They raised two children, Gavin and Tana. Gavin is a rewind mechanic and has worked in Alberta at Fort McMurray and Edmonton. He now lives in the Prince George area. Tana recently completed two years of college education at SAIT in Calgary to become a printing management technologist and hopes to pursue a career in the graphic arts field, preferably in advertising sales.

The Garrett Family

Andrew Garrett arrived in Ferguson, just northeast of Trout Lake, from the United States in 1904 and was joined the following year by his wife, Geneva, and their children Nellie, Agnes, Elizabeth, Ernest, Clarence and Josephine. Two children, Ethel and Floyd, were born in Ferguson. From the stories told, those were happy years, and some family members still like to visit the ghost town whenever they are in the area.

Ethel White of Kaslo remembers that whenever she tried to wander out of the yard as a young child the family dog would tug on her clothes and haul her back. Andy Garrett worked in the mining industry, as did his sons later on. In 1918 the family moved to Kaslo.

They once owned a cow that delighted in causing problems by eating the neighbours' laundry from clotheslines. Clarence and his sister Agnes owned an ice cream parlour in a building that stood where the present-day Kaslo drugstore is. As a young man Clarence played hockey on the local team when the rink occupied the site of the present Kaslo Motel. He still liked to play in his late sixties.

In 1921 Clarence and Gertrude Nordquist were married in their apartment on the third floor of the Langham. They somehow managed to haul a player piano up there. The piano is still in use and through the years has entertained five generations of the family. Gertie arrived in Kaslo from Norway with her parents in 1905. Her father worked in the mines and died of pneumonia when she was about six years old. After their marriage Gertie and Clarence returned to the Ferguson area, he to a mine and she as camp cook. The mine was up a mountain, with no contact to the outside world. She was kept busy looking after her baby and cooking.

From there they returned to Kaslo and the same type of work. Clarence was strong and once carried a heavy cookstove up a mountain trail on his back, travelling on snowshoes. They eventually settled in Retallack, where Clarence became mill manager. They lived there for twenty-five years, moving to Trail when the mine closed in the early fifties. They raised a family of five, Douglas (deceased), Irene Craft (deceased), Bill and Dorothy Philips, both of Victoria, and Bud of Kaslo.

Life in Retallack was not easy—there was no such thing as inside plumbing, the laundry was done by hand on a scrub board, then hung to dry, and bread and other goodies had to be baked almost daily as there was no local store. Quite often in the winter they were cut off from town for long periods of time by snowslides. Gertie once had to deliver a baby when the mother could not get to the hospital.

Meat was kept in a "meat house," refrigerated by mother nature. This was once raided by a bear, which Clarence shot through a window. In 1972 Clarence and Gertie moved back to Kaslo, where they celebrated their 60th wedding anniversary in 1981. Clarence died in 1984 at the age of 86, and Gertie still lives in her own home, having watched her family grow to include sixteen grandchildren, twenty-eight great-grandchildren and six great-greats.

Floyd, now deceased, had two sons, Bob of Kelwona and Barrie of Castlegar. Ernest and his son, Jim, are both deceased, leaving Ethel White, a spry 87-year-old, the only surviving member of the original Garrett family of Ferguson still living in Kaslo; her late husband, Clarence White, was the first baby born in upper Kaslo (and the third in Kaslo); their son, Dale, lives in Campbell River on Vancouver Island.

Agnes Short Hughes (deceased) was mother to the late Marion Norberg, Ethel Yager (formerly of Kaslo and now of Nelson), the late Charles (Chummy) Short, Evelyn Short of Victoria and Ernest (Rusty) Short of Salmo. Nellie Harty moved with her family back to Spokane; she was the mother of thirteen children.

At one time half the population of Kaslo was related to the Garretts by blood or marriage; someone once remarked to a newcomer: "Never talk about a Garrett because the Garretts are related to everyone in town."

The Greensword Family

Charles Henry (Harry) Greensword and his wife, Mabel, arrived in Kaslo in 1946. They purchased the Kaslo Meat Market, which was where the Kaslo IGA store now stands. The Kaslo Meat Market was a small store that handled groceries and fresh meats, where most customers charged their groceries and then had them delivered. Harry operated the store until 1956 when ill health required him to sell the store and retire. He was an ardent stream fisherman and actively pursued that hobby until he died in 1966. Mabel continued to live in Kaslo until her death in 1974.

Harry and Mabel had five children, two of whom lived in Kaslo. After high school Keith, the fourth child, went on to join the RCMP, where he served for fourteen years. He and his wife Amy now own and operate Amy's of Vancouver and live in Richmond. During the Second World War Amy (Matsuzaki) and her family were interned in Kaslo.

Gloria was the youngest child and the only daughter of the Greenswords. After high school she attended college in Calgary and then joined United Airlines in San Francisco as a stewardess; she flew for two and a half years and then married Barry McCarron. They now live in Rancho Murietta, California, where they own and operate a golfwear business. They have two children: Scotty, twice Junior Golf Champion of California, is a UCLA graduate and is employed in the family business; daughter Barri-Lynn, a graduate of the University of the Pacific, also works in the family business.

The Greenswords' eldest son Lewis, served in the RCAF for five years and is a UBC graduate. He retired recently as chief of municipal grants for the federal government. He and his wife, Helen, live in Ottawa. Their son Gary is in the real estate business in Toronto.

Vernon, the second Greensword son, also served in the RCAF. As the sales manager for Remington Arms (Canada) and later sales manager of Gevelot of Canada, a subsidiary of a French arms manufacturer, he was classified as an expert in skeet and trap shooting. He died in Calgary in 1986. His daughter Sherin married George Elder; they operate their own real estate leasing company in Calgary. His son Douglas, a noted collector of WWII memorabilia, is self-employed and lives in Calgary.

The third son, Leonard, was for many years a radio and television announcer, first in Canada and then in the United States. Until his retirement he owned and operated an advertising agency in Spokane. He and his wife, Helen, now live seven miles south of Kaslo. Their son, Charles Henry, is a chiropractor practising in Spokane.

Kaslo remains home to all members of the Greensword family. As one of them said: "Kaslo can be described as not just a beautiful place, Kaslo is also a state of mind."

Harvey and Edna McIntyre

Harvey and Edna McIntyre moved from Field, B.C., to Kaslo in the spring of 1951 with their daughters Judy and Roberta. Harvey worked in several mines in the Kaslo area, such as the Cork Province and Ainsworth Base Metals, and out of town in the Greenwood and Silverton areas. He loved to hunt and fish and tied his own flies on a rather elaborate fly-tying system he developed during a long illness in the late 1940s. Edna still lives in their little house on Eighth Street. She has seven grandchildren and eight great-grandchildren.

The Hewat Family

Ronald Hewat came to Kaslo in 1920 as Government Agent along with his wife, Mary, and sons John A., Ronald W. and Harry C. He was born in Walsgrave on Saive, Warwickshire, England, educated at Mervin College and Harrow and came to Canada in 1888, working as a farm pupil at Moosomin, now in Saskatchewan but then in the old Northwest Territories. He moved to Calgary in 1889, then to Edmonton, and on to Golden in 1890.

After a trip to England he returned to Canada in 1892, ranching near Pine Lake, Alberta, and married Mary Walton in 1897. Later he returned to British Columbia, settling in Princeton. He joined the B.C. Government service in 1905 as a constable and in 1910 was appointed assessor, collector and mining recorder at Fairview, a lively mining camp between Keremeos and Oliver in the South Okanagan.

A son, Cecil, born in Princeton in 1909, was killed by fire in 1912 and is buried at Okanagan Falls. Ronald Hewat was government sub-agent at Wilmer from May 1914 to December 1915, when he was named Government Agent at Fernie and then transferred to Kaslo. He was a Mason of long standing, a past district deputy Grand Master, a life member of Kootenay Lodge of Perfection and a member of Kaslo Lodge AF&AM. He was a vicar's warden for 50 years, 33 of them at St. Mark's in Kaslo. It was worth your life if you sat in his pew at church and when the boys were young he caught them putting buttons in the collection plate instead of the money he had given them. He was also honorary president of the Kaslo Golf Club and the Board of Trade.

Retiring in 1939 he retained the post of stipendary magistrate until 1945. He loved fishing, golfing and lawn bowling and was well known for his English pipes and the saying "by jove." He died in 1959; his wife had died in 1941. His son, John A., was in both world wars. He married Dorothy Kerstead and they settled in Toronto; they had no children. Ronald W. married Pauline Downey and they had five children: Agnes, Pauline, Helen, Michael, and Patricia. Harry C. married Laura La Belle; they had four children: Wilfred H., Ronald F., Kenneth and Barbara Duplisse.

Jack Matthews' Memories

Jack Matthews arrived in Kaslo on September 9, 1919, and lived on B Avenue next to the Garlands, and across the street from Sam Green's. He started in school with teacher Mavis Kane in grades 1 and 2, Miss Hendricks in grades 3 and 4, Miss Whittaker in 5 and 6, Mr. Robson in 7 and 8, Miss Porter in 9 and 10, and Mr. Carter in 11 and 12. Jack Matthews continues his narrative:

In summer we would go picking huckleberries, leaving on the 7 a.m. train and go to 10 Mile, 12 Mile, or Whitewater. Generally 30 to 50 people were on the train for 25 cents each. When I got older, went fighting fires for 25 cents per hour. I got caught at Kokanee Glacier Park and had to come down a rockslide wearing a wet rag over my mouth. Made it down from Kokanee Park and got in a truck and went back up South Fork to the same fire—George Palthorpe was the forest ranger.

Sports

I have played basketball, baseball, and hockey. We played basketball in the old school on C Avenue, baseball in Vimy Park and hockey in the skating rink at Fourth and D Avenue, where the Kaslo Motel is now.

The rink was natural ice. The women would heat bricks in the oven, put them in gunny sacks and stand on them with a blanket over their feet and knees. I remember going to Nelson on the *Moyie* for the final game when Kaslo won the B.C. Junior Championship. The City would lease out the rink every winter. There was one Junior team and four City and School teams. The ice was generally ready the first week of December, and by spring there was nearly two feet of ice to melt. The Kaslo team played Nelson, New Denver, Rossland, and Phoenix—all junior games—after the boat got in at 9. If the boat was three or four hours late games started half an hour after it arrived. Sometimes sailing of the boat was delayed so the visiting players could get back to Nelson.

Every year they had a carnival with nearly 200 people in it. There was lots of snow in those days, and we would have to shovel two or three feet of snow off the roof two or three times a year. It cost 10 cents for hockey practice and 15 cents to skate for two hours. The ice would last until April, and one year we played a team from New Denver twice in one day—baseball in the afternoon and hockey the same night.

Some of the players were Leonard Garland, Bill Zwicky, Harry Hewat, Don Calvert, Russell Tinkess, and Raymond Butler.

One winter day we went to Slocan City in a truck covered with a tent and heated by a coal oil heater. We had to go through Nelson as the road to New Denver was blocked. It took six hours. When we left Kaslo it was 15 below zero. Arrived in Slocan and it was 20 below zero. They gave us two drinks of rum to thaw us out—we lost the game 9-0.

When we went out of town to play baseball we used a city-owned truck with two wooden benches nailed back to back and nailed to the truck floor. Some of the players were: catcher, Sam Gardiner; pitcher, Jack Matthews; first base, Leonard Cadden; second base, Casey MacPherson; shortstop, Lockie MacPherson; third base, Otto Augustine; fielders, Basil Erickson, Gilbert Erickson, Charlie Valance; spares, Tom Allan, Ted Allen, Phil Goodenough. That meant three pairs of brothers on the team.

Victoria Day—Kaslo Celebration. Boat from Nelson with 300 people. Ball team played in school park, two grandstands. We would be on the road by 6th Avenue and get the foul balls and take them back and get 10 cents a ball from the ball players.

Fruit

In summer we would fish on the CPR slip and the King George boathouse and catch suckers and sell them to the Chinese. We picked cherries and were paid 40 cents a crate and would make $4 a day at that rate. The Bing cherries were so big, it took only nine cherries to make a foot. Bill Hendren's house on B Avenue was then a cherry orchard.

I remember picking cherries for J.W. Cockle to send over to the London World's Fair (three-ten lugs). However, I can't remember the year. The cherries took first prize. When I was in England with the army, we would go to the pubs. One day I met a man and got talking to him. He said he'd joined the Canadian Army in Toronto in the First War. He was British, so he stayed in England after the war. He asked me what part of Canada I came from. When I told him Kaslo, he told me that he had looked after fruit at the Wembley Exhibition and remembered the cherries from Kaslo.

The next time I met him, he had a picture of the lugs of cherries and on the front of the box was "J.W. Cockle, Kaslo, B.C." I went home with him and met his daughter; six months later I married her and brought her back to Kaslo. She always said Kaslo was the most beautiful place she had ever seen. We raised our children in Kaslo. Everyone knows how hard Joan worked to build the library in Kaslo to its present state.

I worked on the *Kuskanook* in the summer while the train was being barged from Kootenay Landing to Procter. In winter I played hockey for the boat crew from Sirdar, not far from Kootenay Landing. We skated from Procter to Nelson some years. Most years the boat could not get to Nelson so we took the train from Procter to Nelson. Every summer we went to Vancouver for holidays. Dad would get a pass from the CPR and we would leave Kaslo at 5:30 a.m., arriving in Nelson at 9:30 a.m.; catch the train at 9:30 p.m. to Robson, catch the *Minto* to Arrowhead, and the train to Revelstoke and on to Vancouver. The trip took three days.

During the Second War, nobody was using the skating rink. The city took it down and sold the land to Bill Tonkin and Fred Aydon. They built the

Kaslo Cabins.

When the boys came home from the war, the city built an open-air rink across the creek from the Trailer Court. Every Friday night we had a hockey game against the *Moyie* crew. One day a truck with a high load was crossing the bridge on Fourth Street and took the cables down. The bridge collapsed. The water pipes for the skating rink were on the side of the bridge so they were gone. George Baker and I flooded the bowling green on Front Street so the kids had some skating. We would flood it after we got home from the Florence mine, about 1 a.m.

After the war I had a plumbing and hardware shop in Front Street. I put plumbing in several houses and worked on the school's steam boilers and put the sterilizer into the old hospital. I also put water into the old fish hatchery at the Scout Hall, and put the water in for the three outside ponds and the big pond where the campground is now. The troughs are all filled with gravel now. The hatchery was there from about 1940 to1945. Bob Thompson was the Fisheries man there. The hatchery held the fish in the three ponds for a year. The second year the hatchery people would put the fish in the middle pond (the Camperdown elm tree was in the centre of it) close by the lighthouse in the park. It was always good fishing there because the overflow took the excess food into the lake, and the rainbow trout hung around eating the food.

In 1925 we would walk across the bay on Sundays and drink mineral water from where the Beachcombers Marina is now. We would go through the samples and play with clay pots and old pieces of ore left from the refinery.

One Sunday in 1932, the fire bell rang. The fire was on A Avenue, behind the house across from the Butlers' house, built up on an island with water up to the corner of A Avenue and 3rd Street near the Masonic Hall. The firemen walked through water up to their armpits pulling the hose to get to the island. The sidewalk was built up because the water sometimes came up nearly 32 feet. One day we were swimming in the bathing beach and Leonard Garland came in and pulled the boat on the beach and started to pull in the lines and pulled in a 20-pound rainbow where we were swimming.

Roads

Some winters there was lots of snow. One day I helped Philip Goodenough on the mail bus. We left Kaslo at 11 a.m. for Mirror Lake, and then had to shovel slides all the way to Fletcher Creek. We would shovel out and move the car up to the next slide; behind us another slide would come down. Between 9 a.m. and 4 p.m. we had 24 inches of fluffy snow. We arrived in Nelson at 8 p.m.

Once while I was working for the Kootenay Florence Mine, we left Kaslo at 6:00 am with Cliff Anderson, six people in the car. At 9 a.m. we were at Mirror Lake. The road was all ice and no sand. The highways were

The 1954 Kaslo School Band.
KLHSA no. 988.40.

never sanded or salted in those days. We pushed the car around and got back to Kaslo at 12 noon.

When working for the Florence mine we travelled over a dirt road. In the spring, the roads were all mud. To get up Woodbury Hill, the government had a Cat to pull the cars through the mud.

I worked for Webster's Grocery Store as a delivery boy. For the first two years, we had a horse and wagon; then he bought a Model A Ford. The boss, Charles Webster, drove it until I was 16 and I got my driver's licence without a test. Later, Henry Whellams had the contract to haul the mail from Nelson in his station wagon. He was late so he borrowed the Webster truck and I drove the mail into Kaslo for three days, two days before Christmas. Mr. Whellams went over the bank into the lake between Woodbury and Florence mine. His passenger, Miss Coleman from Argenta, climbed up the bank and phoned from Woodbury. When they pulled the car up the mail was soaking wet. When parcels were picked up at the Kaslo Post Office, water ran out of them. Two days later, the ridge where the car landed was gone into deep water.

I went up Fry Creek with Noel Bacchus one Christmas holiday to his trapline. Every four miles he had a cabin. You couldn't stand up in the cabins. We took six days to go up and back—21 miles on snowshoes. We fished at the last cabin and got nice mountain trout for dinner. He brought out six mink and two marten.

One Christmas holiday I went with Cameron Clarke with a sleighload of groceries to the Florence Mine. The only road was the Back Road—it took all day. John Swords was the cook, and Bill Tonkin's Father, Jack Tonkin, was the mine foreman. A few days after it opened, Mr. Tonkin was busy barring down a chute to get some ore when the crowbar slipped and went through his stomach. They pulled it out and Dr. Barclay patched him up.

Every Labour Day we would go to Sandon to play basketball with the Sandon boys. The miners would make sure we had enough money to buy lunch. We would visit Johnny Harris's hotel. Cleaver's butcher shop, and Black's store. We would walk down to the red-light district and watch some of the customers.

Then there was band music. George Drennan was bandmaster of the Kaslo City Band, and he taught most of us. We would play a for the May Days celebrations in a bandstand that looked like a gazebo between A.T. Garland's store and the Big G store on Front Street. Mr. Drennan used to wear a uniform that came from is days with Sousa's Band, founded by John Philip Sousa, the U.S. march king, in the early 1890s. The uniform looked pretty tired in later years.

In the summer of 1930 there was an added interest in Kaslo Bay. The air division of CM&S—now Cominco—operated a flying school here to train pilots how to land on pontoons. It was the time of bush pilots and of transporting prospectors by air. The instructor was Page MacPhee, son of A. Logan MacPhee, the Kaslo policeman and works foreman. Page's mother was the organist for many years at the United Church. Page, who died in Calgary about two years ago, put in a lot of flying time in the North. His son was also a pilot, who was killed almost 60 years after that Kaslo Bay flying school; he was flying supplies in Nicaragua when he was shot down in 1989.

And there was seamanship. Dr. Calvert was a Methodist minister and also the Navy League commander in this area. He trained us boys how to tie knots and signal with flags. He took us camping and showed how to be sailors. One of us who did become a real sailor was John Stubbs, who joined the navy in 1930 and later commanded the Canadian destroyers *Assiniboine* and *Athabaskan*. John was lost in the sinking of the *Athabaskan* off Normandy.

Then too we used to skate on Mirror Lake when the people cleaned snow off the lake to cut ice. The CPR used the ice on its trains from B.C. to Winnipeg. On holidays the CPR sternwheeler *Kuskanook* took people down for 50 cents. We would build four fires around the lake for lights at night.

During the Depression I worked four days a month widening the road from Mirror Lake to Fletcher Creek with about twenty young people on relief. When the Conservatives were elected I drove the government truck for $2.80 a day in 1932-33.

I worked for the Village of Kaslo for twenty years, with twelve of those years as foreman. I was an alderman for six years. I am now living in Abbey Manor overlooking Kootenay Lake—a wonderful home for retired people.

The Jardine Family

Andrew Jardine Sr. was born in Collingwood, on Georgian Bay, Ontario, the eldest of fifteen children. He went out to Colorado in 1880, later going up to Winnipeg, where he joined the CPR construction gang working right through to Revelstoke. He was present when the Last Spike was driven in November 1885. Later he walked by trail by the Columbia River past where Nelson now stands and arrived in Ainsworth, one of the first settlements on Kootenay Lake. His brother Archie followed him and they both arrived in Kaslo in 1889. Andrew Jardine found a showing of lead and copper ore which he, Jack Allen and Lardo Jack MacDonald staked and recorded in Ainsworth in 1891. This claim—the Beaver—was the first claim staked in the Slocan and it started the great rush of prospectors in this area.

Archie Jardine remained for a number of years in Kaslo where he kept law and order as City Policeman. In the early 1930s he and his wife moved to Vancouver. Another brother, Malcolm, spent a few years in Kaslo; he never married and in 1912 he moved to Tonopah, Nevada, where he died at the age of 97.

Andrew Jardine married Frances Metz from Salt Lake City in 1895. They were the second couple to be married in the Anglican Church in Kaslo. In 1907 a son, Andrew, was born to them. In 1935 Andrew Jr. married Margaret Alexander, third daughter of James and Margaret Alexander of Cooper Creek in the Lardeau. They had two sons, Jim and David, who grew up in Kaslo. Jim married Elaine Gaskell, daughter of Ed and Irene Gaskell. For a few years Jim was employed by Kootenay Forest Products in the area. When T&H Sawmills built its sawmill here Jim worked as woods superintendent for a number of years. For the past 15 years he and Elaine have lived in Clearwater, B.C., where he is logging superintendent for the Vavenby Division of Weyerhaeuser Canada. They have one son, Ronald, an electronic technician, and a daughter, Susan, a nurse at the Royal Inland Hospital in Kamloops where she and her husband, Ken Gerbrandt, and young son Justin live. Ronald has two sons, Michael and Kevin.

In 1957 David Jardine married Alice Ross, daughter of Al and Mary Ross of Castlegar. David also worked for Kootenay Forest Products, and later for Cominco at Riondel before moving to North Vancouver where he was employed by the District of North Vancouver. For the past fifteen years or more he has worked for Sidney Freightways in Vancouver and on the Island.

He and Alice had two daughters and one son. Debra, born in Kaslo, is married and has two sons. She, her husband and sons live in Lillooet, where they own and operate the Four Pines Motel. Jeanette, born in North Vancouver, is a secretary in Port Moody. Glen, born in North Vancouver in 1971, lost his life in an accident in March 1992. His body is in the family plot in Kaslo Cemetery.

Andrew Jardine Sr. served as City Alderman in 1894, 1901, and 1904-05. Jardine Mountain, Jardine Creek and a Kaslo street named Jardine Street are named in honour of him and Andrew Jr.

In the early 1920s Andrew Sr. assisted by the late Sam Bruce, built the pavilion at the park. He hewed the square timbers by hand with a broadaxe for the sills that were buried in the sand for posts for the foundation of the building. This building was officially opened in 1925 by the Governor-General of Canada, Lord Byng, while he was on a tour of the country. The vice-regal party arrived in Kaslo on board the sternwheeler *Nasookin.* Mayor David Kane in his Studebaker accompanied by Lord and Lady Byng led the parade. The park was officially named Vimy Park in honour of the men who lost their lives in the successful battle for Vimy Ridge in France. Their names are inscribed on the monument at the Cenetaph here. Lord Byng, as General Sir Julian Byng, commanded the Canadian Corps at Vimy and later the British Third Army.

By the time of Andrew Jardine's death in 1946 at 86, he had taken out 57 consecutive Free Miner's Licences here. He named the Antoine Mine after an Indian cook named Antoine who travelled with him on a prospecting trip in the Slocan, preparing bannock and beans for the hungry prospectors. Mr. Jardine staked it in Ainsworth, because Antoine, as a native, was unable to do so. The property was sold for $40,000 and for many years it was a very productive mine owing to the high grade of ore in the veins but like many other mines it now lies dormant in the hills. Mr. Jardine was foreman on many of the wharves built along Kootenay Lake from Nelson to Lardeau for the steamers to land.

In 1891 while coming down from prospecting in the hills Andrew Jardine and Jack Allen came across a bear beside a lake; they named that lake Bear Lake. After that the name was somehow changed to Fish Lake. Bear Lake is the first lake on the highway travelling from Kaslo to New Denver; the other lake, closer to New Denver, is Fish Lake. Scotty Mitchell, a bachelor, owned the Bear Lake Hotel and Store, right on Bear Lake, where he accommodated travellers, residents and miners working in the area. He also operated the Bear Lake Post Office on his premises. He is buried in the Kaslo Cemetary.

Andrew Jr. worked for the provincial government as a logger in the Lardeau Valley and at many mines in the Kootenays. To name a few: the Scranton, Utica, Lucky Jim, Noble Five, Yale Lead & Zinc, the Spokane in Ainsworth, and the Cork Province. He was job foreman at several of these mines, and he also owned the Emerald Mine on Emerald Hill. Since his death in 1990, his sons have owned the Beaver and the Emerald. His wife, Margaret, has always taken an active role in the community. She served as Alderman in 1963-64-65-66 and on the Victorian Hospital of Kaslo board for 31 consecutive years, seven of those years as board chairman.

During her tenure as chairman many people urged that an intermediate-care facility be built in conjunction with the Kaslo hospital to ensure that all those in need of such an institution would be able to remain in their home town rather than be placed in facilities elsewhere. Beginning in 1980 much research was done toward this end, and many hours have been spent in committee meetings—but as of today the citizens of Kaslo and area are still hoping and working so that one day this project will become a reality. Mrs. Jardine is also a life member of the Ladies Auxiliary to the Victorian Hospital of Kaslo and remains quite active in 1993.

The Langille Family

On May 25, 1957, George and Doreen Langille and their children Nancy and Larry arrived in Kaslo from Tatamagouche, Nova Scotia.

People have often asked, "How did you find Kaslo?" The answer is practical—George had a brother who was a partner in T&H Sawmills, so he had a job to come to.

After a few months he decided he would continue with his trade of plumbing. He built several houses in Kaslo, and realized the inconvenience of having to buy all the material in Nelson, so he opened a building supply store in 1960—Kaslo Building Supplies. After selling the store, he continued to work at plumbing and heating.

Doreen worked at the telephone office for six years, and was on call at the school for many years. She now operates her own business—Mary Kay cosmetics, colour and figure analysis.

Nancy, who attended Kaslo School and business college in Trail, lives in Kaslo; she is married to Stan Baker and has two children, Corey and Stacey.

Larry, who attended Kaslo School and BCIT in Vancouver, has his own business in Nelson—Nelson Building Maintenance He is married to Diane (Hansen), and has two children, Scott and Sherrie.

The Lawrence/ Leith Family

The Lawrence family first moved to Kaslo in May 1973, when Jean and George arrived. George became manager of the Liquor Store. He had discovered the Kootenays in 1972 when he came with a friend, Bill Thorstad, to visit the Duncan Dam. Mr. Thorstad had worked building the road to the Duncan Dam. For ten years the Lawrences enjoyed the beauty of the Kootenays until George's retirement in 1982, and in 1983 they moved back to the coast, and now live in Abbotsford. During their time in Kaslo, George discovered the joy of fishing for the big ones on Kootenay Lake and was active in curling, becoming a life member of the Kaslo Curling Club.

The second wave of Lawrences arrived in 1978 when Ron and Lynn Leith moved here from Burns Lake with their two children. Lynn, daughter of the George Lawrences, soon found work as a nurse at the local hospital and Ron started work as a carpenter. Lynn can still be found at the hospital but these days Ron can be found waiting on customers at the building supply store. Their children, Reg and Debra, started school here and are now both in high school. The family has enjoyed the country taking part in camping, hiking, and hunting. The children are active in sports both in and out of school.

The third and so far final Lawrence to arrive in Kaslo was George's brother Ben, fondly remembered as Gentle Ben. Ben Lawrence moved here in 1981 and lived at Schroeder Creek, a few miles north of Kaslo. Ben retired in Kaslo and enjoyed puttering around Schroeder Creek Resort. He also was a life member of the Kaslo Curling Club, and died in 1987 while participating in the Seniors' Bonspiel.

The Laybourne Family

Ben and Euretta Laybourne moved to Kaslo in 1948 from Beverley,

Saskatchewan, a small place not far west of Swift Current. They lived in upper Kaslo for a few years before moving to Nelson where their daughter, Eileen, lived with her husband and family. They made Nelson their home until Ben died. Euretta then moved back to Kaslo with her son Arthur, living in downtown Kaslo until she died in 1961. Arthur has made Kaslo his home ever since. He worked in the mines in the area for many years and later was janitor for the post office.

Martin Laybourne and his family moved to Kaslo later in the 1950s. Martin worked as a mechanic in the local garage until his retirement. His wife, Elga, still lives in the area.

Ken Laybourne moved to Kaslo in 1950 with his wife, Faye. They lived with his parents until their house was built in 1951. Ken worked in the Yale mine, for the Village of Kaslo, and later with T&H Sawmills, until illness forced him out. He was a Second World War veteran and an active and honorary member of the Kaslo branch of the Royal Canadian Legion, as well as a volunteer fireman for the village. He and his wife raised three children here, all born in the old Kaslo hospital.

Trudy, the eldest, lives in Nelson with her three children, Bill, Nathan and Erin.

Debbie lives in Kaslo in the old family house where she and her husband, Dale, chose to raise their three children. The eldest, Cass, lives in the area and works for a local sawmill. Rachel, their daughter, lives in Cranbrook with her husband, Shawn, and their son Michael. Waylon has one more year to finish high school and then hopes to become a physical education instructor.

The youngest of Ken and Faye's children, Daryl, lives in Kaslo with his wife, Terri, and their sons Travis and Corey.

The Leathwood Family

Stan and Shelagh Leathwood arrived in Kaslo in the spring of 1959, having come over the Monashee Pass, at that time was not much better than a wagon trail. They were driving a blue-and-white 1953 Chevrolet loaded with all the necessities, five children, and a pregnant Shelagh. After negotiating several of the numerous switchbacks—some of which they had to back up to get around, and dealing with their vacuum shift, which would become stuck in second gear from lack of oil—Shelagh left her fingerprints firmly indented in the window divider after the drive through the hair-raising sheer dropoffs on the roads. Her experience prompted Shelagh to make a prophetic statement then—she told Stan, "Now that you have got me in here you will never never get me back out." This has proved true. Stan was amazed at how three drops of oil repaired the vacuum shift at the first garage.

Shelagh and Stan have always felt it was an act of God that they settled in Kaslo. They both believe there is no finer place to raise a large family or to retire, thanks to Kaslo's unique location, atmosphere and friendly people.

Shelagh was the daughter of a provincial policeman and had moved around the province a great deal. Stan had moved around the country quite a lot as he worked as a contract miner and construction worker. And there was his experience as a Second World War veteran. He worked for Cominco at the time as a development miner to drive the tunnel and shaft raise at Duncan Lake before the Duncan Dam project and flooding.

Once the Leathwoods arrived, they rented the old Morton house on Washington Street, a nice family home. Stan commuted to Duncan Lake for about ten months.

Shelagh noticed the Nomland property for sale and felt it was the ideal place to raise a large family with its garden and fruit trees, so they both decided to let the cards fall where they may and establish their roots. After the Duncan contract was completed Stan moved on to the Bluebell at Riondel and commuted back and forth by boat from Woodbury and car to Kaslo.

Shelagh, in addition to raising and caring for a family of seven (two of whom were born here), became involved in many aspects of village life, serving on many executive committees—May Days, Commisioner to Guides and Brownies, and the Anglican Church. For years she catered the Kinsmen Club's Tuesday night dinners and for the past twenty-one years she has served as a school trustee for School District 86, travelling many miles back and forth to Creston.

Stan worked for around twelve years at Riondel before leaving to become the clerk of works and the future maintenance man at the Victorian Hospital. When the old hospital was torn down and rebuilt, Stan took on the challenge of landscaping the new hospital grounds, shaping them into the aesthetically pleasing grounds we see today. Stan has been heavily involved in community affairs, serving on village council as well as other committees, both cultural and recreational.

For a time, Shelagh and Stan operated a small nursery in Kaslo supplying shrubbery, plants and trees, and Stan has also taught gardening and landscaping classes in the area. Many landscaped grounds in the area stand out as a result of his guidance.

Their children have also become involved in various cultural and recreational developments in Kaslo. Thanks to the academic excellence and influence of the Kaslo School they all went on to pursue excellent careers and there is no doubt that Kaslo, with its unique personality and quality of life, has been a major factor in their success. They will always have a special place in their hearts for Kaslo.

Stan and Shelagh are now retired to enjoy the cultural and recreational life of Kaslo that they have been so much a part of for more than three decades, and also to enjoy their grandchildren—there is now a second and a third generation of Leathwoods in Kaslo. Every family must have a place to start its roots—and Kaslo is that place to the Leathwood family. Stan and Shelagh sum up their time in Kaslo by saying, "Thank you, Kaslo and the Kootenays, the only country God made complete."

Einar and Kay Linn

My family and I came to Kaslo in the fall of 1948. Kaslo was not where I wanted to come to, but we arrived on the 20th of October, a snowy, cold day, and I think it was a long time before I settled in. Anyhow, it was so nice to hear the old train from Nakusp which came in on Wednesdays and Saturdays. The Greyhound bus ran daily to and from Nelson and, of course, the *Moyie*, which stole my heart as I had lived in England and loved the sea and all boats. I used to wrap my kids up and wait for her to come into the bay. When the whistle blew, I was waiting for her—and so were quite a few kids, too.

Kaslo was a busy place then. The mines were going and everyone seemed quite happy. The Royal Canadian Legion was quite a busy place then, too. The first Christmas party we had an invitation to come and bring our kids. Santa Claus was to arrive from the North Pole. I think there were over 100 children. What a party that was! We had platters of sandwiches and cookies, and how we all waited for Santa. The doors were thrown open and there was Santa himself with his reindeer. Each child was given a lovely wrapped gift. Mrs. Claus, of course, couldn't come; she had the flu. Mr. Wardle kept everyone happy with all his piano music and songs. Mr. Webber always was near by to help us out. As we were always short of wood and we had no electricity, we had a huge boiler on the back of the stove for dishes, etc. Then later we had some ladies from the Auxiliary who were receiving their 25-year pins—Mrs. Driver, Mrs. Chandler, Mrs. McGibbon and Mrs. Whittaker.

There were five war brides and it was nice to know they were all from the Old Country so we had many things in common.

We were kept quite busy in those days at the Legion. Lots of work and not much money. We did survive though and had many wonderful times. My husband, the late Einar Linn, and the late Sam Nofield were putting a ceiling in the hall as there was no ceiling. They worked sometimes until two in the morning.

Those were the days, my friend, those were the days.

The McKinnon Family

The McKinnon family, Tom, Elsie, Peter, Ian and Neil, arrived in September 1963 in Kaslo, where Tom was employed by the Government Agents Branch. The family left Atlin, a small settlement in northwestern

B.C., just as the leaves were falling and the reality of winter was approaching. They arrived in Kaslo to warm sunshine, leaves on the trees and what turned out to be a beautiful Indian summer, and the experience became known as the miracle of the two summers. Construction of the Duncan Dam was in the planning stage, housing was at a premium, the hospital was closed and doubts about the transfer to Kaslo were the only clouds on the horizon.

In the years that followed the McKinnons discovered that Kaslo had much to offer—it was a great place for children, with a fine school, a community to feel at home in, and friends and acquaintances with whom they could share life.

When Tom had to leave Kaslo to accept a promotion in New Westminster as Regional Government Agent, the family was greatly honoured at a community party just before their departure. A burl table crafted by Cappy Jacura was presented, and also a plaque inscribed *Presented to Tom & Elsie by the citizens of Kaslo and District in gratitude for years of friendship and exemplary community service, June 17, 1978.*

After retiring from his post as regional manager of Government Agents for the Coast Region, Tom and Elsie returned to Kaslo to retire in a home their son Peter built. Tom became deeply involved in community affairs again, and was honoured with the Citizen of the Year award in 1989.

Peter, Ian and Neil attended school, enjoyed sports and community involvement and today share with their families and friends the good times they had within the community of Kaslo.

The Morris Family

Jack moved to Kaslo from Nelson in 1953 when he bought the G.S. Baker clothing store in Kaslo and renamed it Jack Morris Men's & Ladies' Wear. His first venture into community life was as president of the Bowling Club. He was also the last president as the club folded the following year and Jack was left holding the bowling balls. These he kept until the club was reactivated in 1979 when they were returned.

Jack married Thelma (Dot) Jerome in Nelson in December 1953 and they made their home in Kaslo Bay, where they later built a larger house to accommodate their growing family. This was one of the few new homes built here at that time. Construction has been going on non-stop since.

After a serious automobile accident, Jack had to give up the store. He moved his family to Mirror Lake and developed the Mirror Lake Tent and Trailer Park, which the family operated until 1979, when they moved back to Kaslo.

Jack worked for School District 86 for many years as bus driver and maintenance foreman. Dot was the office clerk at the Victorian Hospital for over twenty years. During this time, Jack's contributions to the community

162

can only be described as monumental—having joined the Board of Trade, the forerunner of the Kaslo and District Chamber of Commerce, in 1953, he is a past president and that body's longest-serving member; he has also served as a fireman, an ambulance driver, a school trustee, a member of PTA, an alderman, the mayor, a director on the RDCK, a District Coroner, the Harbourmaster for the Department of Fisheries and Oceans, Commodore of the Kaslo Boat Club for 31 years, and as a director of many organizations—the Canada Futures Committee, the West Kootenay and Regional Development Co-ordinating Groups, the Regional Economic Diversification Group, the Kaslo and District Health Planning Society, and been deeply involved with the Kootenay Lake Historical Society and its efforts to preserve and restore the *Moyie*, the oldest passenger sternwheeler in existence today, dating back to 1898. That's not all—Jack was also a driving force in organizing the construction of the arena, serving on the Kaslo Recreation Association and the Kaslo Recreation Commission, as well as on the boards of many sports clubs throughout the years.

Jack and Dot have five children.

Don is an instrument mechanic and has his own company. He and his wife, Wendy, live in North Vancouver and enjoy scuba diving and world travelling.

Dale still lives in Kaslo. He was active in drama and gymnastics in high school, and is still an avid sportsman, being active in curling, softball and hang gliding. He is also a gifted magician and is in demand throughout the area. He is a shareholder in Acoustic Sciences Corp. Canada, a company that builds acoustic treatment devices in Kaslo. He and Marianne Johnson are planning a centennial marriage in August, 1993.

Laurel-Ann was was active in the Drama Club in high school, taking the lead in a number of plays, and in 1974, she was crowned Kaslo's May Queen. She and her husband, Elov Simmons, live in Elkford with their four children, Shem, Shurri, Cheylen and Lydon. She is an active leader in her church and the Scouting program there, and in her spare time she keeps busy with her arts and crafts.

Greg enjoyed hockey and curling, and his rink once won the high school district championship. He was in the Drama Club in high school. He has a great sense of humor which is enjoyed by all. He and his wife, Diana, have one son, Kyle, and live in Abbotsford where he is with the Royal Bank. He is active in community service as a member of the Kinsmen Club.

Donna May enjoys sports and was a member of the Kaslo Figure Skating Club, at one time winning a gold medal for freeskate in the West Kootenay Zone Championships. She enjoys curling and horseback riding, and took part in several gymkhanas while in Kaslo. She lives in Vancouver, and after several years in the work force, has decided to upgrade her education; she in attending Langara College in Vancouver.

Jack and Dot are now retired and enjoying a much deserved rest in their home overlooking beautiful Kaslo and Kootenay Lake.

Noble/Bildstein

Frances Evelyn Margaret was born to Albert and Frances Mary Noble near London, England, in 1908. Frances was named after her mother and two Godmothers, and her parents called her Margaret, though in Kaslo she was known as Peggy. Her one brother, John (usually called Jack), died recently in Victoria.

When her father decided to emigrate to Canada, her mother told him, "If you are going to Canada, I am going too." When they arrived in Canada they decided to take a train west as far as it could go and ended up in Vancouver.

After teaching a few years in England, Margaret headed for Vancouver as an exchange teacher to be near her parents. In those days, an exchange teacher could teach for one year in the new country and then had to return to her former school. Margaret's was the Mundella School in Folkestone, Kent. After a year or two she resigned from the school in Folkestone and moved to Canada.

She taught school in Vancouver before accepting a position at Retallack, above Kaslo, because she wanted the experience of living and working in the wilds. She recalls travelling on a rocking, rattling train from Vancouver to Nelson; then by sternwheeler north on Kootenay Lake. The trip took 24 hours. As she was travelling inland she thought she would be lost in the heart of the mountains forever.

William Bildstein was a blacksmith for the Duncan Lake Lumber Company. Some time in the twelve months after Margaret's arrival, the two met and the sparks flew; Margaret and Bill travelled to Vancouver to be married at the Anglican church that was her mother's parish church.

She and Bill moved to Howser, where she worked in the cookhouse as a waitress. In the fall of 1946 she started a school there. She stayed with an older couple, Mr. and Mrs. Greenlaw. They provided one room of their house for a schoolroom. It was very small, and there was difficulty fitting in enough desks for her ten or so students. They used the hallway of the house for their gym where they would dance and play games. She often thought, "This is a far cry from schools where I taught in England."

Peggy Bildstein also taught in Meadow Creek before she came to teach at the Kaslo School in September 1957. She began in the old brick school, and remembers the roof being "rattly." When a fire drill was held and the children were going down the stairs the top of the building would shake. Peggy helped organize many Christmas Concerts over the years she taught in Kaslo, and also helped Marjorie Ringheim with the maypole dance every

May Days. Peggy retired from teaching in June 1973. She had taught in Kaslo for 15 years.

Bill is buried in the Kaslo Cemetery, along with their baby daughter, who died in infancy. Their son, Ted, lives in Tasmania. Peggy now lives in the Gardom Lake Rest Home between Salmon Arm and Enderby, B.C. Two of her former students, Laura Aasen and Nola (Griswold) Bennett, live in the area and visit her occasionally.

The Nomland Family

My name is Sonny Nomland, and I have been asked to write a short history as to when and why our parents decided to locate in Kaslo, and how my three sisters and I enjoyed growing up here.

Our dad, Sam Nomland, was a miner and worked in many gold mines throughout British Columbia after he emigrated to Canada from Norway in 1929.

During the early part of the Second War, we were living in Wells, B.C., where Dad was employed at the Cariboo Gold Quartz mine. However, as lead and zinc were in greater demand for the war effort a lot of the miners moved to the lead mines. Dad came to the Kootenays in the spring of 1943 and got a job at the Kootenay Florence mine near Ainsworth.

After school was out in June 1943, my mother, Johanna, myself and my three sisters June, Jean and Betty followed Dad to Kaslo. Dad had rented a house in upper Kaslo next to the old reservoir.

We all took a liking to Kaslo immediately. We couldn't get over all the fresh fruit that was available and the beautiful gardens that can be grown here with a little bit of effort. Up north we never had the opportunity to have fresh fruit or grow any kind of a garden because of the short growing season.

Another treat to us kids was being able to drink all the fresh milk that was delivered right to your door for 10 cents a quart. At that time there were two dairies delivering door to door—Frank Abey and Henry Larsen's Kaslo Dairy.

One of the biggest thrills of the day for me as an 11-year-old boy was to get up early and ride on Henry Larsen's milk truck to deliver milk. I don't ever remember getting paid for this, but just being able to ride on the truck's running board made it all seem worthwhile.

During the cherry season my sisters and I could always manage to make a few dollars picking cherries. This was before the Little Cherry disease hit Kaslo and the cherry industry was big business here.

We couldn't pick cherries in the afternoon heat, so we spent pretty well all our afternoons at the beach. It always seemed that we were busy all summer—time went so fast. Before you knew it you were back in school again.

We had a good school in Kaslo. Looking back, I often wish that they had never torn down the big red-brick schoolhouse. I always loved to look at the beautiful landmark from downtown. I must say I did much better on the outside of the building than I did on the inside.

In 1944 Dad purchased Mr. Powers' house, one block up from the hospital on A Avenue. We lived there until 1946, when he sold it and we built the house on Washington Street where Stan Leathwood now lives.

We always grew a big garden and had lots of fruit trees. This of course meant lots of work for the whole family as it seems Mom was canning fruit all summer, as well as storing vegetables to last pretty well all winter.

Of course, growing up in Kaslo was not all work. We still found plenty of time to hunt and fish. In those days all the creeks were open and there were always lots of fish to catch.

The most unfortunate part about Kaslo was that after High School there was not much in the way of jobs available unless you chose mining or logging as a career.

Other than my sister June, who married Earl Coad from Victoria, we all married local kids we grew up with. June and Earl had three children. Jean married Gib Lind and they had three children as well. Betty married Merv Carlson and they had four children, and I married Agnes Webber and we've had five children.

Agnes and I are now living in the house on C Avenue in upper Kaslo that Tom Baba built for Mom and Dad in 1964, just a year before my Dad passed away. My mother is now 89 and is living with Jean in Victoria.

Both Agnes and I enjoy living in Kaslo again—it's a great place.

The Nord Family

Gustaf Albin Nord was born in the province of Västerbotten, Sweden, January 14, 1892. Times were hard in Sweden and as Albin matured he realized that for any real hope for a better life, it would be necessary to move to the new land, Canada, which he had heard so much about from his cousin's husband, John Alm, who had already emigrated to a bustling town called Kaslo in the province of British Columbia.

In 1911, when Albin was nineteen, he made the arduous journey by ship, train and sternwheeler. He must have thought that he would drop off the end of the earth. He arrived at Kaslo and probably got work at one of the mines. After five years, he returned to Sweden to fetch his fiancée, Nanny Homstrom. They were married, and the newlyweds sailed back aboard the Noregian liner *Kristianiafjord* from Bergen to New York in September 1916. Less than a year later, the ship was wrecked off Cape Race, the souteastern point of Newfoundland.

Once Albin and Nanny got back to beautiful Kootenay Lake and Kaslo, he promptly found work in Riondel at the Bluebell mine. Nanny stayed with her cousin, Emmy Alm.

Here is a translation of a letter from Albin to his parents in Sweden.

Riondel, B.C. Nov. 15, 1916

My dear parents!

While I still haven't received a letter from Sweden to answer, I still can't resist the temptation to send home a line. I hope this finds you all healthy and happy. I myself am at best health and my wife is getting better too although she has been a bit out of sorts lately.

As you can see, we are now at another place. Nanny is with Emmy and she's staying there for a while. I am working in Bluebell lead and silver mine eight hours a day and, as a beginner, $3.50 per day.

A couple of months this winter I could probably have earned more if I'd gone out in the forest in The Pas. But over the long run, it is better here.

One of the conditions of work here is that almost inevitably, you have to keep two households: one main one and one in the place of work in the mountains.

This place is still one of the few exceptions to this rule since the place is near Kootenay Lake with a mild climate, and beautiful. Not so high up in the snowy mountains so there's a lot of families living here. I rather wanted it like this too because it is nice and cheaper.

Riondel is on the other side of the lake about one hour voyage from Kaslo. The boat leaves daily from Kaslo to Nelson and back and stops here every time.

Now I'm sitting here in room no. 4 in the workmen's dwelling in Riondel, and I can't exactly say that I'm satisfied with myself. I think they call it homesickness.

It was to some extent implanted by being home, even though I didn't think that then. Sometimes my mind wanders so far that it would have been better if I'd taken a loan and stayed in Sweden.

I guess I belong to that kind that dreams, and a person like that misses the right atmosphere here. It's too materialistic for an idealist.

I want to return to the land. I feel it, but I'll have to see what time brings. Not everybody can be Americanized. It feels like I never could feel at home here but as I said: I'll have to see what time brings. As long as I'm healthy I guess it will work out.

I'll have to end this soon because it's only half an hour until I'm going down into the mine again and I'll first have to put on the mine rags. But I'll come back to you later. I hope I've received a letter from you before that. Give my love especially to Vilhelm from me together with mother and all the others.

Yours sincerely,
son Albin Nord
Box 504, Kaslo, B.C. Canada

Albin Nord's grandson, Maurie Nord, continues this report on the Nord family:

In 1917, my father, Alexander (Sandy) Nord, was born in Kaslo. It seems that Albin Nord got over his homesickness and decided to move his young family to Ross Spur in the Beaver Valley. It was not long after this that he got appendicitis and died at the age of 28. This seems so sad and ironic in that he was always making reference to his health and depending upon it to be good.

When her husband died, Nanny Nord returned to Kaslo with her three-year-old son and lived with her sister Emmy Alm and worked as a cook for the road gangs. Andy Jardine remembered her as a good cook and he remembered the young Sandy Nord as being so eager to wash his Model T Ford, for which he was paid the huge sum of 25 cents. Andy said that Sandy would wash it on Saturday and would be back on Sunday to see if he could wash it again.

Nanny Nord eventually married Edwin Leet, who helped to raise the wild young Sandy. Apparently, Sandy was always out fishing and it worried his mother so that the neighbour said that if he had Sandy as a son he would "kill a boy like that!"

When Sandy was about eleven, around 1928, a popular thing was to sleighride down "the cut." He was sleighriding one day and lost control, slamming into a telephone pole. The crash opened up a large hole in his skull, and the doctors didn't think he would live. They put a steel plate in his head and sewed him up and hoped for the best. Sandy lived to have a son and three daughters. The plate in his head exempted him from going overseas in the Second World War. This story has been passed on to present-day Kaslo folklore—the miracle survivor of the sleighride accident.

Nanny (Nord) Leet had a daughter named Myrtle. The Leets spent many years in Kaslo and eventually moved to Nelson.

Going back to Kaslo is always a favourite time for me. I can picture my dad as a little tyke running around in his knee-high socks and knickers getting into trouble and reciting the rhyme about Old Dame Milligan who hobbled on her cane out of Hong Kong Alley into Pollywog Lane.

Sandy Nord is survived by his four children, all in British Columbia: Vivien Moore of Fruitvale, Sherry Kowalchuk of Okanagan Falls, Pamela Krueger of Surrey, and myself, Maurie Nord of Penticton, plus 14 grandchildren and a few great-grandchildren.

Lawrence (Flash) & Darleen Olson

Flash and Darleen both grew up in the Kaslo area and attended high school here but it wasn't until 1955 that they moved to Kaslo to live.

In 1958 they acquired approximately 80 acres at the top of A Avenue, which was known as the MacDonald Addition. They moved a house from Howser onto the property, put on an addition and fixed it up; this was their home until they sold it in 1990. Since then they have lived in the downtown area.

When they came to Kaslo, Flash was mine manager at the Cork Province at South Fork. After it closed he was employed at mines and construction jobs in and away from the area. Darlene worked at several places in town but mostly at the Bank of Montreal. They both enjoyed their years with the Kinsmen and Kinette clubs.

When they moved to Kaslo they already had three of their four children, Susan, Lillian and Carl. Larry was born in the old Kaslo Hospital. All of the children graduated from Kaslo School. Susan has a son, Jesse, and lives in Ainsworth. Lil has three children, Amanda, Erin and Nicholas, and lives in Kaslo. Carl, his wife, Barbara (Smith), and daughter, Micaela, live at Crescent Beach on Kootenay Lake's West Arm, and Larry lives at Balfour.

All members of the family enjoy the outdoor life that the Kaslo area offers and are sure it will continue to be home.

The Pangburn Family

Jean Keilty Alexander Pangburn was born in Broughshane, Ireland, in 1906 and arrived in Canada at the age of eight months. The family lived for five years in Fernie, where her father, Jim Alexander, was a foreman in the coal mines. In the following four years her father and his wife, Margaret, had three more girls, Ellen, Margaret and Elizabeth, and later a son, Ernest.

In 1912 they moved to Cooper Creek in the Lardeau Valley, where Jim had purchased 52 acres of land. The land had to be cleared and cultivated but was very fertile. There were two bachelors living there. Margaret was the first white woman to live at Cooper Creek.

Jean Pangburn relates this story about her childhood: Father had gone ahead to Cooper Creek and built us a temporary shelter. He had built a floor and four-foot walls, and then raised a large tent on the rafters. This served us very well during the summer except for the mosquitoes.

When we left Fernie we travelled by train to Kootenay Landing at the south end of Kootenay Lake, then transfered to a steamer that travelled as far as Procter where we transferred to the *Moyie* which was a smaller steamer. The *Moyie* took us to Lardeau where we boarded the CPR train to Cooper Creek. The train stopped right in front of the tent that Dad had erected for us. He was so happy that we were all back together again. It

169

seemed that we were in the middle of a wilderness. Mother was lonely at first but was very brave and made the best of everything.

We did not have our house built by winter so one of the bachelors offered his very small house to us. We moved in and it was here we celebrated our first Christmas. I can remember it to this day. Mother had brought a cream separator from Fernie, one of those tall cans that could hold three or four pails of milk, and had a glass window where you could watch the cream rise to the top. Well, that first winter it was not used for its intended purpose—instead, mother used it to hide her darning and sewing. On Christmas morning there weren't any decorations or bright lights but hidden in the cream separator Mother had a small doll for each of us four girls. When we were all gathered around, Mother (to her apparent great surprise) reached into the separator and found first one doll and then another, amazed at what Santa had managed to do through the night. We were as happy with those dolls with china faces and either dark or blonde hair as any child could be with a present in the 1990s.

In 1928 Jean Alexander met Cecil Pangburn at the Cooper Creek station and they were married the same year. They also had four daughers and one son; Betty, Evelyn, Jeanne, Cecil and Joy. In 1993 Jean lives in her own home in Kaslo. Her husband died in 1988.

The Porter Family

Betty Porter (née Aldous) moved to Kaslo from Calgary with her parents, Eric and Agnes, in 1938, travelling to Kaslo on the *Moyie*. Eric came to take over the Pat Burns Meat Market, at that time next to the 1896 building on Front Street. The meat market was later moved up the street to where Eric's Meat Market is now. Eric Aldous purchased the meat market from the Burns interests after the Second World War and operated it until his death in 1955.

Andy Porter was hired by Agnes Aldous in 1956 and later married her eldest daughter, Betty. They have continued to operate the meat market since 1957. They have two children, Douglas and Holly. Doug has followed his father's footsteps in the butcher trade. Holly is married and lives in Trail.

The Saalfeld Family

Theresa Saalfeld was born in Munich, Germany, emigrating to Canada in 1931. Work was scarce, and she worked for a farmer in the Moose Jaw area of Saskatchewan. She married Carl and they operated a large farm, about three sections of land. They moved to Kaslo with their six-year-old son, Ron, in 1948. Mr. Saalfeld remodelled and built several houses in Kaslo. Mrs. Saalfeld was a great swimmer and enjoyed swimming in Kootenay Lake. She was an active member of the local Women's Institute and served on the School Board for 14 years. Ron is a independent worker, and can be found working on excavations, roadbuilding, forestry or mining activities. Mrs. Saalfeld, now Mrs. Anders Anderson, lives at Willowhaven, near Nelson.

Shutty Bench

Shutty Bench, the area a few miles north of Kaslo on the west side of Kootenay Lake, was founded in 1898 by Andrew Shutty and his son Andrew Jr. The Shuttys landed on the beach and ventured half a mile up to what is now Erwin and Wanda Ammon's farm. They settled on this spot and built a log house. In 1904 Andrew Sr. sent for his wife, Mary, and their children, Sophia, Mary and John. Andrew Jr. was an older half-brother of the three children.

The family came from Podbiel, a village in a Slovak region of the Austro-Hungarian Empire. The Slovak-speaking provinces became part of the new country of Czechoslovakia at the end of the First World War in 1918. Only recently, on January 1, 1993, the Slovak part of Czechoslovakia split off in a peaceful break to become Slovakia, with the remainder becoming the Czech Republic.

Others who came out to the Kootenays from the same area over the next few years included Joe Surina, John Mikulasik, Steve and Joe Bendis, Louis Furiak and Joe Gallo.

In time, Andy Jr. parted from the family partnership and went farming on his own. He built a house on top of the hill where Stewart and Margaret Dallyn's house now stands.

Andy Jr. worked at a number of things. He was at different times a foreman on the Kaslo & Slocan Railway line and a teamster hauling ore down from the Utica mine to the K&S flag stop of Keen. He worked on the telegraph line between Kaslo and Lardeau. He built and owned a telephone line from Kaslo to Shutty Bench. Later he allowed two other settlers to join his phone line—the Allsebrooks and Wests, both of whom had businesses. The line was built along the lakeshore and the bluffs—at the time there was no road between Kaslo and Shutty Bench.

Andy Jr. was a good farmer and had some modern equipment. He owned two horses, half a dozen cows, two pigs, twenty-five chickens, two dogs and various cats. He built a blacksmith's shop and took some work as a farrier. He kept honey bees and took great pride in grafting fruit trees; on one tree he had seven varieties of apples. He was unmarried and did his own cooking. At one stage, in partnership with Andy Sr. and a partner in Nelson, he leased the beer parlour of the Madden House on Baker Street in Nelson. The Madden, where Woolworth's store is today, was founded as a saloon and hotel by Hugh Madden, a Nelson pioneer.

171

Sophia, the eldest child of Andrew Sr. and Mary, worked on the farm. She was twelve when she arrived in Canada and had little opportunity for schooling. To help make ends meet, she got a job at Halcyon Hot Springs on Upper Arrow Lake. There she met Joseph Surina, and they were married in Kaslo in 1910. Their wedding gift was a twelve-acre piece of property of their own choice. Later they purchased an adjoining lot. She was a family person—she raised ten children and lost two. She took great pride in her family, was a serious church person, and didn't hesitate to lead people on the right path. Apart from her own garden and the unusual amount of work at home, she took on caring for flower gardens. She travelled as far as the Armstead place, three and a half miles away, on foot, and did her own babysitting while working. She told the story of the time she carried on her back a 100-pound bag of flour from Kaslo to her home almost five miles away.

Mary, the second daughter, left home early to work in Nelson and later went on to Spokane. She was married three times—to men named Blondell, Kroening and Larsen—and had two daughters by her first marriage.

John Shutty, the youngest, married Mary Vavrichan from their native land. They raised two sons and a daughter. John built a house and barn above and adjoining the original property. After John's death, Mary married a countryman, John Basista, and they had a daughter.

John Surina, a son of Sophia and Joseph Surina and a grandson of Andrew Shutty Sr., recalls his grandparents and his uncle John: "John Shutty was Grandpa's boy. He was a good provider. Grandpa moved in with John and Mary in later years. John worked casually as a lineman for the Kaslo electrical department. In 1927 he bought the first car on the Bench—a Ford with a two-speed Ruckstell rear axle. We don't know much about Gran and Gramps and their background. On one occasion he rode a pig backwards, hanging on to the tail and hollering for help. He was also mauled quite severely by a big Holstein bull. In his younger days he'd spent a lot of time in the military."

Shortly after the Shuttys established themselves in the area, a forest fire burnt all the benchland and some of the slopes. Andy and Andy Jr. then proceeded to survey and divide the land into lots, and named the area Shutty Bench. Horses, scrapers, picks, shovels and wheelbarrows were used to put in a tote road from Kaslo as far north as the Kemball place (later owned by the Cowans and now by their daughter Robina Haegedorn) and a side road below Arthur Curnock's place (later the Mark Jesty house and now the Pete Tarr place) down to the lake, where a wharf and warehouse had been built as a drop-off and pick-up spot for the sternwheeler Moyie.

The Bench drew settlers from Britain in addition to those from Andy Shutty's home region. Arnold Kemball, a retired Indian Army officer, built a large place at the north end. Rupert Guthrie built a house about half a mile south along the shore. It was later G.A. West's place, and now belongs to Don and Pauline Evers; their three children have houses on parts of that property. Captain West put in what became a famous cherry orchard. Tom Taylor was a farmer from Lancashire who settled where Bob and Barbara Tarr's B&B feed store is now. Maitland Harrison came from Yorkshire. Charlie Nichols was also an Englishman who had come to Canada to settle in the Barr Colony—now Lloydminster—on the Saskatchewan-Alberta border. Some people called the area the British Bench, in spite of the large number of Slovak families and a few others like the Koehle brothers from Germany and a Danish settler.

The first school opened in 1913 in what is now the old cottage on the Steve Bendis property, though there had been an earlier if unofficial school at the Pogson place down by the lakefront. The school remembered by most older residents is the one that opened in 1921 on land donated by Andy Shutty. It was at a bend in the present Highway 31, south of the John Shutty (later Basista) property. The pupils were surnamed Shutty, Surina, Koehle, Nichols and Gallo, and over the years there were kids from the Bendis, Furiak, Williams, Mucha, Jesty, Cowan and Allsebrook families. The school was closed in 1946 and the pupils were bussed to Kaslo School. The building was remodelled into a community hall, but was moved off the highway right-of-way in the early 1950s when the road was straightened and extended northward to Lardeau. The hall was demolished a few years later, and the late Cappy Jacura used the wood from it at his place.

Life was simple in the early days, John Surina continues. "The game was work from morning till late at night. Fieldwork and chores every day, and we really did live off the land. Sunday was partly a day off. After chores we would travel by horse and wagon or sleigh to Kaslo, to go to Sacred Heart, the Catholic church. For the rest of the day, we'd play ball or shinny for an hour or so and then get back to chores."

The early Shuttys are buried in the Kaslo Cemetery. Andy Sr. died at 89 in June 1936; his wife had died at 64 in September 1929; John Shutty died at 46 in a hunting accident at his farm in September 1932; Andy Jr. died in Nelson at 73 in March 1953.

Shutty Bench has changed; perhaps the benchmarks in its conversion from a separate community into a northern suburb of Kaslo were the closing of the school and the loss of the community clubhouse.

The Westerhaug family

Wayne Westerhaug was born April 22, 1948, at Yorkton, Saskatchewan, son of Arthur John and Frances (Schultz) Westerhaug. In 1953 his parents, Wayne, and sisters Ruth and Lenore moved to Matsqui, in the Fraser Valley, where they operated a dairy farm. Wayne received his education in Matsqui before moving in 1964 to Kaslo, where he was mainly employed in the logging industry. While in Kaslo he met Sharon Hansen, and they were married in 1969. They have two sons, Arthur David Westerhaug, born in 1970, and Kevin Wayne Westerhaug, born in 1973.

Wayne and Sharon bought property in the Allen Addition in upper Kaslo where he built his home and raised his family and where he still lives. Wayne has worked for the Village of Kaslo since 1981, and Sharon has been with the Credit Union in Kaslo since 1976.

Arthur and Kevin received their education in Kaslo, graduating from J.V. Humphries School where their mother also graduated. Arthur now lives in Nelson and Kevin in Kaslo.

As the family is very active in outdoor sports, Kaslo has been the ideal community for the Westerhaugs—it has everything to offer with its beautiful scenery, lakes and mountains.

Tom Humphries

Kaslo in the '50s and '60s—when I grew up here—was the same in many ways as it is now. Much of the village is as it was then, and the same small-town friendliness is still alive. Our mountains, all possible shades of green and blue through the seasons, are still as beautiful as they were when the Kane brothers were pounding their first stakes into the shores of Kaslo Bay. But some things have gone that will never come again; we did some things then that we will never do again.

We will never walk along the gravel road that was A Avenue, down the old trestle joining the upper and lower parts of town, go into Larry Potter's store, fidget in front of the long row of candy jars on the endless polished wooden counter and finally buy three cents' worth of penny candy (all different). Or, in later years, go into Keohane's Red & White and wonder at how many groceries could be crammed into such a tiny space. We will never again wander into Grandma and Grandpa Osopowici's drugstore with its unused soda fountain and its magazines and mystery tonics, or into Alfie's shoe shop with its pungent smell of shoe grease and woodsmoke, and Alfie himself perched amid the friendly clutter.

Unless time takes a twist, we will never run into the water on a hot summer day to swim out and meet the four-foot waves pushed aside by the *Melinda Jane* as she heaved into dock at the slip pushing her barge with its cargo of empty rail cars. Our teenage children will never sweat it out on that same hot summer day loading those same rail cars with lumber down near what is now the parking lot for the boat club dock.

We will never by welcomed by the cool interior of the CPR station down beside the rail cars, with its low overhanging chalet-style eaves, its slat wooden benches, and with Norm Miller sitting in the corner office under the green cone lampshade, working out the figures for the next shipment.

And the lake will no longer bring the pure, wet fun of frogs and logs as it floods in the springtime, right up to the Scout Hall.

The oiled floorboards of the "old school" will no longer creak under our feet; we will no longer smell that lovely old building's years of wax, chalkdust and sweat on a sunny autumn afternoon.

In those days past we ran and played in the hollow spaces of the old Langham, virtually abandoned for years (the father of one of my friends owned it). In January we flooded ice rinks with garden hoses in our back yard, or with firehoses on the school field, and in August, bare-torsoed and brown, we pedalled our one-speed bikes along the bumpy road to Mirror Lake, with the blue flowers of the chicory lining the hot, still ditches.

In one way or another all or those things have gone. With the paraphernalia of modernization and our attendant shift of perspective, something else has gone, too. That something was an almost innocent unconsciousness of ourselves as an "attraction." As a community, we were largely unaware of our own charms. I think that was a good thing.

Kaslo is not quite the same town it was back then. But don't get me wrong—it's still a wonderful place to be. Unless we all lose sight of why we're here, Kaslo will always be Kaslo.

Pat Dooley *(née Leathwood)*:

Memories of My Youth
The Green Forest
The path between the two houses was well-worn . . . out the back, through the hospital, and in minutes she was ringing the Humphries' door bell. She and Mary walked up the street and picked up Trudy. The next several minutes was spent answering the question, "What shall we do today?" On this particular day, they decided to go to the green forest. It was a special place for them out the New Denver road. The green forest was lush and hidden, with huge trees and moss covering everything. They pretended that moss-covered logs were luxurious chesterfields and chairs in a mansion . . . . For several hours that day and days to come, they played in a fantasy world of wealth and romance.

There were many special places in Kaslo where friends spent their time being together and playing games that didn't require many toys or material possessions... Mostly, our games involved using our imagination and getting to know our friends. The nature of the games changed over the years, but I remember vividly how important it was to be with friends. Easter Lily, the clearing overlooking Kaslo about a third of the way up Mount Buchanan, locations on the New Denver road, the beach and numerous other spots provided us with places to fantasize, plan and share secrets. Many of them gave us the kind of solitude that allows friendships to develop free of the distractions of physical toys.

When looking back on my youth, it seems fitting that green forest comes to mind immediately as one of our most special places. Green forest was alive, lush with moss and protected by trees. In Kaslo, we were able to grow up in a safe place that offered us many opportunities and left us with many memories.

A Place Called School

It was a daily routine. . . .She stopped to pick up Trudy, picked up Mary and then the three of them usually met up with Bonnie. Their final stop was for another Mary and then they walked the few blocks to Kaslo School. In the schoolyard, small children and older children were engaged in a range of activities befitting their age. As the bell rang, the 300 students entered the building using a number of entrances to begin another school day.

Kaslo School (now J.V. Humphries Elementary-Secondary) was a special school. It was special because everyone knew each other, because the school spanned kindergarten to grade 12, because the school held that special place in the community that schools hold in small towns and because of a host of other things that made it a wonderful learning environment. I remember several teachers to be as much a part of Kaslo School as the physical structure itself—Mrs. Ringheim, Mrs. Bildstein, Mrs. Huber, Mrs. Higashi, Mr. Douglas. What gave Kaslo School its uniquely special character, though, had a great deal to do with the principal—Jack Humphries. His presence was evident in so many ways—as a teacher, as a community member and as a disciplinarian. Mr. Humphries went home for lunch and we learned to recognize his return by his whistle as he walked along the road. The English and Law classes he taught were alive with discussion and thinking. When I later obtained a degree in English from university, I would remember Jack Humphries as the best English teacher I ever had. He was able to develop in many of us a love of literature and helped us make the connection between what we were reading and the themes in day-to-day life.

When I look back on my education, I remember my years as a student in Kaslo School with pleasure. When I reflect upon people who had an impact on my life, I acknowledge the role Jack Humphries played in helping me to believe in myself. To this day, his picture sits on my desk in my office.

Thank God for the Rummage Sale

The Anglican church ladies were in the process of preparing for another rummage sale. Calls came to the house that someone had something to pick up and the stuff was stored on our porch for weeks and months before the actual event. It seemed as if there were some months that might be classified as "pre-rummage sale" months and others as "post-rummage sale" months.

In any event, the rummage sale was a major event and we never knew

A typical Kaslo scene (looking east on Front Street) previous to the advent of motorized vehicles. Circa unknown. KLHSA no. 988.40.470

The Bear Lake Store with proprietor Scotty P. Mitchell (on the right) with a friend. Photo courtesy of Margaret Jardine.

what would show up in the house that had been purchased at the rummage sale. Clothing, dishes, tools, furniture and just about anything else just might have came from there. Years later, the rummage sale became one of many memories we laugh about at family gatherings.

The rummage sale was one of many things that I associate with our family as I look back on growing up in Kaslo. It came to be a joke in our family, as did the chickens, ducks, turkeys with names and numerous other things we remember about growing up. Kaslo was a special place for our family and our yard was constantly full of kids who enjoyed swinging on the trees, sleeping in the tent and generally enjoying being part of a crowd. We have lots of memories and things we laugh about now . . . our family gatherings include many "remember the time when . . . " and we all have a special place in our hearts for what Kaslo offered us as a big family.

In adulthood, our family has a unique kind of closeness. Our parents were totally devoted to us and, as parents ourselves, we have now come to appreciate how special it was to grow up together, in our house, in a village like Kaslo.

•••••••••

Dateline: Incidents through the years

1892—Wagon road to Fish Lake completed.

1892—*The Kaslo-Slocan Examiner* starts up with Mark Musgrove as editor. The newspaper lasts until May 13, 1893.

1893—*The Kaslo Claim* is started by R.T. Lowery on May 12, 1893; the paper lasts until August 25 the same year.

1893—John M. Burke's bank closed.

1893—Millington Brothers brick manufacturing plant is in operation; these local products built several long-lasting structures, including the 1896 Building.

1894—Another newspaper, *The Times*, was operating during this year.

1894—Fire in February; flood in June

1895—K&S Railway built by English and American capital; a huge raft of logs is brought from Bonner's Ferry to Kaslo.

1895—R.T. Lowery reopens *The Kaslo Claim*. In 1896 he sold it to David W. King, who renamed it *The Kootenaian*. The paper and printshop was sold many times in the ensuing years and many names appeared on the masthead. The editors were David King, 1896 to July 1906; J.G. Potter, July 1906 to May 1911; H.W. Power, May 1911 to July 1919; Jas W. Grier, July 1919 to February 1921; M.B. McClaren, February 1921 to May 1922; Frank S. Rouleau, June 1922 to

The 1901 City Council, from left: W. N. Papworth, Dr. G. Hartin, Angus Campbell (owner/skipper of the tug, Hercules), A. Jardine, F.E. Archer, A.W. Allen, W.E. Hodder, and Mayor G. Carlson. KLHSA no. 988.40.504

November 1940; C. Roy Fahrni, November 1940 to September 1954; Allan Stanley, September 1954 to August 1962; Mabel Robinson, August to November 1962; W.H. Bell, November 1962; Bill Staats, December 1962 to February 1963; Ernest R. Smith, February 1963 to March 1963; Art Stanley, March 1963 to January 1967; Denis Stanley, January 1967 to 1969.

There was almost as many publishers as there were editors during the company's life. They were: David King, 1898 to 1899; The Kootenaian Printing & Publishing Co. from December 1899 to August 1901; Blackburn & Webster from August 1901 to July 1912; Kootenaian Printing & Publishing from July 1912 to 1923; Frank S. Rouleau from April 1923 to October 1940; C. Roy Fahrni from November 1940 to September 1954; A.B.S. Stanley from September 1954 to August 1962; Graphic News & Publishers from August 1962 to March 1963; Art Stanley from March 1963 to 1969. The Stanleys, owners of the *Arrow Lake News,* moved the business to Nakusp in 1963 and published *The Kootenaian* from there until they closed the Kaslo operation in 1969.

1896—Electric light plant and waterworks project completed; ice rink built.

1896—In January, the Holland brothers set up a cigar factory on Front Street. On February 1, their license to manufacture the cigars is refused; on February 15 the refusal is revoked; the deal is on again.

1896—German bakers Riedel and Küster announce their intention to build a brick store on Front Street. Charles Kapps begins excavating for a large building at of A Avenue and 5th Street, to be occupied by the Kaslo Bottling Works when completed. This building becomes the Langham.

1897—A Avenue trestle built; many new houses erected.

1897—*The B.C. News,* a weekly paper was started. It changed its name to *The Kaslo Morning News* in April, 1898, but lasted only a short time.

1897—Columbia Comic Opera Company gave a performance *Said Pasha* to an appreciative audience, the first performance of its kind in Kaslo.

1898—Kaslo Board of Trade was incorporated on February 8 with G.O. Buchanan as chairman.

1898—A two-foot high Camperdown elm tree is brought to Kaslo by C.W. McAnn from "down south." It is planted at his residence at the southwest corner of B Avenue and Fifth Street.

1898—City Hall built.

1899—Board of Trade publishes an illustrated book extolling the magnificence of Kaslo, the "Lucerne of North America"

1900—The first in-town curling match takes place at the Kaslo Skating Rink on February 15.

1900—Sailing boat races were held to the great excitement of residents and visitors; they became an annual event.

1901—Queen Victoria's funeral procession in February; Drill Hall built.

1902—Cost of cordwood increases to $4.50 per cord to $4; ping pong craze hits Kaslo.

1903—Victorian Hospital of Kaslo opens.

1904—The West Kootenays produce nearly half the total tonnage of ore mined in the province.

1905—On June 29, bids for sale of the St. Pancras Hotel (later the King George) are called for, with bids over $2,500 being considered.

1906—First fruit fair held in Drill Hall.

1907—Logs in the sawmill boom in Kaslo Bay are frozen in; work is shut down temporarily.

1907—*The Kootenaian* laments on March 9, "...There are fewer narrow-minded people in Kaslo than any other place. IF THESE FEW STIFFS could be kicked out what an ideal community this would be to live in. ..."

1907—Kootenay Lake Farmers Institute holds formal inauguration on July 15.

1907—Winter finally drops its first frost on December 19, ending the longest rose-growing season so far.

1908—From the April 10 *Kootenaian:* "...THEY'LL DO IT SOMETIME! A local clever guy placed some dynamite in the oven to thaw out— yes, it happened but luckily he was only slightly hurt. Damage to the stove and kitchen cannot be properly estimated since they have disappeared. ..."

1908—Sunshine Lodge No. 57, Independent Order of Odd Fellows (IOOF) was instituted with charter members Walter LeGallois, B. H. Strobel, J. W. Power, J. M. Carney, J. N. Dally, Robert Hendricks and G. O. Buchanan. The Lodge garnered a a large membership in the following years, and the yearly excursion picnic to Procter, together with other lodges in the district, was one of the main events of the summer for many years. The three-storey Odd Fellows Hall, near the west end of Front Street, had the Lodge rooms on the top floor, rooms on the second and a store on the ground floor. The building was in continual use until destroyed by fire in 1950. The building known as the Alexander or Commission building, located on the southeast corner of Front and 5th, was then purchased by the IOOF.

1908—Earl Grey, Governor-General of Canada, wrote a long descriptive letter to Premier Richard McBride about his recent trip up Hamill Creek and over to Windermere. He intended to return, bringing a party for a longer stay. In his letter he notes, "...I am convinced that if this route were made accessible and the necessary action taken to

This group portrait was taken to commemorate the laying of the cornerstone of the Provincial Government Building. It

advertise its attractions, you would bring to this part of your Province a steadily increasing stream of people. . . ."

1910 —Women's Institute was formed.

1910—A fire originating near New Denver Siding was neglected and gained headway on July 15 and 16 until it spread to a point beyond Whitewater, destroying the buildings of the Rambler-Cariboo mine, the Payne mine, the Lucky Jim mine, the settlement of Whitewater, the Whitewater mine, much of the K&S Railway and a large quantity of excellent timber. Unfortunately, at the Lucky Jim, five men—Col.S.W. Pierson, Charles A. Norman, W. A. Chesley, Edward Lucas and David Patterson—did not have time to escape and lost their lives while taking shelter in the workings. A beautiful baptismal font was presented to St. Mark's Anglican Church in Kaslo in their memory. A sixth miner, Gus Gustavson, died on July 24, the day a memorial service was being held for the other five men.

1910—Charles Caldwell moves the Camperdown elm tree to his residence at A Avenue and Washington Street.

1911—On June 22, Coronation Day, the cornerstone to the new provincial building was laid by Thomas Taylor, Minister of Public Works. The program included exercises by the school children and massed choirs, speeches by several Kaslo citizens, including Mayor Archer and Archdeacon Beer, and an address by Mr. Taylor. The articles

The brick Kaslo School 1913 to 1969.
KLHSA no. 988.40.421

183

placed in the memorial stone were a copy of *The Kootenaian,* some coins and various "knick-knacks of local interest." The government building was constructed during the next year and has been in continuous use ever since.

1912—A miner was attacked by a huge eagle on May 3. After a fierce struggle he captured it. It was sent to the municipal zoo in Spokane.

1913—Kaslo School was constructed at a cost of $31,990. The bonds were all purchased locally, which gratified the local School Board of that time.

1913—The first appearance in public in uniform of the Kaslo Cadet Corps under George Hindle; Mary Caroline Davies, formerly of Kaslo, won prizes for poetry and short stories in California; Fred Archer's new "flivver" was frightening the horses on Front Street, and Mr. Strathearn's pony cart was the delight of the local children.

It was about this time that the first motion pictures were shown in the Eagles Hall. Those sponsoring the venture were Allan Anderson, and J. Riddell.

1913—Kaslo's new telephone system was in operation by August.

1913—Kaslo man invents improved cultivator; powered by gasoline and granted U.S. letters patent.

1914—The electric light plant was purchased by the city. This served until 1931, when the citizens voted to build a new plant as more power facilities and modern methods were necessary. This gave twenty-four-hour service and could be operated by one man. Frank S. Chandler was city electrical supervisor for thirty-six years.

The Buchanan sawmill had been closed for some time after the owner became Inspector of the Lead Bounty. It passed into the hands of W. Cook, who operated it unsuccessfully for a short time until it was taken over by the bank. It closed down for many years until it was operated by the Lambert Lumber Company.

1914-18—Kaslo people did their part in the war effort of the First World War. The 54th (Kootenay) Battalion was recruited in the Kootenays in 1915, trained at Vernon and went to England in November of that year under Lieutenant-Colonel A.H.G. Kemball, CB, DSO, of Shutty Bench. On the organization of the 4th Canadian Division at Bramshott, England in April 1916, the 54th Battalion became the senior unit among the four battalions the 11th Brigade under Brig.-Gen. Victor Odlum. The 54th fought at Ypres, the Somme and Vimy Ridge, where Col.Kemball was killed. Many Kaslo men served in the 54th—among them F.H. Abey, S. Bostock, Augustus Carney, T.H. Carney, J.W. Chadwick, E. Cook, A. Coombs, Alexander Fraser, L.A. Gillis, Howard Green, H.A. Hansen, W. Herron, T.H. Horner, J.W. Kellett, G. Koch, J. Koch, C.Lingard, C.McIvor,

The Kaslo Cenotaph at the 1992 Remembrance Day ceremony.

M.McLeod, G.A. Palmer, E. Reader, J.H. Skillicorn, A.A. Taylor and A. Taylorson. (It should be noted theat the records of the 54th show next of kin for several of these men to be in places far removed from the Kootenays.) And there were many other Kaslo men in other regiments and branches of the services. Those on the home front worked hard for the Red Cross and other patriotic associations, and even the school children did their part—the older girls helped with the knitting and sewing, while the young children grew potatoes in a huge patch behind the school.

In the Second World War, the effort of the Kaslo people for the Red Cross was outstanding, as it was in the First World War.

1917—New dam proposed to catch overflow from Mcdonald Creek. Arrangements to be made with Allen and McDonald. A bylaw to raise the height of the power dam on Kaslo River, assuring a better supply in winter. Both bylaws passed on Sept. 24, 1917.

1918—In January Grace Caldwell and Catherine Hughes successfully ran for city council, becoming the first women elected to a civic council in B.C.

1920—Public Library Association is formed on September 30 with founding members A.T. Garland, A.W. Anderson, R. Hughes, Vidler Papworth, L. Hanna, S.H. Green, John Keen, Ronald Hewat, Helena Nash Keen, W.H. Burgess and Sarah Carney. The library was in the provincial government building and run by volunteers. Records indicate that Miss S.M. Fawcett was librarian until her death in 1938.

1921—Fifth Street bridge condemned. Bridge to be repaired.

1921—A beautiful cenotaph on Water Street overlooking Kaslo Bay was unveiled by Judge John A. Forin on November 11, 1921. It is dedicated to the memory of Kaslo men who gave their lives inthe First World War. The names inscribed on the monument are Thomas H. Carney, Alexander Fraser, Harold L. Hanna, Harry O. Hansen, James W. Kellett, Arnold H. G. Kemball, John H. Skillicorn, James A. Sweeney.

After World War II, the following names were added: John R. Dryden, Clifford S. McHardy, Norman F. Meers.

1922—A memorial plaque to Lt.-Col. Arnold Kemball was unveiled at the government building by Premier John Oliver.

1922—Shade trees planted on Water Street.

1922—Sidewalks - Front Street, 4th and 5th Streets.

1922—Dr. George Carruthers Read, who had come to Kaslo from Trout Lake ten years earlier, was drowned in Kootenay Lake while on his way to see a patient at Riondel. A room in the Victorian Hospital was furnished in memory of Dr. Read, a well-known and respected man

The original Fire Hall. It was also a bonded whiskey warehouse for a time.
Photo courtesy of Dan Pasemko

who was noted for many kind deeds and unselfish acts.

1924—Vimy Park was opened with an impressive ceremony by the Governor-General of Canada, Lord Byng. Previously, the only recreation park was up the hill on the school grounds. Largely due to the efforts of Alderman Samuel H. Green an City Council, a large piece of lakeside property land was purchased in the city's east side from the McQueen, Butler and Whittaker families and is ideally situated for a park. Later, a pavilion was built by C.H. Goodwin, and fireplaces, benches, a ballpark and tennis court added.

1924—Kaslo Public Library is moved to the third floor at City Hall. Membership fees were $1.25. In 1925, 237 adult books, 12 non-fiction and 7 juvenile books were in circulation, and there was no funding from provincial or municipal governments

1925—Kaslo Golf Club, directly south of the city, was opened. Although the course is small, it affords a great deal of pleasure to Kaslo residents and visitors. The Rainbow Trophy event is open to all members of a golf club and is one of the highlights of the year.

1926—The road between Kaslo and Balfour was finally completed, linking Kaslo and Nelson with forty-four miles of narrow, twisting, unpaved highway. The highway was much needed—the only prior means of transportation was by boat. Among the first to drive this road were Mr. and Mrs. Fred Speirs, Laura LaBelle (Mrs. H. Hewat), Mr. Archer and Mrs. McQueen.

1926—Resolution by Board of Trade to petition Government to make beavers wards of the government. Among reasons given are that beavers dam creeks and rivers, irrigating large areas, increasing air moisture and providing better water supplies for fighting and preventing forest fire.

1928—Sidewalks installed downtown. Homeowners shared costs under home improvement bylaw.

1928—Tenders for annual skating rink operation.

1931—New light plant installed; contract let for dam. Pipeline, control panel, and surge tank generator make it a most modern plant.

1932—Fifth Street bridge condemned.

1932—Kaslo's second brick manufacturing plant was at A Avenue and Washington Street where the main reservoir was later situated. The plant later moved down to Valley Flats because of clay deposits.

1934—Board of Trade protests the closing of Kaslo's liquor store as it served a wide area.

1934—The high-speed boat, Lady Bird, owned by L.T. Gilbert, makes a 50-minute trip from Nelson to Kaslo.

1935—Board of Trade petitions council to develop Kemp Creek water supply; petition by ratepayers to develop Kemp Creek water supply at a cost of $15,000 By law passed by rate payers in September 1935. Job completed June 1936.

1935—A former Kaslo woman gets U.S. patent for permanent (Finger Wave) curling machine.

1937—Council approves motion to tear down 40 year-old skating rink, terming it a dangerous eyesore.

1937—Kaslo contracts with Provincial Police in April to police Kaslo at $30 per month.

1938—Kaslo Bowling Club organized; first playing surface was at Henry Giegerich's tennis court on Nob Hill.

1938—Rod and Gun Club given permission in May to shoot crows in city limits.

1938—Rod and Gun Club opens a fish hatchery in Kaslo River; Frank Chandler and Bud Thompson oversee the project. The headworks of the electrical plant dam are initially used for the project; Mr. Chandler and his son Bill catch coarse fish to grind up and feed the thousands of Kamloops (rainbow) trout in the hatchery. The "Chandler-Thompson Diet" becomes legendary.

1939—Annual membership fees for the tennis courts were $1 for juniors, $2 for visitors and $3 for adults.

1939—Kaslo Bowling Club moves to Front Street; it is still there in 1993.

1939—The first airport is built at Fletcher Creek. 3,700 feet long and 300 feet wide, with a additional taxi surface of 300 feet. The airstrip was surveyed by H.D. Dawson and levelled by Thom Sleep, operating his bulldozer.

At the same time, J.J. Bjerkness, a Norwegian-born fishing enthusiast, used his own funds and Mr. Sleep's bulldozer to construct five ponds for rearing Kamloops rainbow trout on his property near the Fletcher Creek airport. He eventually turned the ponds over to the Fih and Wildlife to be run concurrently with the Kaslo program.

1940—A.L. MacPhee moves the Camperdown elm, now about eight feet high, to the centre of the Trout Rearing Pond under construction at Vimy Park. The Kaslo Rod and Gun Club began building the 60 by 40-foot two-storey log building with volunteer labour. Designed to house fish hatching troughs, a number of large windows let in adequate light, and good-sized dormers were incorporated into the second floor.

1940—Fish and Wildlife, at the suggestion of the Kaslo Rod and Gun Club, released a good number of hen and cock pheasants on the Golf Course.

1941—The Trout Rearing Pond is in operation at Vimy Park; the circular pond is shaded by the small but dignified Camperdown elm. Interest in the Kaslo program is province-wide; the Chandler-Thompson

A view from the golf course. There doesn't seem to be much traffic from the look of the roads. KLHSA no. 988.40.341

diet raises fingerlings to eight and ten inches in ten months. Spawned redfish, or Kokanee land-locked salmon that have completed their life-cycle, now account for a major portion of the diet. This free-for-the-taking food source made the diet affordable, although storage was a problem; it took three tons of food to raise about 750 pounds of trout. However, in fall 1941 there was over seven tons of redfish in cold storage, ready for winter feeding. Approximately 100,000 fingerlings were released from the Kaslo pool in 1941; in June, 10,500, and in October 70,000 were released into the North Arm; 13,000 were released into the West Arm from the Bjerkness pond; and 12,000 were sent from Kaslo to the Slocan Lake rearing ponds in New Denver.

1942 —City of Kaslo donates a German gun, a trophy from the First World War, to the Dominion Government. A shell casing is kept at the light plant.

1942—Over 1,000 Japanese-Canadian people from the coast were relocated in Kaslo after the outbreak of hostilities with Japan. Initial resentment by residents soon vanished as the internees proved to be quiet and law-abiding.

The B.C. Security Commission (BCSC) requisitioned the Fish Hatcheries building, the Langham and a number of other buildings to house the internees. Throughout the war years, improvements

Fire Department circa late fifties by the look of things.
KLHSA 988.40.767

were made to many of these buildings by their occupants to make them habitable, or at least usable.

One of the most outstanding Japanese o come to Kaslo was Dr. K. Shimo Takahara. During the war years he worked among his own people, but as their numbers became less, he took on more non-Japanese patients, treating all his patients so successfully he became known all over the Kootenays. So great was his reknown that patients from as far south as San Francisco and as far east as Winnipeg would sometimes seek him out. His untiring devotion to duty and unselfishness endeared him to all who knew him. He worked until the night of his death, which was a great shock to the community. In his memory, the Kaslo Board of Trade refurnished the children's ward of Victorian Hospital.

1944—The Women's Institute recognizes and establishes the need for a Senior Citizens' home in Kaslo and area, however, provincial and federal governments of the day did not fund such projects. Although several attempts were made in subsequent years, the project did not get off the ground until 1979.

1945—The BCSC relinquishes its holdings in Kaslo, among them the fish hatchery building. It is leased to the Rod and Gun Club on a twenty-five year term at $1 per year to carry on the hatchling program. A waterline is installed.

1945—Kaslo Recreation Association (KRA) starts up with a mandate to promote,organize, and supervise all sports, crafts and cultural affairs in Kaslo. The KRA worked closely with city council and other community groups, organizing May Days, Babe Ruth and Little League Baseball, swimming lessons and much more. Its members repaired and maintained the recreational equipment and facilities, organized teen dances and Halloween parties, all with volunteer labour. For funding the association organized a full month of fundraising campaign in October, sharing profits 50/50 with the Legion on dances, and taking the profits from the May Days Midway and gate receipts.

1950—A fire destroyed three large buildings on Front Street. Those destroyed included the Odd Fellows Hall, with Grayling's Shoe Store, Morphet's Hardware, the Seven Taxi office and the Arkaid, all of which had apartments upstairs. Working in sub-zero weather, the volunteer Kaslo Fire Brigade contained the fire to those three buildings with great difficulty and no casualties, much to their credit.

1951—A very well-attended public meeting was held at the King George Hotel on January 25 to explain the new Gas-Ice product. Charles F. Gorse, president of the company, ". . .spoke in some detail of the

192

field opening up to Gas-Ice market, relating of its value to railway
and truck refrigeration; the fishing industry, and many other com-
mercial and domestic uses. . . ." P.E. Poulin, in charge of stock sales
in Nelson, gave a short speech in which he urged Kasloites to invest,
". . . assuring them that he had made close enquiry as to the reliability
of the company, and was completely satisfied that this was an A1
investment, and control of the company should be kept in Canada for
Canadians. . . " Mr. Gorse speculated earlier that month on January
4 that "there is no limit to the demand for this gas-ice, and the entire
output of the plant is already spoken for many times over. . . " The
company had leased property four miles west of town on Kaslo
River, and Mr. Gorse, with assistants A. Gardner and George Leet
set up a rotary drilling system there.

1953—Kaslo celebrates its Diamond Jubilee year. In the small city of 1,000
to 1,200 inhabitants, mining is still the main industry, and there are
several small logging camps operating successfully in the area.
Kaslo Bay is used as a log dump to form booms of logs which are
towed by tugboats to Nelson. Some farming and fruit growing is still
carried on.

1953—Tourism has increased—in fishing season, when the big Kamloops
trout are biting, out-of-town cars are almost as numerous as local
ones. In the summer months, different types of tourists arrive—
families on holiday, former inhabitants renewing old acquaintances,
golfers and older people who come to enjoy a quiet holiday amid the
magnificient scenery. The fishermen return again in the fall, as the
run of the big fish takes place, sometimes lasting until late in
November. Hunting is also an attraction for the fall visitors.

1953—Citing lack of use, Village Council asks the Rod and Gun Club to
relinquish its lease on the former hatechery building, and permission
is granted to the Boy Scouts to use the building twice a week.

1953—Kaslo's modest civic improvement program is carried out as fi-
nances allow. More concrete sidewalks are replacing the old wooden
ones, a new fire hall has been equipped with a modern fire truck. City
Hall has been renovated, a large truck and bulldozer have been
purchased and construction has been started on a garage to house the
city equipment.

1953—The new Lardeau road opened up a large expanse of new country and
Kaslo is poised to become the trading centre of the district. With a
slight increase in the price of metal, many prospects could reopen;
there remains an untold wealth of metal lying undiscovered in the
surrounding mountains.

1953—Interested citizens reorganize the library with hopes of obtaining
provincial funds under the direction of Mrs. Doris Drayton and Mrs.

W. Walker; they approach the Public Library Commission, which sends its superinendent, C.K. Morrison, to look this situation over. In a book about his tour of B.C. libraries he writes, ". . .I toiled up the steep stairs leading to the room under the tower and found a gracious library lady holding fort. Shelves were filled with an unhappy conglomeration of moth-eaten books serving little purpose but gathering dust. . . ." As a result of his visit a provincial grant of $250 a year was given if council would match it, and the library moved from its "Ivory Tower" to offices on the main floor of city hall vacated when the Bank of Montreal moved to Front Street. That year's annual report shows 3,507 books borrowed.

1953—A week-long celebration was held in August to commemorate Kaslo's Diamond Jubilee year, the sixtieth anniversary of Kaslo's incorporation as a city. Hundreds of letters had been sent to members of pioneer families, resulting in people attending from points all over North America. Reunions of friends who had not seen one another since "the Nineties" were many and varied. Mrs. David Kane, widow of the first permanent resident of Kaslo, was present as were many others who had been prominent in Kaslo's early history.

Entertainment was varied and among the most outstanding was an excursion from Nelson aboard the sternwheeler *Moyie*. Arrangements had been made for Nelson members of the Board of Trade to re-enact the pirate raid of '93. Fittingly dressed for the part, they landed on the beach as in former days.

The Bonner's Ferry Sheriff's Posse treated the crowds to an excellent musical ride, and each day a band from neighbouring cities Trail and Nelson was in attendance. A monster parade was held. Early history was re-enacted at a giant outdoor concert in the evenings. The Jubilee Queen, Jeannette Cousins, was crowned in a colourful ceremony at a specially built platform at Vimy Park. Many pioneers were introduced at this time by Mayor Roy Green.

Old-time races such as drilling, mucking, log-sawing and pie-eating competitions were held, and the winners of the various categories in the beard-growing competition were announced. A books of early history compiled by the Historical Committee was on sale. A flower, fruit and vegetable show was held in the Legion Hall. Dances, teas and private entertaining were the order of the day. Every possible effort had been put forth to make the celebration outstanding.

The city was decorated as it had been at first celebrations. Residents of Kaslo and district, many in authentic old-time costumes, participated and assisted in every possible way. Visitors were billeted in almost every home and every available bed was occupied. The weather co-operated perfectly and the Jubilee was successful even beyond the hopes of the hardworking group of people who made it possible.

1954—Kaslo Recreation Commission (KRC) formed to assist and promote adult recreation.

1954—Bowling Club folds; Jack Morris ends up with the bowls.

1954—Boy Scouts and Roy Green given permission to erect stone fireplace and insulate the ceiling with sawdust in the former fish hatchery (Scout Hall) building; the KRC assists with funding.

Mid-1950s—The Rainbow Square Dance Club starts up, taught by Marg Ringheim.

1955—New fir floor installed in Scout Hall with donated lumber and labour.

1956—Kootenay Lake has near-record high water; the Scout Hall floor is cut into sections and raised in order to save it.

1956—The Kaslo Credit Union is incorporated on September 12 with Charter #357. Charter members were E.H. Morphet, A.W. Riley, V. Leclair, B. Leclair, J.H. MacKinnon, Lilo Fleing, Audrey Barraclough, Ray Barraclough, Robert Wallace, H.C. Prout and J. Bartelme. Ace Bailey from the Rossland Credit Union was instrumental in setting up the Kaslo credit union, along with several others in the Kootenays. On October 10 the first meeting was held at the

The last council of the city—in 1959 the city changed to a village. Standing, from left: Herman Carlson, Ernie Augustine, Jack Humphries and Jack Morris. Seated, from left: City Clerk Percy Dunn and Mayor Roy Green. KLHSA no. 988.40.507

Antique fire carriages from Kaslo's past in the 1 9 5 3 Diamond Jubilee parade. KLHSA no 988.40.157

Oddfellows Hall, where E.H. Morphet was elected president, Ray Barraclough vice president, Alf Watson treasurer, E.M. Dunn secretary, and Reg Mossman, Alex Riley and F.C. Yoxal directors. After six months of existence, the neophyte Credit Union could boast assets of a whopping $301.96, and was gauged a success.

1957—The CPR retired the *Moyie* from service and Kaslo acquired the ship for $1; the Kootenay Lake Historical Society was formed.

1957—T&H Sawmills moved its operation to the bench just south of Kaslo, operating there for 15 years until the mill was moved to the Dairy Beach. The mill left a pile of sawdust about 75 feet deep covering almost three acres. Since then this sawdust has proved to be an enormous benefit to landscaping and soilmaking projects in the area; the pile has diminished considerably and as of 1993 Village Council charges a nominal fee for the privilege of taking sawdust away.

1957—Television cable service was installed.

1958—B.C. Centennial celebrations were held.

1958—Boy Scouts lease the Scout Hall for $1 a year.

1959—The City of Kaslo became a village on January 1st—66 years after its incorporation.

1959—Kinsmen Club starts, beginning a twenty-year history of good deeds and fun.

1962—After owning their own light plant for over fifty years, Kaslo taxpayers voted to sell the Kaslo Electric Utility to West Kootenay Power and Light Company.

The Moyie on her final voyage—to the beach at Kaslo. Note the high water conditions. KLHSA no. 988.40.775

1962—A new alarm system and siren were installed for the Fire Department which has served Kaslo on a volunteer basis since 1892.

1962—Renovations commenced on the Scout Hall (the former Fish Hatchery building) by the Kaslo Kinsmen Club. It was renamed the Kaslo Community Hall, and is used extensively by various organizations.

1962—Almost 300 dial telephones were installed and the new service was located in a portable building on A Avenue. The conversion cost $108,984, made up of land, $2,270; buildings, $4,600; central office equipment, $48,700; toll equipment and outside plant, $41,000; equipment and rewiring, $12,414. All phone numbers were changed to include the 353 prefix.

1963—A new post office was erected at the corner of A Avenue and Fifth Street. Highways Minister Philip "Flyin' Phil" Gaglardi, arrived in Kaslo, promising to widen the road through Coffee Creek bluffs and to look into improving the road north to Lardeau.

1963—Bridge Hill trestle removed and replaced with fill.

1963—Kaslo Kinette Club formed.

1964—Dr. Marion Irwin and Dorothy Wolfe open a coin-operated laundromat on Front Street. The laundry included six Speed Queen single-load washers, four triple-load driers and one double-load extractor, a soap dispensing machine and a change machine.

1964—The road between Kaslo and Meadow Creek was improved and paved, and work commenced on the Duncan Dam twenty-five miles north of Kaslo. This brought many new people into the area, traffic increased enormously and business conditions improved.

1965—School Districts 5 and 6 amalgamate to form School District No. 86.

1965—Regional District of Central Kootenay with headquarters in Nelson, incorporated on November 30. It covers an area of 9,000 square miles and included ten municipalities (later reduced to nine when Castlegar and Kinnaird amalgamated) and eleven electoral areas.

1966—Kaslo, with a population of under 1,000, is the centre of extensive logging and sawmill activity. T&H Sawmills installed modern dry kilns on the Dairy Beach on the south side of the Kaslo River and moved to this location in the fall. The mill employed 55 to 60 men and logged all around the lake.

Mining activity has diminished, with a few mines, including the Antoine, Utica and Blue Star still active. Optimism prevails—there is a renewed interest in mining in the district this year with over 870 mineral claims registered. The total for 1965 was 620.

The tourism industry continues to increase, and local facilities now include a hotel, a café, rooming house, three motels, three trailer parks and a marina in Kaslo Bay, with several other motels nearby. The federal government has installed free docking facilities

198

for boats and a loading ramp, and fishing and hunting continue to draw large numbers of sportsmen each year.

1966—New playground equipment installed by Kinsmen.

1966—The Kaslo and District Board of Trade sponsors a 4,300-foot-long gravel airstrip at the base of True Blue Mountain. Built entirely by volunteer labour, the project was spearheaded by Wilf and Clare Higgins and Board of Trade president Jack Morris. The airstrip is 300 feet wide at an elevation of 2,354 feet and there is enough level land there to extend the airfield to 6,000 feet if need be.

1966—The village commission (council) continues improving facilities. $25,000 has been spent on renewing water lines, and mercury vapour lamps have replaced the old incandescent type.

1966—Tentative approval is received to form a Hospital Improvement District with a new hospital to replace the old one built in 1903.

1966—Fire Brigade given permission to purchase an ambulance.

1968—Front Street is paved for $5,000, the first pavement in village limits except for the highway.

1968—The Village leases the Kaslo Airfield and begins a twenty-year struggle with the Air Transport Assistance Program (ATAP) to have the strip paved.

1968— Kaslo celebrates its 75th birthday, paying tribute to pioneers. On Sepember 14, a dinner in their honour was held in the United Church hall, at which presentations were made to Howard Green, Ray Goodwin, John Vallance, Henry Newcomen, Frank Abey, Harry Abey, B.F. Palmer, Cameron Clarke, Arvid Tapanila, Clarence White, J.B. Fletcher, Flora Green, Elizabeth Giegerich, Mrs. Ross Fleming, and Mabel Schroeder. Mrs. Green was presented with the Freedom of the Village, as was Mr. White. These presentations were made by Mrs. W. V. Drayton and Mayor Drayton, respectively.

1968—The old brick school was torn down and replaced, after serving the community since 1913.

1969—Recreation Commission #2 approved by RDCK.

1969—Kaslo Riding Club is formed in May.

1970—A group of volunteers and donated equipment under the Kinsmen banner smashed down and removed the back of the old hospital. They demolished and burned it in one weekend in order to clear the site for the new hospital.

1970—Ainsworth School building was moved to Kaslo for use as a music room.

1970—Mirror Lake Post Office moved to the S.S. *Moyie* site in Kaslo. The little building was in the *Guinness Book of World Records* as the smallest post office.

1971—Sod was turned in January for the new hospital. Practically 98% of

Mayor Jack Morris (in the middle) cuts the ribbon at the opening of Kaslo Riding Clubs' gymkhana grounds. Norma Turner on the left and Barb Douglas on the rignt assist.

Photo courtesy of Joyce Davidson.

The Kaslo and district arena, seen from the south. Note the tennis court in foreground.

the concrete work at the Victorian Hospital—sidewalks, curbs, stairs, patios including the dentist's office—was poured with a 2 1/2 cubic foot mixer using local Three-Mile (Highway 31A) gravel.

1972—A grant from New Horizons allows Kaslo Seniors to buy four carpets and bowls, resulting in the formation of the Kaslo Carpet Bowling Club.

1974—Roy E. Green was made Freeman of the Village of Kaslo.

1975—Kaslo and District Arena is finally opened. A dedicated Arena Committee, after several years and three referendums, was successful in having the arena built. It was a true community effort; volunteers once again rose to the occasion, backed by the committee's dedication and resolve. Raw logs were cut, transported, and milled by donation; the timbers were sized and transported back to the arena site to be put up by volunteers. The whole area participated— young and old, boys and girls, got together in workbees and raised the building from foundation to roof in a job well done. The hardworking committee was made up of Jack Morris, Bob Howlett, John Morrow, Morley Hyatt, Pat Remple, Kurt Thomas, Cappy Jacura, Shelagh Leathwood, Stan Leathwood, Albert Edwards and chairman Glen Allen.

1975—Council endorses restoration of the Langham Cultural Centre.

1975—The Canadian National Hangliding Championship is held here.

1975—Patty Wenger starts *Pennywise,* a weekly buy-and-sell advertising publication, still thriving in 1993.

1976—A landslide occurs on April 26 at the Jones Boys Marina on Kaslo

Lorne Nicolson and Lyle Kristiansen at the opening of Abbey Manor.in 1984.
Photo courtesy of Isabel Butler.

Logging sports competitors Colin Jacobs (with wedge) and Russell Semenoff.
Photo courtesy of Gordon F. Brown.

Bay.

1976—Kaslo Credit Union assets reach $930,000.

1976—B.C. Government offers to purchase the ambulance for $1,370.83 and equipment for $152.

1976, '77, '78—Kaslo Hang Gliders held their Kaslo Cup Fly-in, featuring a target landing competition on Kaslo Beach. The 1976 cup was won by Kasloite Dale Morris; the 77 cup went to Dave Chernoff, also from Kaslo; and in '78 the cup went to Wayne Mundy of Nelson.

1978—B.C Provincial hanglinding championship is held in Kaslo; local pilot Dave Chernoff takes 4th place in the World Hangliding Championship competition in Tennessee.

1978—An accident involving several teenagers prompts the Kaslo Senior Citizens Association to establish a Tranportation Committee to look into starting a community bus service between Kaslo and Nelson. The Kaslo Community Services Society was formed and fundraising began, digging as usual into the deep pockets of the community. In short order donations from individuals, businesses and clubs raised enough to purchase a 12-passenger bus. Volunteers drove and maintained the vehicle, and increased use soon made it apparent that a larger bus was needed. Again, donations were successfully sought and a 22-passenger bus was acquired. The service is run on a totally volunteer basis until the late 1980s, when a shortage of upkeep and

The pavilion in Vimy Park, now inhabited by the Kaslo Day Care Society.
Photo courtesy Isabel Butler

Maypole dancers, 1988. Photo Courtesy Gordon F. Brown

The 1988 May Royalty. From left: (rear) Karen Thomas, Heather Handley, 1988 Queen Nicole Unrau, 1987 Queen Alison Hamper, and Liz Tarr. Not shown: Connie Strilaeff. Photo courtesy Gordon F. Brown.

The Camperdown elm tree as it appears in 1992. This tree, now around 100 years old, once shaded the trout-rearing ponds that were here. This tree is not true to seed, apparently—seeds taken from it have produced true elms in the past. The tree in and of itself never fails to gather sharp-eyed horticultural aficionados around it each year. Plans are underway to commemorate its distinctive history with a plaque.

maintenance personnel prompts the seniors to open negotiations with B.C. Transit to take over the service.

1978—First Logging Sports held during May Days at the beach.

1979—West Kootenay Power terminates lease in Village Hall in preparation to move into new premises on Highway 31 just south of Kaslo.

1979—A chain of events was set in motion that ended with the completion in 1984 of Abbey Manor, the Kaslo senior citizens home. David Abbey approached Mayor Isabel Butler about the need for one and Mayor Butler contacted the Kinsmen, who already had an extensive body of research establishing the need for such a facility. The Kinsmen sank their teeth into the project, overseeing it to its completion. The Central Mortgage and Housing Corporation (later the Canada Mortgage and Housing Corporation) bought the property and funded the project, and a landscaping project was set up. The grounds were prepared for landscaping and turfing with around 100 truckloads from the arena sawdust pile. In total, almost 27,000 cubic feet were mixed with approximately 30 truckloads of sand. Volunteers designed and laid the garden, lawn and trees. About 43,000 square feet of turf was laid and an automatic sprinkler system installed.

The one-floor, ten-apartment building was designed to accommodate an additional ten units without obstructing the existing views.

1980—Kaslo Day Care Society was formed, born of a need for quality care for pre-school children of working mothers. With the Village Council's permission, the society moved into the pavilion at Vimy Park, restoring the building with the help of the Katimavik program and much donated time, labour and materials. Supervisors are qualified daycare personnel, and provide many activities for the children including local field trips, crafts, colouring, nature, stories and social interaction.

1980—Kaslo Carpet Bowlers lease present property on Front Street and begin landscaping.

1980—Fire Department receives new ambulance.

1982—Lawn Bowlers back in action on new greens.

1982—New public library facilities opened August 14 in the renovated basement of the Village Hall.

1983—A $175,000 riprap dike is constructed along Kaslo River, guarding the town from future floods.

1984—The senior citizens' home is officially opened, named Abbey Manor in honour of the Abbey family, who made a generous donation to the building fund. Operations are managed by directors who serve two-year terms administering the budget and attending the needs of the facility.

1985—Kaslo Credit Union directors decide to merge with the Kootenay

Gordon Portman, Jennifer Handley and Sarah Sinclair lead the crowd in 'Oh Canada' during the official opening of the S.S. Moyie Visitor's Interpretation Centre. Photo courtesy of G.D. McCuaig.

208   Sharon Winsor, Sherry Fenton, Billy March, Barb McKinnon and Mayor Jack Morris unveil a plaque commemorating the donors that enabled the adventure playground to become a reality in Vimy Park. Photo courtesy of Karen McCuaig.

Savings Credit Union to provide products and services that only
larger organizations can provide to members, joining a nine-branch
network. The Kaslo credit union will grow from just over $3 million
to $9 million and serve 1,800 residents and businesses as of 1992.

1986—Carpet Bowler and Lawn Bowler clubs merge.

1988—Kaslo Village Hall dedicated as a National Historic Site. The 1898
building is the oldest remaining Municipal Hall on the B.C. mainland and one of the only wooden-frame municipal administrative
buildings in continuous service since the turn of the century.

1988—Kaslo is the first community in Canada to officially recognize the
injustice of the Japanese relocation program of the Second World
War. A plaque was unveiled at the Langham Cultural Centre on
August 6.

1988—Howard Dirks, Minister of Tourism and Provincial Secretary, an-
nounces a long-awaited $135,000 grant from ATAP to pave the
Kaslo Airstrip.

The budget:

Grade existing base	$1,400
Place and compact 3,500 tons gravel	$14,000
Place 2 inches compact asphalt	$108,269
Apply 52,000 litres of magnesium chloride	$9,531
Apply 37,600 litres of primer	$18,800
	$152,000

This left a shortfall of $17,000, which Mr. Dirks was able to get
from ATAP's 1989 budget, when the job was completed. The Kaslo
Airfield now boasts a 3,700 by 60 foot paved runway and a 250-by-
150-foot paved parking lot; in addition a specified helicopter
landing and fuel storage site was approved by village council and an
airport development plan is now in place.

1989—Spearheaded by Barb Legg, Leah Honkanen, Billy March, Barb
McKinnon, Sharon Winsor and Sherry Fenton, canvassing begins in
late September to raise money for a new Adventure Playground in
Vimy Park. The initial fundraising effort raises almost $12,000.

1989—S.S. *Moyie* is declared the oldest intact passenger sternwheeler in
North America.

1989—Kaslo Victim Support Service is formed on January 5. Made up of
of RCMP members Corporal Brian Roberts and Constable Barry
Shannon, Anglican minister Ken Bond, Catholic lay minister
Adrienne McMillen, Community Church pastor Olaf Sorensen,
United Church minister Shelley Stickel-Miles, Maranatha pastor
Dan Walton, community counsellor Suzanne White, and seniors'
counsellor Garfield Belanger, the service was designed to deal with
victims of crimes with special needs, specifically spousal assault,
and assisting the RCMP, the community and all clients wherever

possible. The service also provides aid and comfort to families that must face sudden death situations.

1989—George McCuaig and his wife, Karen Semenoff, begin publishing *The North Arm Voice,* a news and views monthly newsletter for North Arm residents. Published on recycled paper, it is the first newspaper to be actually printed in Kaslo since *The Kootenaian* was moved to Nakusp in 1963.

1990—Long negotiations between the Kaslo Senior Citizens and B.C. Transit System conclude successfully, establishing a regular Nelson-Kaslo-Meadow Creek Bus Service with a 12-passenger bus. As of February 15, 1990, the bus runs to Nelson and back once a week on Wednesdays, and on every first and third Thursday of the month from Meadow Creek to Nelson and return.

1990—On December 3 Jack Morris is awarded a Civic Award by the City of Nelson in recognition of outstanding service to his community.

1991—Jack Morris is again honoured on January 22, this time being given the Freedom of the Municipality by the Village of Kaslo (the term "Freeman" had been deemed politically incorrect by this time.)

1991—The 12-passenger B.C. Transit bus is replaced with a 16-passenger bus; in October in-town and local service is set up to run Fridays on a trial basis.

1991— Official opening of the new S.S. *Moyie* Visitors Centre.

1991—Bed Races instituted at the May Days Celebration

1992—Public information meetings are held in Kaslo and other Kootenay Lake communities by the B.C. Ministry of Environment's, Fish and Wildlife Branch to inform residents about the North Arm fertilization project to enhance the fishery. Fertilization begins in the summer, with initial results promising.

1992—B.C. Transit adds weekly in-town and local service to the bus run on a one-year trial basis.

1992—100th May Days celebrated.

1993—B.C. Transit adds weekly in-town and local service on Fridays permanently to the schedule. In addition to the Nelson-Kaslo-Meadow Creek-Kaslo runs, the bus now goes to Shutty Bench in the morning, returning at noon; to upper Kaslo four times; around Vimy Park twice; and out to Mirror Lake by demand. Kaslo's bus service is established, thanks to the hard work and perserverance of the Kaslo Senior Citizens Association

•••••••••••••

The Past Queens of the May ride the float one more time—this time to commemorate their own participation as V.I.P.s in Kaslo past. Definitely a pretty picture.

A rare photograph of Lardo Jack McDonald, one of Kaslo's intrepid pioneers.
Photo courtesy of Margaret Jardine

The Mayors of Kaslo
—1893 to 1993—

R.F. Green	1893, 1896, 1897
George T. Kane	1894
John Keen	1895
Charles W. McAnn	1898, 1900, 1906, 1907
Dr. Gilbert Hartin	1899
G.A. Carlson	1901
A.W. Goodenough	1902
Fred E. Archer	1903, 1909, 1911, 1919, 1925, 1930, 1931, 1937, 1938, 1939, 1940, 1941, 1942
W.E. Hodder	1904, 1905
Sam H. Green	1908
J. W. Power	1910
A.T. Garland	1912
D.C. MacGregor	1913, 1914, 1915
James Anderson	1916, 1917, 1918, 1921, 1922, 1923, 1929
W.G. Robb	1920
David P. Kane	1924
William H. Burgess	1926, 1927, 1928
W. J. Murphy	1932
W. Vilder Papworth	1933, 1934, 1935, 1936
Roy E. Green	(from May) 1942, 1952, 1953, 1956, 1957, 1958, 1959, 1976, 1977
Edward Latham	1943, 1944
Charles Webster	1945
George S. Baker	1946, 1947, 1948, 1949, 1950, 1951
William V. Drayton	1954, 1955, 1962, 1963, 1964, 1965, 1966, 1967, 1968, 1969
Charles Lind	1960, 1961
Wilfred R. Higgins	1970, 1971(to August, 1972)
John V. Humphries	1973, 1974
A. Nelson Colter	1975
Isabel Butler	1978, 1979
Angus J. MacLellan	1980, 1981
Jack D. Morris	1982, 1983, 1984, 1985, 1986, 1987, 1988, 1989, 1990
Gordon Gaskell	1991, 1992, 1993

•••••••••

Kaslo Aldermen/Commisioners/Councillors
—1893 to 1993—

British Columbia municipal elected officials were called Aldermen from 1893 to 1957; Commissioners from 1958 - 1968; back to Aldermen from 1969 - 1993; and in 1993 they became known by the current politically-correct term, Councillors.

Cameron, Alfred -	1893
Devlin, Thomas E. -	1893
Green, Samuel H. -	1893, 1894, 1906, 1907, 1921 ,1922,1923, 1929, 1930
Kane, David P. -	1893, 1894, 1909, 1910, 1911, 1919, 1928, 1929, 1930
MacKay, Adam -	1893, 1894
Beattie, Francis -	1894
Jardine, Andrew -	1894, 1901, 1902, 1904, 1905
McMillan, Daniel -	1894
Stone, O.T. -	1895, 1903
Retallack, J.L. -	1895
Byers, Hamilton -	1895
Fletcher, A. McL. -	1895, 1902
Cameron, J.R. -	1895, 1897
Murchison, Colin -	1896
Goodenough, A.W. -	1896, 1897, 1898, 1900
Whiteside, George -	1896, 1898
Moore, D.W. -	1898
Kane, G.T. -	1899
Fawcett, S.H. -	1899, 1902, 1903
Papworth, W.V. -	1899, 1901, 1903, 1904, 1905, 1906, 1907, 1909, 1910, 1911, 1912
Twiss, E.D. -	1899
Campbell, Angus -	1899, 1904, 1905, 1906, 1907, 1908
Archer, Fred E. -	1898, 1900, 1901, 1902, 1905, 1926, 1927, 1928, 1934
Carlson, G.A. -	1900
Hartin, Dr. Gilbert -	1898, 1900, 1901, 1905, 1928, 1929
Hodder, W.E. -	1900, 1901
Kennedy, T.L. -	1901
MacGregor, D.C. -	1902, 1911, 1913
Young, D.J. -	1902
Holmes, W.J.H. -	1903, 1906,1907
Adams, A.F. -	1903, 1932
Watnee, Nils M. -	1903

Power, J. W. -	1904, 1905, 1906, 1907, 1908, 1909, 1933
Giegerich, Henry -	1904, 1905, 1906, 1910
Allen, J.M. -	1906
Strathearn, D.S. Osborne -	1907, 1913, 1914, 1915
Augustine, Otto -	1908
Desmond, O.E. -	1908, 1911, 1912
McAndrew, M.P. -	1908
Walsh, P.H. -	1908, 1909, 1910
Cockle, J.W. -	1909
Latham, E.H. -	1909, 1910, 1913, 1914, 1918, 1942, 1945, 1946
Speirs, James -	1910, 1911, 1912, 1914, 1915, 1916, 1919, 1923, 1924, 1928, 1931
Robb, W.G. -	1911, 1912, 1916, 1917, 1929
Fingland, J.J. -	1912, 1914
Goldsmith, Alexander -	1912
Anderson, James -	1913, 1914, 1920
Strachan, John -	1913, 1914, 1915
Abey, F.T. -	1915, 1942, 1943
Alpaugh, Ephram -	1915
Murphy, W.J. -	1915, 1932
Curle, A.J. -	1916, 1917
English, William -	1916
Hunter, S.A. -	1916, 1917, 1918, 1920
Riddell, J.A. -	1916, 1917, 1919, 1920, 1921, 1922, 1923, 1925, 1926, 1927, 1934, 1935
Cadden, Jack -	1917, 1928
Caldwell, Grace -	1918
Hugh, Catherine -	1918
Menhinnick, L.C.S. -	1918
Hendricks, Robert -	1917, 1918, 1919
Timms, E.F. -	1919
Noble, W.E. -	1920, 1921, 1922
Stott, George -	1920, 1921, 2922, 1923
MacKenzie, D.A. -	1921, 1922, 1932
Stubbs, J. H. -	1921, 1922
Drennan, G.B. -	1923
Hendricks, Walter -	1923, 1924, 1929, 1930
Beck, Harry -	1924, 1925, 1926, 1927
MacPhee - A.L. -	1924, 1925,1930,1931 to October
Reuter, S.J. -	1924, 1925, 1930, 1931, 1947, 1948
Burgess, W.H. -	1924, 1925
Sutherland, Alexander -	1925, 1926
Tinkess, J.H. -	1926, 1927, 1942
Cosgriff, D.P. -	1927

Exter, Herb -	1929, 1930, 1934, 1935
Paterson, James -	1931, 1932, 1935, 1936, 1964
Ward, Edward C. -	from November 1931
Palmer, George A. -	from November 1931, 1932
Milne, R.B. -	1933
Archer, Charles Francis -	1933, 1934, 1935, 1936
Brett, C.F. -	1933
Grayling, A.L. -	1936, 1937, 1938, 1939, 1940, 1941, 1942
Sandilands, Mrs. L.M. -	1936, 1937
Larsen, Henry M. -	1937, 1938, 1940, 1941, 1945, 1946
Rudkin, W.P. -	1938
Hewat, Ronald -	1939, 1942
Webster, Charles W. -	1941, 1942, 1943
Tinkess, G.W. -	1942, 1943, 1944
Whittaker, Margaret -	1943, 1944
Sutherland, G.K. -	1944, 1945
Bowker, Gordon D. -	1944, 1945, 1953, 1954
Tonkin, W.H. -	1945, 1946, 1947
Morton, George L. -	1946, 1947
Bavington, Arthur -	1946
Holliday, M.A. -	1947, 1948, 1950
Logan, W.R. -	1948, 1949, 1950, 1951
Drayton, William V. -	1948, 1949, 1950, 1951, 1960
Leveque, Eugene J. -	1949, 1950
Carter, L.F. -	1949, 1953
Carlson, Herman -	1951, 1952, 1953, 1954, 1955, 1956, 1957, 1958, 1959, 1961, 1962
McGibbon, Fred -	1951, 1952
Patterson, Ralph -	1952, 1953, 1956, part of 1957, 1964
Shillington, Ruby -	1952
Lind, Charles -	1954, 1955
Miller, Norman S.	1953, 1954, 1955, 1960, 1961, 1962, 1963, 1964, 1965
Augustine, Ernest -	1955, 1956, 1957, 1958
Morris, Jack D. -	part of 1957, 1958, 1959, 1960
Hand, Jack -	1956, 1957
Humphries, John V. -	1958, 1959
Gilker, Robert -	1959, 1960
Nomland, Sam -	1961, 1962, 1963
Higgins, Wilfred R. -	1961, 1962, 1963, 1964, 1965, 1966, 1967
Jardine, Margaret -	1963, 1964, 1965, 1966
Edkahl, Ivan -	1965, 1966, 6967, 1968, 1969, Part of 1970
Tompson, Fred -	1966
Hewat, Ronald -	1967, 1968, 1969, 1970, 1971
Jones, W. Robert -	1967, 1968, 1969

Rota, Sam -	1968, 1969
Aydon, Fred -	1970, 1971, 1972
Keohane, James -	1970, 1971, 1972, to June 1973
Riley, Orval -	1970, 1971, 1972
Frie, Kenneth -	1972 to August
Leathwood, A. Stanley -	1974, 1977, 1978, 1979, 1980
	from September 1988, 1989, 1990
Hartland, Clifford -	1973, 1974
Matchett, William J. -	from August 1972, 1973
Bildstein, Frances -	1974
Colter, A. Nelson -	1974, 1980, 1981
Van Horn, James -	1975, 1976, to March
Butler, Isabel -	1975, 1976, 1977, 1986, 1986, 1987
Belanger, Garfield -	1975, 1976
Herzig, A.K. -	1975
Jones, Terry -	1976, 1977
Semenoff, Molly -	from March 1976, 1977, 1978
Cheyne, R. Irvine -	1978, 1979
Smith, Richard -	1978, 1979
Huggins, Ring -	1979
Cox, Orlando -	1980
Scarlett, Donald -	1980
Chappell, Charles	1981
Moser, George -	1981, 1982
Watson, Karen G. -	1981, 1982
Budde, Lutz -	1982, 1983, 1984
Matthews, John -	1982, 1983, 1984, 1985, 1986, 1987
Forbes, Alex -	1983, 1984
Ward, Jack -	1983, 1984
Linn, Michael -	1985 to June
Kuzyk, Taras -	1986, 1987
Wickware, John -	1985, 1986
Onions, Gladys -	1987, 1988
Scarbo, Joseph -	1988, 1989, 1990
Watson, Eric -	1988 to July
MacLellan, Angus J. -	1988
Bagger, Paul -	1989, 1990
Gaskell, Gordon -	1989, 1990
Humphries, Thomas -	1991, 1992, 1993
Kisch, Kenneth -	1991, 1992, 1993
Mackle, Patrick -	1991, 1992, 1993
Pickard, Douglas -	1991, 1992 to December 31
Gevers, William -	1993

•••••••••

Some of the seniors that made this book possible.

From left: Isabel Butler, Jack Matthews, Bob Swanson, Jack Morris, Dot Morris, Catherine Douglas, Betty Swanson,